COUNTERPREDATORS

SURVIVAL RESPONSE CONDITIONING AND THE PARENT / CHILD CONNECTION

BILL KORTENBACH

Copyright © 2012 by Bill Kortenbach

All rights reserved. This book or any portion thereof may not be reproduced or used in any manner whatsoever without the express written permission of the publisher except for the use of brief quotations in a book review, or unless the total amount of quoted text does not exceed 100 words in length.

First edition, 2012

ISBN-13: 978-1-4566-1428-7

Published by eBookIt.com

DEDICATION

To my lionhearted children, Brandon Michael and Alana Marie—
my motivation throughout the adventure that became this book.

"The world breaks everyone
and afterward,
many are strong at the broken places."

–Ernest Hemingway

CONTENTS

What is a Counterpredator? 1
Introduction 3

PART I: THE CULTURE OF PROTECTION 11
1 The Currency of Fear 13
2 "Houston, We Have a Problem…" 20
3 The Victim Factory 35
4 Ordinary People—and Heroes 66
    Part I Endnotes 76

PART II: THE ADRENAL ADVANTAGE 79
5 Welcome to My World 81
6 The Foundation 88
7 This is How We Roll 98
8 Training Day 104
    Part II Endnotes 121

PART III: BODY CHESS 123
9 The Passive/Aggressive Strategy 125
10 Alarms and Triggers: Your Internal Radar 130
11 The Power of a Decisive Choice 137
12 A Line in the Sand 146
13 The Art of Misdirection 157
14 "Thank You, Sir, May I Have Another?" 172
15 The Third Arena 178
    Part III Endnotes 196

PART IV: THE WOLVERINE CLUB 199
16 Basic Instincts 201
17 The Bones of the Earth 211
18 What Powerful Children Know 227
19 What Powerful Children Do 248
20 When Bullies Meet Hard Targets 278
21 Mouse Jockeys: A Fresh Perspective 301
22 Adopting the Empowered Mind 316
    Part IV Endnotes 328

    List of Tables and Figures 331
    A Note on Sources 332
    Recommended Reading 333
    Links 336
    Acknowledgments 337
    About the Author 341

What is a Counterpredator?

Since this is a word that the reader may not commonly encounter and because I define it narrowly for the purpose of this book, a brief explanation will be helpful.

A counterpredator is an individual who has the will and the skill to confront and defeat a predator and who will engage an aggressor without hesitation when necessary. There are two types of counterpredators. Public counterpredators are usually professionals, like policemen, soldiers and bodyguards, whose job requires them to seek out aggressors and put them in check. They are in the public eye and pursue their professional objectives openly. Because of this, predators avoid public counterpredators whenever possible and it is usually easy for them to do so.

Private counterpredators may have less formal training then public counterpredators, but they are just as committed and have a formidable skill set. A private counterpredator is an aggressor's worst nightmare, because it is hard to distinguish these individuals from potential victims until they are engaged, and then it is too late. A private counterpredator could be anyone: a parent, a martial artist, or even a street-smart civilian who learned his or her skill set in the school of hard knocks. Either way, they have superior motivation, courage and the will to retaliate when provoked. While they do not consider themselves to be heroes, they perform heroic acts, and will often intervene to rescue a stranger.

Counterpredators are society's guard dogs, and no civilization can survive without their presence. As Richard Grenier said, *"People sleep peaceably in their beds at night because rough men stand ready to do violence on their behalf."*[1]

In every culture, the part that private counterpredators play is an incredibly important role. The greater their numbers, the healthier, safer and more compassionate a society is. Therefore, the transition of vulnerable citizens into private counterpredators is the focus of this book.

Introduction

What you are about to read on the subject of child safety may shock you. It is written from a perspective that is the polar opposite of the way it is commonly addressed. This "counterculture" approach is necessary because the society we inhabit and the culture it has adopted is one of the leading causes of our vulnerability. Modern civilization is driven by human desire. We want instant gratification/deferred payment and to this end, we visualize ourselves obtaining more and achieving more. We want to experience the good things in life, and this is normal—as long as provision is made for life's unpleasant surprises. The root of the problem is that the search for the good has crowded out the preparation for the bad. As a result, we become immune to threat *because we become blind to its proximity*.

I believe it is important to put this trend toward unnecessary vulnerability in check. Allow me to suggest another visualization exercise. Imagine your child has disappeared. The authorities have caught the perpetrator, and he has led them to her body. Imagine the agony, the grief… the guilt. Imagine reviewing the events leading up to the *end of your life as the parent of this child* and coming to the conclusion that it might have been prevented. What could you have done differently? How will you conduct yourself from this time forward with your surviving children, or others you may have in the future? Would you be willing to take action to arm yourself with a more effective skill set, one that gave you the advantage over a predator if he targeted you? Would you be willing to take the time to pass that skill set on to your children?

Bear in mind that this hypothetical scenario is real to parents all over the world. It could happen to you. The purpose of this book is to confront vulnerability. We must first become counterpredators ourselves, and then pass on this advantage to our children.

When it comes to the subject of child safety, society gives parents what I call porthole perspective. Our view of the subject is limited by our social mores, ideology and lack of exposure to the world of predator and prey. It is helped down that path by denial and complacency. Like a stowaway in the hold of a ship, we see only what is visible through the porthole. The real tragedy is, unlike the stowaway, many of us do not recognize the situation. We do not realize that our perspective is limited. We believe the view through the porthole frames the whole horizon.

In this analogy, the ship's hold represents the prison of politically correct thinking. This auto-programming directs our focus away from the creative, critical thinking so necessary to independence and self-sufficiency. "Group Think" with regard to child safety is a deadly threat to our children. It is robbing them of the tools nature intended them to possess and it is responsible for vast numbers of adults becoming victims in waiting—meals ready to eat.

What we need most is to come up out of the hold and onto the deck. From there, we can climb through the rigging, into the crow's nest and address reality from a 360 degree view. We need to stop surrendering control to others and begin steering our own ship. Before this can take place, it would be wise to acquire the knowledge that will allow us to become proficient navigators.

When we decide to take action to improve our children's training, we attempt to find resources for *them*, when what we need to do is begin with ourselves. This reminds me of the pre-flight safety instructions flight attendants give passengers regarding deployment of emergency oxygen masks. In the event of crisis, they instruct us to fit ourselves first. After our oxygen supply is secured, we help our children with their own masks.

Instinctively, we sense that we are the weak link in our children's safety. We surrender leadership in this field to the "experts," because we believe it is the best and safest choice. We replace ourselves with someone we believe is a better mentor than we are. I strongly urge you to reconsider. Preparing your children to survive—and thrive—in a harsh, unforgiving environment begins with you. To that end we will be taking a different approach toward the goal of making your child a hard target: First and foremost, *you must become one yourself.*

You are the key to your child's safety. How you view the world, what you think is possible, and the choices you make based on your knowledge and experience will vastly impact your children. For their sake, you must be willing to expose yourself to the widest range of ideas and experiences available because only then will you be equipped to choose the best and right path. I cannot over-emphasize the importance of a parent having first-hand knowledge of this subject.

I want to encourage your exploration of and familiarity with effective methods that you can trust, not because of the opinion of an expert, but because they have worked for you. Your child's right to proficiency in the arena of self-preservation is crucial. You cannot in good conscience take a short-cut. You invested in this book because you want to ensure his or her safety. Grab your own oxygen mask first. Without the advantage of personalized knowledge, *none of us* have a point of reference in deciding what is real and effective. We cannot choose the best training for our children when we fail to see all of the options. That is porthole perspective.

We must discover for ourselves what the truth is, what works and what does not. We need to know what we can trust. We must question assumptions that even the experts rely on, because both society and the individual are predisposed to accepting an expert opinion, rather than evaluating evidence on its own merit.

Trusting an expert is easy and comfortable. Occasionally we get lucky. My question to you is, *"Are you willing to gamble with your child's safety and future?"*

Nearly every parent who has lost a child due to circumstances involving human negligence or malevolence started with the belief that it wouldn't happen to them. They played the odds, believed the experts, engaged in "group think" and lost their child.

The problem with an expert mindset is that it arrives at a conclusion and stays there. Forward progress stops because the energy it took to arrive at "truth" is now used to reflect that truth back to others. This is a luxury no parent can afford. For our children's sake, we must be continuously receptive; open to the signals, nuances and clues intuition sends us. There is no stopping place, no point at which we arrive. Instead of depending on expert opinions, we need to become experts ourselves, the kind that believes anything is possible, in any circumstance, at any time. We need to be reconnected with the primal instincts that lie dormant within us. We need to know by direct, personal experience that <u>we</u> have all the advantages a predator has because *nature has equipped us to become predatory ourselves in the defense of our children.*

To affect this course correction, it is not necessary to have a degree, to be successful in business or to have a brilliant child psychologist on retainer. What is essential is replacing the attitude of denial with acceptance of reality, and adopting an open mind. What you think you know can be every bit as damaging as what you don't know. The two in conjunction could have disastrous results for you and your children.

I wrote this book because I have witnessed the benefits of **Survival Response Conditioning** and they have been spectacular. I refer to these benefits as "the adrenal advantage," —*knowledge of and experience with all of the primal assets nature has equipped us with—gained under high stress in a very short period of time.*

The positive changes in the lives of those we train using this method are so profound that I felt compelled to seek a wider audience. I want to share this experience with as many as possible, that they too may share in these wonderful benefits. The thing that has intrigued me most is what can happen to at-risk children—and what their true potential is. They have become my greatest motivator. I have seen the holes and cracks our young people fall through, and I know there is a way to plug them. This solution is labor-intensive and edgy, but the reward is worth the labor and greatly outweighs any incurred risk. I want to share my success in these endeavors with you. I have learned personally that if what you are doing is not working, there is nothing to lose and everything to gain by considering an alternative approach. Your investment in this book proves you are willing to consider that you may lack the specialized knowledge essential for your family's safety. This is a good start.

I have three objectives as this material is presented:

First: To motivate parents and others concerned with the safety and security of our children to a positive acceptance of reality. I want you to recognize and understand the root causes of apathy and disempowerment: how they infect our society and create victims. To avoid these pitfalls we need a crystal clear perspective.

Second: I want to underscore the importance of having an intimate, working knowledge of what it takes to protect *yourself* against human threat, by regaining a close connection with the abilities and sensitivities nature has bestowed upon you. Once these assets are identified, and their value appreciated, the desire to possess this connection will take charge. You will become receptive to methods that will quickly give you the requisite experience. I want to encourage you to obtain this education yourself, as soon as possible, and I will show you how to do it. Without this experience, you cannot reach your full potential as your child's protector, and you cannot excel in the role of mentor/hero to your children that they need you to assume.

Third: Having obtained the "adrenal advantage" and armed with a fresh perspective, you will be able to use this book to examine and become familiar with the most effective and empowering survival lessons for your children. Together, we will explore the training that supports those lessons: a conditioning process that begins with their becoming a hard target and results in their becoming an adult counterpredator. Thus, you will reclaim the title of expert with regard to your children's safety that has been forfeited to the authorities by default.

To achieve these goals, I have divided the body of this work into four parts. In the first three, the focus is on the experience and preparation of the parent. The last section is devoted to children's safety issues and how parents can bond with them in training.

Part 1: The Culture of Protection defines the victim/threat problem from several different angles: individual thought patterns and habits, society, culture, human dynamics, etc. It is a reality check, directed at the predatory environment that we have physically, mentally and emotionally attempted to keep at arm's length. In the endeavor to guarantee our safety, our culture has made us vulnerable by minimizing the importance of exercising the skill set nature meant us to have. It is vital that we see this right from the outset so that what follows retains its impact.

Part 2: The Adrenal Advantage is a look at the physical program itself; the process that gives parents—and other interested adults—a conditioning experience that can reconnect them with their own personal power.

Part 3: Body Chess is an exploration of the strategies that support the physical program. Once instilled, these strategies dictate timing and tactics, allowing the graduate to outmaneuver a predator. For those unfamiliar with the threat environment, this section will explore the winning combination of emotional conditioning and superior strategy that makes Survival Response Conditioning such an effective solution.

Part 4: The Wolverine Club explores a unique training format designed for children, based on the five sources of danger/threat to every child: familiar adults, strangers, situations, peers and themselves. The text examines the basics of imprinting the adrenal advantage in children, how the process differs from what adults experience in like circumstances, and what the impact of owning this potent skill set and outlook will be for our children. We will discover what powerful children know and what they do, how to handle bullying and Internet predators. Last and of greatest import, we will learn how to train children to think in a way that will eventually make them impervious to negative thoughts, depression, boredom and all the other internal and self-directed enemies of a child's emotional health.

As a parent, you can use this book in two different ways. You may choose to treat what I have written as you would treat any other book: a source of information. If you do, you will know more intellectually about the subject of personal safety in general and child safety in particular, but that is as far as the benefit will go for you. Knowledge alone cannot save you, or your child. This is where so many programs fail: They leave the participant with an intellectual knowledge that is guaranteed to desert them in the moment of crisis, when adrenal influences shut down the brain's cognitive processing.

The other choice is to use this book as intended: to obtain the adrenal advantage for *yourself*. This benefit, this edge, will give you the ability to respond to crisis with stunning clarity and precision, to act simply and decisively in the moment—*to choose powerfully.*

You will find, as you explore what I have written, that there is some repetition. This is with purpose. My father once told me that good arguments are worth repeating. You need a better than even chance of *retaining* this lifesaving information. The common F.Y.I. approach is unlikely to effect the necessary changes to your thinking, especially when measured against the goal of preserving human life. In addition, some of the topics are connected by multiple links, and to deal with them all at once would interrupt the flow of the point under discussion. Because of this we will occasionally revisit a previously mentioned topic to explore a new facet that is central to the context. The importance of the objective demands maximum retention.

Some of the strategies and techniques I present may repel you. It may occur to you that your child might be traumatized by the exercises that I suggest; that you don't want your child to be exposed to the world of predator and prey; that the cure I'm suggesting is worse than the disease. I understand. Accordingly, I want to urge you to test these methods yourself, and become familiar with the full array of the fabulous arsenal of defensive weaponry that nature has implanted within you. Once this has been achieved, you will no longer be reluctant to expose your children to the adrenal advantage. I believe you will commit to *bringing it to them.*

I congratulate you on your willingness to consider new and alternate approaches. Your open mind is your greatest asset. While this may be a bumpy, emotional ride, I will remind you that all real progress is measured against sweat equity. You are on the right path. Now, with all the courage you can muster, I challenge you to confront this truth: **What you fail to expose your child to, in a controlled, compassionate environment, could take place without you, alone, and at the hands of a predator, under the most vicious and unforgiving conditions.**

I invite you to consider that nearly every parent who has lost a child for any reason, would do anything to have just five minutes more with their child, if within that time just a tidbit of information giving them a fighting chance to live, might be imparted. There is no ideology, philosophy of childrearing, or any other high-minded principle that they would not instantly abandon in exchange for that one small window of time with their child. Many, if not all parents would risk their own life to have it.

Just ask them.

I

The Culture of

Protection

Chapter 1

The Currency of Fear

"It is the capricious nature of tragedy that is so bewildering. Like the toss of a coin, the process by which some escape and others are struck down seems random and arbitrary."

–R. Raven

Heads

(Inside the mind of a Psychopath)

Like a body in traction, he feels the pull: at first just an occasional tug, but now with the passage of months, steady pressure; looming, malevolent—filling every corner of what he has become. The blissful rapture of having another under his absolute power has nearly bled out. Memories and fantasies no longer curb his hunger. He needs a meal and food is everywhere. Little girls and sometimes boys, riding bikes, swimming, playing in the park, laughing, screaming, and chasing each other: innocent and clueless. He feels powerful, God-like, knowing he can separate them at any moment from their frail cocoon of happy security. They are opportunity, electricity, a jumpstart-jolt of pure adrenalin—but most of all they are MREs: meals, ready to eat.

He commits to taking action soon, but not too soon. Timing is everything. It is the reason he and those like him are seldom caught. He has an eye for detail. For him, planning an acquisition is just as exhilarating as the actual snatch. How he loves outwitting the authorities! They think they know so much, but they are no match for him. Contemptible! That's what they are... just like the parents: a more careless and brain-dead sector of society would be unimaginable! If they were half as intelligent as he is, they might produce a challenge for him once in awhile... and as for challenges...

This time he's going to make the grab right in front of Mom and Dad—who won't even realize what is occurring! In fact, he's going to ask their permission, and they will say "yes" with a smile! The time to do this will be just after lunchtime on a sunny day; a picnic day on a weekend in a park: Right after they eat, when they feel sluggish, relaxed and sleepy. He will wear a uniform of some sort, from a service industry—nothing official of course, maybe a security guard or... a delivery driver! Yes... on a warm day, he will blend in with short pants, and he knows a uniform will make his face forgettable.

He will acquire a puppy; an adorable, irresistible little scrap of bait, and a leash to hold her. He will select an appropriate facial disguise from his extensive collection. He revels in the feeling of power a convincing disguise gives him over the unknowing. He can walk among them, smile, and even converse with these fools, who are unaware of his true identity[2]. There is no longer a difference between who he is and what he does. He is a shadow, an obsidian blade. He is *"the Edge,"* slicing his victims from the Book of Life, but until he finds a worthy subject—until he is ready to make his selection—he will spare them.

Where to park his vehicle? Behind a building or a grove of trees, the closer the better, provided it is not directly visible from his hunting ground. He will stroll through the park, paying no apparent attention to the playing children, picking up "Fluffy's" poop like a good, responsible pet owner. All the while he will be taking mental notes: which children belong to which picnic blanket, which parents are attached to which children and how attentive are the parents. Who is engrossed in the latest novel? Whose vision is limited? Are they lying flat on their back, or on their stomach? Who is sleeping, who is tanning, etc., etc., etc.

When he spots a situation that pleases him, he will gradually work toward his little mark, close enough that they can see how cute and playful Fluffy is, close enough for them to want to touch or hold her. He is exceptionally patient. It is the most significant ingredient in his recipe for success. He never forces a situation to fit his needs. He is a chameleon, blending with and becoming a benign component of whatever environment he enters. His presence and demeanor are designed to avoid alarm.

Within view of the parents, he will not initiate a conversation with a child. That is the reason he brought Fluffy. Like a moray eel, coiled into a hole, he waits for the little MRE to come to him, smooth skin glowing, eyes sparkling with curiosity, oohing and aahing over the dear, sweet puppy; asking all kinds of earnest, yearning and wistful questions about Fluffy. Such a ripe little peach to pick! With just the right mix of gentle humor, he will answer those questions, hinting sadly that he might not be able to keep Fluffy permanently. This will trigger hopes that Fluffy might be able to change owners with *just* the right family...

It is critical this conversation take place in proximity to the parents. Too far away could cause them to worry about a strange adult talking with their child. Close in, they will see that *he* did not initiate this conversation, and the protracted patience that adults display toward children when they would rather be elsewhere will be obvious. Besides, what could happen? They are right there! Because he broadcasts disinterest, he will be viewed as harmless.

So far, the part he has played has been passive. The stage is set. Act two is about to commence. This is the part he loves. He is so close. The anticipation is delicious! He can see that he has the confidence of both the MRE and its parent. He has succeeded in portraying himself as a pleasant, harmless individual, someone *just like them*. He asks his first question: "How long do you folks plan to stay at the park?" Now, shyly, and with measurable embarrassment, he admits he is in something of a fix. He cannot take little Fluffy to his next appointment and is loath to leave her in the hot car. He will only be gone half the time they plan to stay at the park. He can see how young Jamie loves animals... maybe she will be a veterinarian someday? Why not start her career right now? (Big wink at Mom and Dad) He will pay Jamie $20 to watch Fluffy and (he produces pen and paper) on the off chance he is late, here is his address and phone number. Would it be alright to pay $10 now and $10 on his return? Yes? Wonderful! (His relief is evident.)

He passes the leash to the MRE and reaches for his back pocket. *A puzzled look*. He pats all his pockets... "Well! It looks like I left my wallet with Fluffy's water! (Big smile) Be back in a sec!" He takes three or four steps toward where he has parked (out of sight), looks back over his shoulder and, without pausing, gives three sharp lilting whistles: international dog owners language for, "Come here! I have something good for you!" Fluffy tugs at the leash and the MRE holding it follows him without hesitation. Mom and Dad feel the first twinge of uneasiness but brush it off... "After all, he volunteered his contact info, and he has trusted us with his precious puppy. It would be rude to exhibit distrust... wouldn't it?"

Jamie, Fluffy, and the kind pet owner are never seen again.

Afterward, when he has extracted all the terror, pain and horror possible from her young, tender little self, he will discard her remains on some remote wooded hillside, where wildlife and the elements will complete the task of erasing her. Fluffy can join her, too. It will be fun to strangle the little mutt right in front of her eyes. She will cry—and scream and scream and scream! He can't wait to lick her tears...

The beauty of this plan from his perspective is the lack of risk. He has all the power, because he is the only one who grasps what is happening. If the parents intervene, or if he gets to the car and anyone can see him, he does exactly what he agreed to, gives the MRE the $10 and comes back in a half hour. They never know how close to *the Edge* they came. Best of all, he has built a bridge of trust that can be used with the same family at a later time. This strange blend of audacity and patience is his most potent weapon.

Tails

(The Crystal Judson Brame Story)

She will be dead in less than a month but it is not possible to know this, sitting in my office, sharing coffee. She is poised, well dressed, cultured and attractive. If you passed her on the street, there would be no hint of darkness, no portent of tragedy to convey her hidden struggle. You would not imagine her as a prisoner of fear or any other vice. She appears successful and in control. Every outward indicator suggests nothing other than an ideal existence. She has a beautiful home, two healthy, happy children, does community service work, and has a husband who is a pillar in the city government.

As the sound of her voice breaks the silence of my office, a note of discord becomes apparent. Even before her words reveal her secret, a subtle nuance, unidentified, radiates primal fear. Her eyes become haunted, and her posture crumbles. She is transforming from the woman she wants the world to see, to the reality beneath the surface.

She has existed, for more than a decade with this dual identity but few if any are aware of her secret. She is talented, intelligent. She married well, or so it seemed. Her dreams of a happy home and family were coming true. And then, he hit her and her world changed. It was easy, the first time, to forgive him. When he made his tearful apology, blaming a high-stress job, it seemed genuine. This is a man she admires and loves, someone she has given her heart to, and the bond is permanent. Hope dies hard, when you believe in dreams, and has a willing partner in denial. Besides, he swears it will never happen again.

But it does happen again, accompanied by humiliating verbal abuse. She finds her love and loyalty exact a high price in pain and suffering. She is humiliated at her own naivety. I comfort her by pointing out that this process is seldom seen in its true light by the people engaged in it. It is like standing too close to an oil painting. Clarity is only possible with distance. Failure to accept reality, **to see what is** rather than what we desire, makes us weaker and blinder with every excuse we accept. It is a natural process, like the stumble before the fall.

Over time, her love for her husband is eclipsed by fear of him. She is all alone, and like a shell-shocked veteran, feels lethargic and helpless. He is a well-known, respected public servant, in a position of trust. Who will believe her story, when weighed against his record of service? She is trapped. Since he controls the bank accounts, she is only allowed a tiny amount of money at a time. He checks the mileage on her car and requires her to keep a daily log of all her movements. He allows her no privacy, accompanying her even in the examination room when she visits the gynecologist. He watches her when she uses the bathroom. He requires her to step on a weight scale every morning in his presence. He monitors all her phone calls. His job gives him access to sophisticated surveillance equipment. She senses he uses it to track her movements. She can never be sure when he will appear. He rarely tells her his schedule, and more than once, on days he is supposed to be at work, she has glanced out her window only to find him standing there, staring in at her. This frightens her nearly out of her wits.

The first time he threatens her life she is too numb from the beating that accompanies the threat to assign it its true significance. Later, as the hidden bruises he inflicted heal, she begins to suspect that his capacity for violence might be far greater than she has been willing to accept. On the surface, he appears to be a decent father and is protective of their children. Yet his rage has been so irrational, so out of proportion to the situations that ignite it… There are guns in the house, and he is an expert marksman. What if he should truly snap?

From this point on, fear—deep fear—overshadows her every waking moment. She cries a little, describing how he senses her fear and how it fuels his anger, fanning it white-hot regularly and often. Because of this, she is extremely careful to show no sign that anything is awry; not to him, not to anyone. She strives to become a mirror, reflecting only images that are normal—deflecting any possible suspicion or question about what is behind the glass. Her home gradually becomes a maze of trip wires, with a conflagration inevitable. Finally, after years of it, more in fear for her children than herself, she decides to confide in family members. They convince her to file for divorce.

Now that she has moved in with her parents, his behavior has become more abusive, sinister, and malevolent. She truly fears for her life. That is why she is here, in my office, pouring out her heart. Friends told her about my Survival Response Conditioning program and because of the unique circumstances surrounding her case I decided to interview her personally.

I advise her to gather all available funds, including donations from family and friends; take her children and disappear for a time. I tell her that her husband is in a politically appointed position, and a threat to his job (such as revealing his vile treatment of his wife) is often viewed by personality types like his, as a threat to his own life. I validate her concerns and suggest she do all in her power to de-escalate the situation by reassuring him that she won't publicize their problems.

She doesn't think she can escape; she feels his reach is too long. She feels helpless, not knowing how to extricate herself from the trap he has constructed. She knows she has done the right thing in leaving him, but fears the consequences. I know that statistically, the most dangerous time for a woman in an abusive relationship is just after she leaves her partner. I tell her that her instincts are on point.

I also know that what this woman needs more than anything else is to rebuild her sense of self, lost during twelve years of abuse. Being lost is a state of mind. According to Laurence Gonzales, author of "Deep Survival: Who Lives, Who Dies and Why," it is caused by *"the inability to make the mental map match the environment."*[3] This definition is particularly accurate in cases of long term disempowerment.

I look at her, and see a brave woman and a desperate one. I see a woman in a situation where she needs an advantage; the leverage that comes from experiencing a new facet of the power locked within her. I have given her the right advice, but it is not enough. She is afraid to risk choosing options that she feels are beyond her ability to execute. Realizing this, I suggest enrolling her in the Survival Response Conditioning program, because I know that undertaking it will be one of the most empowering experiences of her life. Afterward, possessing new-found clarity and resolve, she will be better prepared to make powerful choices. She agrees, signs the necessary paperwork, and enrolls in the program for the calendar date of Sunday, April 27, 2003.

I call her twice during the next two weeks to uplift and encourage her, and her responses are cautious but optimistic. It is Saturday, April 26. My staff is making preparations for the program the following day. I send one of them to the local hardware store to purchase necessary items. He returns; face ashen with news of a murder/suicide in front of the hardware store, seconds before his arrival. Instantly I remember her situation—and in my heart I know. The story makes national headlines, because she is not instantly killed. For nine days, she hangs on, fighting a losing battle for her life from a hospital bed. Her name is Crystal Judson Brame and her husband, the man who shot her and then killed himself is David Brame, Chief of Police in Tacoma, Washington.

Chapter 2

"Houston, We Have a Problem..."

"We don't see things as they are. We see them as we are."

–Anais Nin

I will never forget the first time I held my newborn son in my arms. As his faint but firm pulse beat through my skin and his tiny fingers gripped one of mine, I felt a powerful, primal current surge through my body. In that moment, *I assumed a new identity.* An unexplored facet of myself leaped out and enfolded my son in a protective shroud of energy. I knew then, without doubt or measure, I would sacrifice my life to keep him safe. I am sure my experience is shared by the vast majority of parents.

Nature equips us with a fierce and implacable resolve to stand between our children and anything that would harm them. This drive is so powerful that it replaces and supersedes even the survival instinct—our prime directive before we become parents. Animals in the natural world possess this same drive, and it is in perfect accord with their instincts and abilities. An animal's life in the wild conditions it to its environment from birth, by repeated exposure to hazard under terrible pressure: stakes that have life–and–death consequences. In spite of this, animals succeed in raising their offspring to self-sufficiency much more often than not in spite of the vastly hostile environment they inhabit.

At defining moments in our lives, like the birth of a child, a close brush with death or an intense, shocking surprise, we briefly revisit the sub-text of our will to survive. Ironically, it is an alien place to most of us, especially considering the elemental role it plays in our nature. Most of us seldom, if ever, ask ourselves why this should be, yet it is a very significant question when exploring the subject of personal safety.

Our society has produced an environment where many of us have—to one degree or another—lost connection to our primal abilities. We spend most of our life within what we would consider "normal" parameters. We *rarely* confront circumstances that require familiarity with our absolute limits. Over generations, we have been weaned away from dependence on our primal skill set: the instinctive ability to sense and avoid harm from an outside source, or to confront and defeat it. Luckily, this is not a permanent loss. The survival instinct is hardwired into all of us, and it is impossible to erase it entirely. The problem: Whatever is not used regularly loses effectiveness, accuracy, and speed. Subconsciously we sense this, and it affects our perception in subtle but profound ways.

Heads or Tails?

"Through the Eyes of a Predator" and "The Crystal Judson Brame Story" are examples that highlight two aspects of our perception of the threat environment. Predators like *"The Edge"* exist, but they are statistically rare despite the extensive media coverage they receive. They cannot be ignored but to place undue emphasis on them detracts from the energy and focus needed to overcome the regrettably familiar abuse from more common sources. What happened to Crystal has become a regular occurrence. The only thing that attracted national news coverage was the fact that her husband was the Chief of Police. Caught between scenarios both unlikely and commonplace, we focus on the first while we are auto-conditioned to the second. This can only happen because we are profoundly unfamiliar with the predatory environment. Before we dig into that subject, however, it is necessary to have a more accurate picture of what causes us to be internally vulnerable as individuals. This is what we will focus on in this chapter.

When we think of vulnerability, our focus fastens reflexively on action: What we do, don't do or should do. This is because survival has to do with *results* and the actions that produce them. Our attention is attracted to visible, tangible outcomes. Yet, *vulnerability is directly linked to an intangible: what and how we think*—and the mental programs that drive these thought processes. I believe that the slow divorce from our natural assets has made many of us prone to weakness and imbalance in four vital areas. All of them are mental programs that help shape our identity.

Mental Programs

1. Self–concept
2. Energy projection
3. Default emotional state
4. Self–determination

It would be helpful to view these programs as scales, with high and low ends. How each of us fits within these parameters is unique. The objective is to create a framework that will help us grasp what has happened to us as individuals in this culture, especially regarding our connection to the predatory environment.

Imbalance in Self–Concept

Self-concept is pivotal to personal safety. This has to do with our personal and internal identity, the *"who I am and how I work"* part of our relationship to others. Self–concept, self–image, and self–esteem are terms that have come to be used interchangeably. This is unfortunate because each of them were intended to clearly define a different aspect of our emotional machinery. For our purpose here, it will be helpful to view **self–concept** as *the story we tell ourselves about ourselves*. **Self–image** is *what we think of ourselves, based on how closely our life reflects our story*. **Self–esteem** is *a measure of how our personal judgment between self–concept and self–image makes us feel about ourselves*. Taken together, they function like gauges on the dashboard of an automobile, giving us the advantage of monitoring our emotional fitness.

On the low end, poor self–esteem (the de-valuing of self) leads to self–doubt, submissiveness, vulnerability and helplessness. People with poor self–esteem are often ashamed of how they feel about themselves and occasionally attempt to disguise this by projecting defensiveness or arrogance. Think of the last time you witnessed a customer treating a waiter poorly for no apparent reason, or a woman who consistently makes derogatory comments about an acquaintance who dresses better than she does. Without realizing it, these people are broadcasting their lack of self-esteem to those around them. A superiority complex, the other end of the spectrum, can be fatal because it leads to deadly errors in judgment. In the "Heads and Tails" stories, the contrast between Crystal, a victim, and *"the Edge,"* a predator, could not be more pronounced, but in reality, they are opposite ends of self–concept out of balance.

The ability to resist pressure to conform is directly linked to self–concept. Those who have a strong sense of self have very little need for validation from outside sources. These individuals think for themselves, act for themselves and do not waste too much emotional real estate worrying about what others may think of them. They are highly resistant to group think, because they correctly interpret it as an unhealthy control mechanism. This clarity and personal power result from acceptance and satisfaction with their own identity. They are not smug; they are real. Their identity is not in doubt. We all know people like this and are attracted to their courage and authenticity. Clearly, these individuals are outnumbered many times over by those who lack personal power. This occurs because the mainstream influences in our culture make it socially acceptable to surrender to the momentum of mediocrity. Given the choice, the majority of us follow the wide, beaten track—because it's easier.

How is it that so many of us find ourselves emotionally and physically vulnerable, not just in a moment of crisis, but on a day–to–day basis? This question plagued me for years, especially after I began to understand how exceptional our natural ability to navigate the threat environment truly is. After studying this contrast from numerous angles, I began to see the outline of an explanation. It is apparent that from a very early age, society exerts a powerful influence over all of us. Eventually the majority are molded to fit within it. How deeply this process is imprinted on an individual basis depends on many variables, but it is safe to say that no one is untouched.

Alice Miller, who wrote *"The Drama of the Gifted Child,"* discovered that many of her patients experienced a "split" in their loyalties early in life. She posited that children were forced to choose between an honest expression of their feelings and the approval of their parents. This choice between authenticity and parental love had devastating consequences for these children, who experienced a loss of their true selves because of *the fabrication of a false, political self that was acceptable to society*. The approval of others became the pivot on which a child's validation turned, leaving no anchor for healthy self–esteem, which is based on acceptance of all your thoughts as your own.

In *"Reviving Ophelia, Saving the Selves of Adolescent Girls,"* Mary Pipher, PH.D., built on and expanded Miller's hypothesis, stating,

> "...this process of creating false selves in children follows a continuum that ranges from basic socialization to abuse. It is present in all families: All parents accept and reject some of their children's behaviors and teach children to sacrifice some wholeness to social acceptability."[4]

Miller placed the responsibility for this traumatic split on parents, but Pipher, in her study of adolescent girls, zeroed in on modern culture as the culprit:

> "With puberty, girls face enormous cultural pressure to split into false selves. The pressure comes from schools, magazines, music, television, advertisements and movies. It comes from peers... In public they become who they are supposed to be ...This is where girls learn to be nice rather than honest." -Ibid. 38, 39

I believe the dynamic that Miller and Pipher bring to light has an even more subtle and universal application. They are correct in identifying the groups they studied as being particularly affected, but it doesn't stop there. *Everyone* is molded by this process and to a degree loses both identity and confidence in the process. This "baggage" is carried into the adult life, and the problem is compounded as parents re-enforce the cycle in their children. When it comes to the assets most needed in hazardous situations, our culture has a significantly weakening influence. Some fight back and regain the lost ground. Others are partially healed. Many never reclaim their lost self and the empowered life that should have been theirs to live is gone forever.

Imbalance in Energy Projection

The force field of energy you project is significant in at least two ways. It either attracts or repels those with predatory intent and it regulates the level of success or failure of your interaction with them. *Disempowerment is caused by a lack of belief in self.* Overconfidence, the opposite extreme, is caused by a lack of knowledge and experience in combination with an overinflated ego. In the same way that a shark smells blood, a predator senses the energy signature of a disempowered individual. Self-defense instructors tell their students to have good eye contact, along with erect posture, and to broadcast their awareness by frequently looking around them. These are good tactics, but they are of limited value without true confidence (belief based on knowledge and experience). Predators are extremely sensitive to discrepancies in behavior and it is not wise to rely on trying to fool them in this way.

Confidence comes from *doing*. The majority of us possess the vague outline of what we *think* we might do in a given situation—in spite of never having had the experience. This is another reason we are vulnerable. Like a person who becomes accustomed to living on overextended credit, we sail along until our boat begins to sink. Our lifestyle and sense of security do not accurately reflect reality. Subconsciously, we recognize this. Ergo, false broadcast, which a predator picks up instantly.

To avoid this trap, you must be reconnected with the full array of your assets. Nothing else will suffice. It's that simple. The disempowerment Crystal and many others experience is caused in part because we feel overwhelmed—unable to extricate ourselves from situations we have failed to prepare for and do not fully understand. Additionally, as Miller and Pipher discovered, we often yield to social pressure and reject a part of whom we are in order to manage fear in a way that is acceptable to society. The problem is the approval of society has little real value in the arena of survival because society itself cannot protect us. Was the Brame tragedy preventable? Yes, but not by society—only the individual has that front-line opportunity and responsibility. The community's role is primarily supportive. It is not designed to initiate action, but rather to respond to it—as evidenced by the fact that even dedicated police officers rarely prevent a crime *in commission*. Mostly, they attempt to achieve closure in the aftermath. All of this leads us to focus on the following basic principle:

> *Those who do not use their natural gifts to preserve and protect themselves risk the eventual loss of everything, including their own life.*

Society, community, friends and family are greatly limited in aiding individuals who expect protection to come from an external source. Like prisoners shuffling down gray corridors, we have become conditioned to dependence instead of exercising self-reliance.

Imbalance in Default Emotional State

This term describes the "at rest" position of our emotional intensity meter, when we are in a frame of mind that is natural to us. Where is this mark between anxiety and complacency? Are we hyper-vigilant or unconcerned to the point of carelessness? What is normal? In the next chapter, we will address anxiety and complacency individually. Right now our focus is the relationship between the two, and where we (the average individuals in our culture) park our comfort envelope on this scale.

Anxiety and complacency rise and fall over the tipping point of fear. Most of us live our daily lives without devoting much conscious thought to threat. Meanwhile, beneath the seemingly calm exterior, deep currents of emotion, many of them fear-based, are in constant movement. Signals, both subtle and overt, tap into and trigger our subconscious, emotional body. It is the *frequency* of our response to these triggers that determine our level of daily stress. If the signals are constant *and continually ignored*, we gradually become conditioned to even the most extreme circumstances. This was Crystal's experience. It was the reason she took so long to exit her situation, first because she could not accept the reality of what her relationship with her husband was becoming, and later, precisely because she grew accustomed to it.

How many of us are ensnared in the same process? At core, fear is one of the most basic common denominators of human experience. Fear of rejection, fear of abandonment, fear of failure, fear of separation and fear of death are normal for human beings. We have all tasted them at one time or another in our lives. We listen to the evening news and hear of predators like *"the Edge."* We are inundated by sound-bytes that inject us with anxiety regarding our children's safety, but they seldom focus on effective safeguards and solutions. At the same time, we accept the occurrence of spousal abuse—episodes of domestic terrorism—as commonplace, hardly worth a ho-hum on our alarm meter. In spite of this, the majority of us are convinced we are protected from these dangers as if we live some sort of charmed life. Like a watermark, this manufactured security subtly influences both our perception of the environment we inhabit, and our attitude toward it. Our personal comfort level demands that we feel secure. To achieve this, it bullies us into believing *"things like that don't happen to people like us."*

It is the complacency of parents in a sunny park that a predator like *"the Edge"* will seek to exploit. Although the story is fictional, *"the Edge"* is a composite character constructed from actual situations. Everything he did has been attempted in the real world at one time or another, often with success.

The ordeal and demise of Crystal Judson Brame should be a reality check for us all. If anyone ought to have been able to feel secure, it was her. She lived in one of the safest communities in the Pacific Northwest (as far as crime rates go). She was the wife of the Police Chief in a large city. She had loving, concerned parents. She should have been able to turn to an army of officers and their families. Instead, many were in willful ignorance of the situation, and some actively participated in covering up what they knew. This reminds me of a statement by Helen Keller, who was blind, deaf and dumb from the time she was nineteen months old:

> *"Security is mostly superstition. It does not exist in nature, nor do the children of men, as a whole, experience it. Avoiding danger is no safer in the long run than outright exposure..."*[5]

For me, this is the crux of the matter: In our fixation with security, we are grasping for evidence of something that exists solely in our minds *and subconsciously, we know it.* That is why we ride the teeter-totter of anxiety and complacency. We want to feel the comfort and provisional stability of the latter, but like an impudent demon, the world we live in keeps us in the air by jabbing us with the sharp end of its pitchfork.

Self-determination

By definition, apathy is the absence or suppression of passion, emotion or excitement. It can also mean lack of interest in or concern for things that others find moving or exciting. *It is the state of emotional disconnection.* This is significant because emotion is the fuel that produces action. Without it, we are lethargic, unmotivated and easily victimized. On the other side of the spectrum, frantic activity wears us down and results in emotional burn-out. People caught in this back eddy are afraid to be afraid, but since they have no viable strategy for dealing with fear, action—any action—becomes a distraction from unease, instead of the solution it was intended to be.

We become easily discouraged because our culture has led us to have an unrealistic level of expectation. Success is expected to be readily attainable, especially for our youth, and when they enter the school of hard knocks and get a black eye, they are shocked. They look around, see that the same thing is happening to their peers and conclude this is the status quo: that they have been lied to. Disillusion leads back to apathy. The result is that in many areas, especially preparation for unfamiliar, hostile environments, *little is achieved because little is dared.*

Of all the fears common to us, fear of the unknown is the most prevalent, and arguably the most limiting. It is the death of all our dreams, the chalk outline of all our aspirations to greatness; it throttles our creativity and stifles our joy. The woman who stays with the abusive spouse does so because it is easier to experience emotional and physical torture than to face an unfamiliar future alone. The man who endures a job he hates sticks with it because it is familiar: he fears being unable to find something better. Years ago, I heard Zig Ziglar, the famous motivational speaker tell his audience, "We become trapped by what we do know and don't like because we are afraid to try what we don't know and might love."

In all four of these areas, an imbalance causes us to miss the all-important central positions. Accordingly, we often find ourselves ensnared by positive or negative extremes, with the high end (complacency, overconfidence, arrogance and aggression) frequently projected to conceal the shameful low. Both extremes are actually supported by society, *and this support revolves around risk.* Those who experience low self-esteem, disempowerment, anxiety and apathy tend to be risk avoiders, while those plagued by complacency, overconfidence, superiority and aggression are often risk takers. Popular culture showcases risk takers as brave, gritty heroes, while the establishment and academia reward risk avoiders with the mantle of intelligence. Our society cultivates victimization by distracting us with assorted fears and then dividing us into separate camps in the same way a boxing referee pushes fighters into opposing corners at the end of a round. The media feeds off these imbalances and "entertains" us with our own weakness and destruction.

Whether we find ourselves mired in an imbalanced extreme or closer to the center of the dial, a majority of us share the resulting two deficiencies: complications with our perception of reality and a knowledge deficit regarding both the predatory environment and our ability to navigate it. Without a clear understanding of these two common denominators, how is it possible to choose wisely between avoided and accepted risk?

Perception of Reality

Our culture *has* painted a false picture of fear and done a splendid job of convincing us that it is real. It has done the same thing with rage and guilt. Each of these emotions is designed to do a specific job that benefits us under certain circumstances, but *because they don't feel nice*, it's easy to broad-brush them as negative and to shun them. The result? When activated, these emotional alarms do not receive the critical focus they deserve and consequently cannot execute their function in preserving our safety. In modern society, reason and logic are given more credibility than our intuitive powers. The truth is they are turtle-slow and often arrive at mistaken conclusions in the initial trauma of a survival situation.

One of the underlying causes of this reality disconnect involves the manner in which we define positive and negative. For most of us, emotion exerts a powerful influence on logic. The vast majority of people in our society reveal this subtle bias in their language. When asked whether we view something as positive or negative, our reply often revolves around the way we feel. This is a very interesting response. It clearly indicates that emotion colors perception to an astounding degree.

For example, while certain individuals are reluctant to fly on commercial jets, which are statistically safe, they are enthusiastic about piloting their own small aircraft, a much riskier endeavor. The issue for these individuals is possession of direct, personal control over their immediate situation. They feel safer, even though the action they are taking is statistically much riskier. *Their emotional safety trumps their physical safety.* By degrees, we are all affected by this ingrained impulse. How we view reality can become more important than what might actually be happening. This is the principle upon which denial works. If we view something as negative because of the way we feel, when that same thing actually has a positive outcome, then our perspective may not be in our best interest, no matter how reflexively we cling to it. Not surprisingly, the more degrees of separation we succeed in placing between ourselves and awareness of danger, the safer we *feel*. In certain respects, we are better at protecting our comfort zone than we are at protecting our life.

In spite of this, occasionally an event takes place that is so shocking that it forces a reckoning. The Brame tragedy is a case in point. For a brief moment, it was both a wake-up call and a catalyst for reform, specifically within law-enforcement circles and more generally on the subject of domestic violence. Even so, the focus of public shock centered on corruption and cover-up in the local police force, rather than the violent actions of a trusted public servant. This is an eloquent example of the tenacious nature of denial. Individually and collectively, we are willing to go to great lengths to avert our attention from even a hint that violence can touch us personally.

Knowledge Deficit: Our Assets

One of the central themes of this book is that *fear itself is not negative*. Given its proper place and balance, it is often a powerful signal intended to warn us of the presence of danger. Fear is designed to enable us to make life-saving course corrections. Fear is not the enemy that so many believe it is. Instead, *ignorance* of our assets and abilities, of our superb capacity to navigate threat and the *lack of experience* in using these mechanisms lead us to distrust the very safeguards nature built into us.

Part of the problem is that we have failed to recognize these assets as *gifts*. We are not acquainted with the advantages nature has blessed us with, because we are no longer intimately acquainted with nature itself. Most of us don't even know we have them, never having had the occasion to use them. These advantages are further disguised by the fact that the circumstances that reveal them are often extremely unpleasant and thus avoided like a bad smell. But is that what we really want? Have we considered the real meaning of avoiding an experience *at all cost* or has this become just a figure of speech? Do we weigh the positive benefit of having the experience itself and what that experience can do for us in terms of knowledge and empowerment—with the resulting growth in quality of life? No? What a tragedy! No wonder we are so easily victimized, and so filled with debilitating fear!

Imagine the effect of having a different relationship with fear, one based on respect and appreciation for the accuracy of the radar we possess, an understanding that is intimately familiar with how our mental, physical and emotional machinery functions. What would happen to our level of confidence, our sense of vitality and control?

These are some of the topics we will explore in the following chapters. My objective is to introduce you to the Adrenal Advantage, and facilitate your acquisition of the vibrant, personal power that is your birthright. Once this is achieved, you will possess a profound desire to transmit these gifts to your children.

Knowledge Deficit: The Predatory Environment

Even with its softening influences, our modern, civilized society has not diminished our intent or our potential to act decisively in the best interest of our children. However, our lifestyle has overwhelmed our instincts. We lack the specific conditioning that would develop survival skills gained by direct immersion in a rugged environment. When we think of a predatory environment, many of us flash straight to the wilderness, jungle or even the ocean. We think we understand them; after all, we have been exposed to them hundreds of times on the History Channel. We take vacations there. We go camping, boating, hiking and skiing, with some idea of the hazards. We have special gear to make our explorations more enjoyable and... safer, but we go with this *"vacation state of mind,"*[6] as Laurence Gonzales points out. We don't really expect trouble; it is not a part of the entertainment. We are twice removed from real danger, first in our level of expectation and second in our level of engagement. Even within the natural predatory environment, we are rarely, if ever, the *target* of predators. We do not match wits with them; our life is not forfeit if we fail to escape, and we only engage in life or death contests with savage beasts in our most vivid, sweat-soaked nightmares.

Yet, the predatory environment that we actually inhabit is much more dangerous. Unlike our excursions into the wilderness, we make no preparation, have no special gear and have very little idea of the real hazards. There is zero expectation of danger, because we seldom view the human environment as predatory. Worse, the predators who troll the human environment have equal and sometimes better intelligence than we do. They are not afraid of fire, and they combine intellect with the natural, intuitive assets that civilization has largely conditioned out of us. By and large, we are completely vulnerable to the human predators who wish us harm. We are in our world until they step into it. Then we are in theirs.

Once we reject playing the odds as a viable option in pursuit of increased safety, the only solution that has any chance of real success is a preparation that *conditions* our primal assets back into us, along with environment-specific knowledge.

In 1988, while on a family vacation in Hawaii, I had an experience that underscored the importance of having specific knowledge of my immediate environment. My wife and I, along with our young son, decided to go body surfing at Sandy Beach on Oahu. We had never been there before, and were anxious to try a new experience.

After the initial novelty of body surfing began to wear off, I paddled my boogie board beyond the breakers, for a relaxing float on the swells. I remember how peaceful it all was—the warmth of the water, the hypnotic rising and falling, the silence. I had experienced the numbing cold of the Pacific Coast, where the water was my enemy every moment I was in it, and this was so... wonderful. I was gazing out to sea, mesmerized by this new world, when I casually glanced back. To my horror, the shore was just a thin line in the distance. I was caught in a powerful riptide and being carried farther out to sea with each second.

Knowing I was not an exceptional swimmer, I was instantly terrified. I could feel fear draining my energy. My first panicked impulse was to turn and paddle for the shore with all my might, but then a curious thing happened. My mind became very still and very clear. I remember distinctly hearing the voice of a friend who had been a lifeguard, and his description of riptides: *"They are rivers in the ocean, Bill. To get out of the riptide's current, you must cross the river."*

I began to paddle parallel to the shore, but I was so far out that I knew I had to conserve my strength. In an attempt to work with the waves, I allowed each swell to carry me to its peak. I paddled only on the descent. Within five minutes, it became obvious that I had escaped the riptide and eventually would make the shore.

When my feet finally touched sand, I was at least a mile down the beach from where I started. After this experience, I began to understand the hidden danger of riptides. Feeling helpless against the mighty power of the ocean prompts knee jerk panic that results in a direct struggle with the current, a struggle few can win. Had I not known exactly what to do and been able to perform those actions under terrible emotional pressure, I am sure I would have drowned. The turning point in this experience happened when fear pushed everything out of my mind but my friend's two life-saving sentences. I have never experienced such clarity, before or since.

If I were unfortunate enough to find myself caught in a riptide again, the situation would be much less alarming to me. I know this as surely as the sun rises and sets. The *experience* conditioned me in a way I can't ever forget. My response would be instinctive and automatic, and fear, while present, would not have nearly the same hold over me. This is the experiential format of learning. It is pure. It is simple. It can change your life, if you are willing to accept its challenges.

*   *   *

Years ago, I got my first taste of Survival Response Conditioning under Dr. Jeff Alexander, the founder of Warrior Spirit. In his presentations, he often referred to the flow of energy and emotion in human beings as "expansion" or "contraction." Expansion is descriptive of joy, inspiration, the positive, vitality and enthusiasm. Contraction is descriptive of grief, the negative, boredom, lethargy and discouragement. It's like breathing. As you inhale oxygen, you accept life, and you expand. As you exhale, you are emptied of the source of life and you contract.

Our connection to nature and natural processes has become fragmented, imbalanced and contracted. We have been smothered, primarily by our society and culture. Like new politicians, we enter the arena with good intent and at length discover that we have been corrupted, without being aware of it. This is the default position *and condition* for large numbers of our society. Ensnared, weakened and vulnerable to forces that can victimize us, we are unaware of our actual level of exposure. Yet, we feel entitled to a safe, protected existence! This is our reality. It is normal. Why is this sad state of affairs readily accepted, and how did it sneak up on us?

Chapter 3

The Victim Factory

"The best way for the shepherd to protect his sheep…
is to teach them not to be sheep."

—Unknown

I would like to offer you a formal introduction to a Club. This fraternity has a long and venerable history, extending back to the days immediately after shoes were first invented. In that far-off time, a man (whose name has been lost in the mists of antiquity) making a pilgrimage, gradually became aware that his right foot had begun to ache. As the traveler considered the way that the pain caused a limp, he noticed another traveler with what appeared to be a similar malady.

The two travelers became engaged in conversation and noticing a conveniently situated resting place, stopped to take advantage of it. At length, they discovered that they did indeed have something in common. Each traveler had a small rock in his right shoe. They discussed all the reasons why the rock caused such irritation and strategies for managing the discomfort. During the discussion, they noticed other travelers with a limp, and wondered if their strategies might be of some use to these folks.

To make a short story shorter, they went their separate ways, and each ultimately started a self-help group designed to deal with the negative effects of the "rock in the shoe" syndrome. As time wore on, offshoot groups with different management philosophies developed. Some took the "position theory," that the rock was better situated at either the front or back of the shoe, rather than the middle. Others insisted that positioning didn't matter at all; it was mental conditioning that would give the strongest relief, and yet others felt that communicating about the problem was the key. Creative thinking abounded: thicker socks, softer shoes; exercises to promote tougher feet.

Some advocated the rhythm method: switching the rock from the right shoe to the left and Vice Versa. For a while, many were persuaded that loving the pain was the answer, but that idea had a short history. There was a movement to embrace and accept your rock, and seminars like "7 Proven Ways to Turn Your Rock into Success." Serious money began to change hands. A whole industry of products and support networks grew up around the rock dilemma. Eventually even the government became involved, and taxes were levied. Books were written and discussed on talk shows: arguments and fights broke out, and the only thing that anyone could agree on was the established FACT that rocks were there to stay.

As ridiculous as this little story appears, it serves to remind us of the power of an *entrenched assumption*. All of us, at one time or another, encounter individuals with opinions they hold with unshakeable faith, which we *clearly* see are inaccurate. No amount of reasoning, evidence or argument budges them. The more confidence these individuals have in their position, the more stubborn they become. I encourage you to consider that we are just like them. "They" is "us." Human beings have a profound psychological need to be right. All of us are susceptible to this mental programming, and when it is combined with the equally powerful desire to be accepted, it's easy to see how the phenomenon called "group think" is adopted.

Pre-conceived ideas, especially those common assumptions generally accepted by society as a whole, form a complex and layered mental construct. Inside this structure, we form opinions, make decisions, choose friends, think, create, react, respond etc. For the sake of argument, let's call this structure our personal comfort zone. This zone, this state of awareness and acceptance, is linked to the zones of everyone within our sphere of influence. Like the World Wide Web, it is a network connecting the social consciousness of our society. We are highly resistant to any change that would force us to alter this cocoon of assumptions. This narrative is so widely accepted, so completely relied upon, that few, if any, ever question the foundation upon which it rests.

An entrenched assumption is very difficult to dislodge, because doing so requires an original moment of clarity, followed by a monumental shift in thinking. Compounding the problem is the fact that often an incorrect assumption is obscured by layers of reasoning which by themselves are accurate and sound. If we don't dig deeply enough, if we stop short of the foundation, we will never know if it supports the structure. The whole body will appear to uphold a conclusion that is actually faulty. It is hard work to correct these flawed ideas. It goes against our nature. People who engage in this type of fact-finding receive little co-operation from their peers and quite often they experience determined opposition. Anything that erodes our comfort zone is immediately and automatically viewed as a threat. Theodore Roosevelt once said, *"The men with the muck-rake are often indispensable to the well-being of society, but only if they know when to stop raking the muck."*[7]

Boat rockers face the possibility of being pitched overboard if the other passengers become fearful or are aroused to anger. Knowing this, it takes great courage to challenge an entrenched assumption. It often entails significant risk and we are addicted to taking the path of least resistance.

In addition, it is hard to imagine we may have been in error about something that we have never questioned before, and more difficult when the issue revolves around a commonly accepted belief. We tend to doubt ourselves, tortured with the thought, "How can I be right when so many others think I'm wrong?" Ironically, once it becomes clear that we have been in error, we wonder how in the world we didn't "get it" sooner.

Sometimes the truth is not buried deeply at all, but hides effectively in plain sight. It is a proven fact that the mind interprets what the eye sees. Our understanding of an issue or an event can alter or re-invent what we actually experience. Consider the following statement:

> *"We fail to see things, not because they are hidden, but because we are accustomed to them." –Unknown*

One of the most powerful and valuable principles that I have personally internalized was first introduced to me by Dr. Phillip C. McGraw in his book "Life Strategies." This principle is the title of Chapter 7: "There is No Reality, Only Perception." In other words, what we believe we see becomes real to us; moreover, it defines our perception so completely that the "seeing is believing" mode becomes our default setting. Our limited concept of reality can actually impede our progress.

In the time of Christopher Columbus, the entire population, from king to peasant, believed the earth was flat; that if you sailed too far, you would go over the edge, never to return. For hundreds of years, this assumption kept the medieval world small, because no one dared to examine it. All the edges of their maps said, "Here be Dragons."

In the field of medicine, physicians treating stroke victims routinely prescribed a maximum of six weeks of physical therapy following the stroke, because it had been accepted for decades that this was the post-stroke window of recovery. Thanks to the science of neuro-plasticity, we now know that in many cases, regardless of elapsed time, partial and even full recovery is possible with therapy of the right type and duration. Dr. Norman Doidge in his excellent book, "The Brain that Changes Itself," details a number of examples of recovery so astounding that we are tempted to think of them as miracles, all brought about as a result of research that was "outside the box."

Why am I bringing all this up? Over the years, I have discovered a number of roadblocks in the way the subject of personal safety in general and child safety in particular is commonly taught and understood. These roadblocks are incorrect, entrenched assumptions which are, at best, misleading and, at worst dangerous.

It is my desire to be absolutely straight with you. My observations and methodology are outcome-based. I care not one wit about political correctness or whether an ideology is popular. My staff and I are committed to doing what actually works to keep children safe and to train them to be as powerful and aware as their maturity level will allow. We have discovered that, with the proper training methods, a child's awareness, ability and skill level can be improved far beyond what is currently acknowledged to be possible by society.

What is presented here will directly challenge the thinking behind a number of assumptions our society has fostered—and you may be comfortable with. In order to achieve this objective, it will be necessary to expose the shortcomings and weaknesses of the methods and programs that are presently in vogue. You need proven and viable alternatives, so that you can make intelligent choices regarding your children's safety.

To accomplish this, it will be necessary to take a good, hard look at what we have become as parents and as a society in general, and where it has led us. This is a reality check, and it will not be easy or pleasant. However, it will be an honest examination of the truth, based on long experience and hands-on training, as well as specialized study and research. I challenge you as a parent, as the only responsible guide and mentor your children may ever have and solely for their sake, to do the hardest thing imaginable: to keep an open mind in the face of long-standing idealistic prejudice. I am a father myself and consider it my duty to question everything remotely connected with my children's safety, from a pin on the floor to society's most hallowed precept. I have that divine and inalienable right as a parent, and so do you: *The buck stops here.* Are you with me?

Are you willing to take a fresh look at your own beliefs and behavior patterns? Are you willing to re-examine what society claims are politically correct methodologies? If not, I would ask, "What are you afraid of? What do you stand to lose? Does maintaining your *comfort zone* fill your horizon so completely that becoming a more informed parent is not worth the effort to expand it?" Presented in this light, the answers to these questions are obvious and clear. It is time to remove the rock from your shoe.

Modern society believes with unquestioning certainty that its members have the right to be safe. Central to that theme is the safety and protection of our children. We pride ourselves on our advanced civilization, on our ability to negotiate differences, on our skill at compromise. We believe in the power of community and in united effort, especially with regard to our children's safety. We expect cooperative effort to be expended by those we have elected at local, state and national levels of government. We have adopted the concept that it takes a village to raise a child who will be a productive member of our society. A profound and deep level of expectation has led us to feel entitled to these community benefits. It is the American Way.

The ability to unite around a common cause opposing a common enemy has from time immemorial been a yardstick by which we measure cultural health and viability. If we are able to circle the wagons and point the guns outward, directed at a perceived threat, we feel stronger, both individually and collectively. As long as the threat is actually outside the perimeter and our united focus remains vigilantly upon it, the model retains its integrity. However, it begins to degrade the moment the wolves get behind the wagons, especially if they are able to cloak their appearance so that they are indistinguishable from the rest of us.

Stop and ask yourself honestly which is the more accurate and realistic interpretation of our society: wagons circled, guns pointed and wolves circling the periphery, or wolves that look like men within the circle, as families gather peacefully around the cook fires? Now, imagine you had been trained all your life to believe that you have the right to be safe—that you are safe—*because you are inside the circle of wagons*, rather than outside of them. Which is more important at this point, a reality check or maintaining our precious comfort zone?

Collectively, our society is terrified of openly confronting this truth: The wolves are not just among us; they are members of our most trusted inner circles. They are our fathers, our brothers, our sons, our uncles and our best friends. They are our coaches, our counselors, our teachers and our priests. The wolves among us all follow nature's law of attraction: Wherever game is plentiful and easily available, they will congregate.

Luckily, Mother Nature provides all of its creatures with incredibly powerful and accurate defense mechanisms. Her means of keeping these 'tools" sharp is to *use them regularly*. Survival depends on practical, instinctive exercise of these skills. It is crucial that we acknowledge the power of this process. There are no shortcuts because what falls into disuse fades with time and becomes only the faintest memory. Like a "safe house," our modern society has sheltered us to the point we are no longer familiar with the assets that nature has blessed us with. We have brainwashed ourselves into believing there is a civilized approach and we want methods that are kind, gentle and humane. We have come to believe our children should be shielded from not only what would harm them, but from what *might* harm them. To illustrate this point, allow me to make a comparison and then draw a parallel from it. Consider the following question: From the perspective of a parent, which environment would you consider safer in pioneer days: a city in the colonies or an isolated farm in the wilderness?

What would your response be? The great majority would automatically choose the city as the safer environment, because it is what most of us are familiar with, and we tend to fear what we do not know. However, a closer examination of reality presents a different picture. In the cities of this era, it was common to find heaps of rotting garbage lying openly in the streets, infested with rats the size of cats. Raw sewage contaminating both running and ground water was common place. The crowded, squalid living conditions led to frequent epidemics of fatal communicable disease. High crime rates involving thieves, murderers, rapists and child molesters, as well as the practice of throwing debtors into prison, often left children without the protective hedge of a complete family circle. Child slave-labor, or conditions very close to it, ensnared large numbers of children in a hopeless cycle of poverty and despair. The callous scramble to get to the top of the social heap or die poor was justification for all manner of terrible habits and the resulting decay of moral character.

Now consider the frontier: clean air and water, very little risk of communicable disease, no crime to speak of, the lack of evil influences, the wholesomeness of family, the value of hard work and daily visible progress in labor. The risks here were very clear cut: unfriendly natives and wild animals (who generally fear and avoid human beings). The availability of convenient medical care was a moot point because the practices of the day led to almost as many deaths and maimings as doctors prevented. Children raised in this environment became strong, healthy and self-reliant. They were trained *by exposure* to skillfully navigate in and around hazardous circumstances. This bold and courageous outlook on life, in combination with the familiarity of experience in their environment produced individuals who carved this nation out of the wilderness with their bare hands.

The irony here is that we often accept obvious hazards just because we are used to them, while we avoid the very circumstances nature and "primitive" societies have always used to prepare their youth to reach their powerful potential. Modern parents who deliberately expose their children to threatening circumstances would be considered grossly irresponsible. What for? We live in a safe and civilized culture! There is no need! Accordingly, our children grow up with virtually no adaptation to the threat environment: They are unprepared for it, and so are we. The odds insulate us from contemplating the consequences of being unprepared, until we become a statistic, and then they cannot be ignored. There was a reason why our great-great-great-grandfather's told their sons, "Go west, young man!"

Right here I want to draw a line in the sand. If what follows seems harsh, please bear with me—my intent is redemptive. It is imperative that we have a way to test the accuracy of our beliefs regarding the threat environment. We raise our children with the beliefs and values that are the building blocks of the safe house. We shelter them and guard them; they are surrounded by a protective web of family, community, government and society. We call this a civilized culture. This is our reality. Yet, in the briefest moment, all this can collapse like a house of cards in a puff of wind: the instant a child ends up in the crosshairs of a predator. Everything familiar disappears and nothing remains but *predator and prey*. In a twinkling, the social mores we pride ourselves on are replaced by what was lurking below all along: nature's law of survival. Nor does it have to be a child: Many adults who are suddenly and personally exposed to a predatory environment are unable to extricate themselves and become victims twice over—vulnerable because of faulty ideology and easy prey for those who would take advantage of this weakness. Our concept of the world may be comforting, but the moment we step outside the lines we have created, whether or not we realize what we have done, the rules change.

Make no mistake about it: The real world is the one that has been in existence for thousands of years. This world is the open spaces between cities; it exists in every street and its tunnels and passageways wind invisibly through each and every home. It is a sub-text in the mind and heart of every man, woman and child who has ever lived and ever will live. The imposter here is the construct we have created called culture. It is a thin veneer woven of gossamer strands, as insubstantial as cotton, but it is soft, comforting and helps us sleep at night. So for most of us, it appears to work out to our benefit in the short term. The safe house that society has created and our mind has adopted, fits our concept of ourselves neatly; it helps us, indeed it encourages us to live in a state of denial.

We have believed the pleasant fiction that because we live in a "safe" society, when something does happen it won't be happening to us. But what is a safe society? Is it a place where bad things rarely happen because the statistics are on our side? Or is it a place where bad things rarely happen because we are vigilant and if something does occur unexpectedly, we have some skill in dealing with the consequences? I invite you to consider—which definition gives you true peace of mind?

The "safe house mentality" I have been describing is based on a number of entrenched assumptions. I call this structure the "culture of protection." Let's look at some of the planks that support this platform. This is not intended to be an exhaustive list, but for now will serve to get the point across.

The Culture of Protection

1. I have the right to be safe and so does my child.
2. Children are helpless against the power and persuasion of a predator.
3. What is difficult for adults is overwhelming for children.
4. Our duty as parents is to shelter our children from harm.
5. It is the duty of community and government to ensure that daycare businesses, the school system and society in general are safe and secure.
6. Strangers are a significant threat and should be avoided.
7. Violence is wrong and should be shunned in all its forms.
8. Civilization is not subject to the laws of nature; it is a separate and distinct environment.

This is familiar, comfortable territory that you will recognize. At face value, it seems pleasant and positive: a calm and reasoned approach that is in accord with what we hear from councilors, psychologists, educators and authority figures in general. As long as society follows the rules it creates for itself, the system will work for a majority of its participants, most of the time. Yet, we all admit that there are those who flaunt the system, break the rules and whose characters are opportunistic and predatory.

This cocoon, this safe house we have grown up around us like a garden, is dependent on the general public's ability to maintain an ideology of separation between individuals who support our rules and those who ignore them. It is "them" or "us." The culture of protection revolves around this division.

Let's briefly examine these eight entrenched assumptions that support the culture of protection mentioned above:

1. I have the right to be safe and so does my child.

You may have that right theoretically, but in the natural world, safety is not a right, but a condition that is carved out by watchfulness, vigilance and conditioning. It is more helpful to think of it as an obligation to act continuously and pro-actively in the best interest of yourself and your children, with the ultimate goal of *pre-*

paring them to survive and even thrive *on their own* in an unfriendly environment. The real problem is, when exposed to a predator, many parents feel just as vulnerable as their children. A significant percentage of modern parents cannot hand down anything of real value in this arena because they cannot give what they do not have. The truth is *we are the real problem here*, the weak link. Even when we realize this, we turn to the "experts" instead of making the necessary changes and getting the experience ourselves.

2. Children are helpless against the power and persuasion of a predator.

Very young children (ages 1-4) have virtually no awareness of their vulnerability, and during this period in their lives, the above statement is true. However, we greatly underestimate the stunningly effective radar that is hardwired into all of us from birth, waiting to be activated. Because we are unfamiliar with these mechanisms, we fail to open our children's awareness to their own abilities and to train them to use their resources effectively. To a great degree, we facilitate their level of helplessness by our own ignorance.

3. What is difficult for adults is overwhelming for children.

According to the science of neuro-plasticity, children have four to five times the number of brain cells that adults do. They acquire information faster, process it more completely and have a much higher level of comprehension than we give them credit for. Dr. Norman Doidge, whom I alluded to earlier, says it like this:

> *"Younger children often progress more quickly through brain exercises than do adolescents, perhaps because in an immature brain the number of connections between neurons, or synapses, is 50 percent greater than in the adult brain. When we reach adolescence, a "massive pruning-back" operation begins in the brain, and synaptic connections and neurons that have not been used extensively suddenly die off—a classic case "of use it or lose it."*[8]

As an example, consider the ease and rapidity with which children become bi-lingual and compare this with the difficulty adults have in acquiring fluency with a second language. If they are trained early enough, they learn to speak the new language *without accent*, something adult learners in the same environment find nearly impossible. We judge children by our own limits and those limits seldom apply. The result of this flawed thinking is that we don't challenge them beyond what **we** think they are capable of. Consider the following story:

On Friday, January 12, shortly before 8 a.m., commuters walking through the L'Enfant plaza station, D.C. witnessed a solo violin concert. During the next forty-three minutes, 1,070 people passed the performer, who played six of the most beautiful and technically difficult pieces ever written. It was six minutes before the first person stopped; during the entire performance, a total of seven people gave $32.17.

Gene Weingarten of the Washington Post was the originator of this social experiment, conducted to determine how people would respond to witnessing something extraordinary in a commonplace setting. Are people able to recognize and appreciate beauty, to perceive the remarkable? How does the average person respond to an unusual event at an inconvenient time? Many demographics were represented by those who passed by, but the only definite pattern of behavior that emerged was indifference. The vast majority passed by as if the violinist were invisible. Few seemed to notice him, and no one applauded.

The only people who consistently recognized that something rare and unusual was taking place were the young children. In that unexpected context, every single one of them noticed, wanted to listen and tried to stop. In several instances, the parent had to pull them away.

The musician was Joshua Bell, a virtuoso violinist who performs 200 times a year all over the world. He was playing a Stradivarius violin made in 1713, worth over $3.5 million. People regularly pay in excess of $100 for an average seat in a sold out auditorium to listen to him perform.[9]

What made these children respond so differently than their parents? The default setting of a young child's mind is curiosity. They were wide open and recognized an *interruption* in the normal kaleidoscope of events, a beautiful and unusual aberration striking enough that it first arrested and then captivated their interest. Unlike their parents, *they acknowledged reality and focused their attention on it,* and without exception, it was their parents who attempted to prevent them.

4. Our duty as parents is to shelter our children from harm.

This is a blatant half-truth, which left un-amended, leads us down a wrong path. Our duty as parents is to shelter our children from harm *and to transition them from the innocence of childhood to fully aware, self-sufficient, powerful adults.* To a large degree, we have abdicated that responsibility in favor of an educational system that teaches our children to be reflectors of other men's thoughts instead of thinkers for themselves. The policies school administrators and lawyers have created to keep our children safe within this environment not only disempower; they actually punish children for following nature's commands. Having been trained to believe it is uncivilized to engage in assertive self-defense when faced with a real threat, our children accept a certain level of victimization as normal and, in turn, peddle the same pablum of disempowerment and helplessness to their children. So it goes "unto the third and fourth generation."

5. It is the duty of community and government to ensure that daycare businesses, the school system and society in general are safe and secure.

Even though this is true, it is dangerous to rely on the assumption that these entities are actually doing their job, and it does not absolve us of our duty to oversee, direct, prepare and protect our children through and within those institutions. It is up to us to thoroughly interview and vet every person we entrust with the care of our children and then to check regularly that they continue to be secure. It is also necessary to begin to partner with our children early in this task, so that they gradually assume responsibility for themselves—but it is impossible to do this safely unless the utmost vigilance is exercised. This is not only difficult, it is decidedly inconvenient, which is why so many parents cheat by playing the odds.

6. Strangers are a significant threat.

Dead wrong. Ninety-three percent of all the children who become victims of adult predators know the perpetrator. The reason this misconception is so prevalent is that the media is voraciously hungry for sensational headlines. They are adept at tapping into society's deepest fears in order to attract readership, *while soothing us into inaction*—yet they remain trusted and popular. Every incident involving a stranger abduction is splashed across the front page and highlighted on the 10:00 news, while domestic incidents get fourth page coverage. The belief that strangers are a major threat is psychologically convenient because it helps us to deny that the problem is much closer to home. It establishes and strengthens the ideology of separation that supports the culture of protection.

7. Violence is wrong and should be shunned in all its forms.

Violence is neither right nor wrong; it is a fact of life. Denial of this reality is one of the most basic problems we face as a society. Accepting the reality of violence places us in the position of doing something to prepare ourselves to face it, survive it, overcome it and limit its effect on those we love. Gavin De Becker, the nation's leading expert on predicting violent behavior recommends we become familiar with what he calls *"a universal code of violence"* and concludes *"...the resource of violence is in everyone; all that changes is our view of the justification."*[10]

Nature provides us with this resource for our own protection, and in the hour of extreme need, we have the ability to tap into our primal instincts and become dangerously effective in our own defense. We should be thanking God for a survival instinct that works, instead of worrying that its occasional exercise will somehow traumatize our children or make them prone to violence.

8. Civilization is not subject to the laws of nature; it is a separate and distinct environment.

It is the height of arrogance to think that any part of nature can become greater than the whole. As advanced as human civilization is, we are powerless when confronted by nature unleashed. We can't even accurately predict the weather. This delusional thinking is a perfect example of the safe house mentality gone awry. For thousands of years, the world has functioned in the same way. Nothing is new except this set of ideals that we have conjured out of thin air and clothed ourselves with. Nature smiles and says, "The emperor has no clothes, and uh, by the way, the rest of you are naked, too!"

Interestingly, we sense this on a very subtle level; so subtle that most of us can't readily identify it, but we feel it just the same, as tiny ripples of unease on the surface of our consciousness. This is one of many reasons for the feelings of insecurity and fear we feel, when we focus on the safety of our children. Our culture is a culture of convenience, and it is second nature to attempt to pin the blame for anything that goes wrong as far away from us as possible. I believe the best way to begin a course correction is with responsibility and honesty.

*   *   *

If we fully commit to the goal of making our child a hard target, there are five mental road blocks each of us must confront. Even though we may not be bound by them all, there are well-meaning friends, relatives and acquaintances who will attempt to erect them across our route, and we will be forced to negotiate them anyway.

Mental Roadblocks

1. Confused Priorities
2. Denial
3. Complacency
4. Pro-Passive Bias
5. Protection without Preparation

Confused Priorities

For most of us, the world we live in is a confusing swirl of competing draws on our time, interests and pocketbook. We balance our careers, families, hobbies, home maintenance, vacations—when and if we have time for them—church, health and fitness concerns, and countless personal issues. We have been led to believe and we *want* to believe, that we are achieving the American Dream. In bygone days, this meant owning our own home and living a comfortable life. Today, it has come to mean much more. The American dream has evolved into the belief that we deserve it all and we can have it all. We can successfully balance and achieve excellence in *all* the afore-mentioned pursuits. The underlying premise is the belief that we do not have to give anything up. Yet, there are still only twenty-four hours in the day and seven days in a week. For each new thing crowded into our already over burdened schedules, something else must have less attention paid to it.

> *It is a law of the mind that what we possess is less important to us than what we desire, in terms of focus, attention and directed effort.*

In other words, the moment we get what we want, our mind becomes intent on achieving the next thing we think we lack. As the novelty of acquiring what we have intensely desired begins to wear off, we emotionally adjust to possession of it and we begin to take it for granted. This does not mean we are thoughtless and self-centered; rather, it highlights our busy lifestyle. We don't feel we have the time to meditate on the things that are truly important to us because we are caught in the current of achieving, increasing and enlarging our own lives. This is what the American Dream has become. I challenge you to take a good, hard look at your life and ask yourself to what degree this applies to you personally. If you view it pragmatically, you will see that this snare directly affects you and everyone you know. It has become a cultural constant.

This next thought is likely to be one of the hardest concepts in this book to grasp, accept and act upon. It surely was for me. If you can make this adjustment to your perspective, all the other things we cover together will become easier to consider, accept and implement. I invite you to consider that this same law of the mind applies to the parenting of our children, with equal or greater force than any other issue we face as adults. As our children develop from infants, to toddlers, to young children, our focus subtly changes. We shift from providing direct care, (feeding, clothing, bathing etc.) to establishing a healthy environment (nice home, good school, fun activities) for them to explore and grow in. Somewhere in this transition many of us shift our priorities from them to us. It happens gradually, and often we don't notice it at all. In many ways these changes are justifiable. After all, the reason we focus on our career, get the second job, buy the bigger house is for them, isn't it? We know that it is—that's how we view it. My question to you is, "How do you think *they* view it?" How do you think your child would answer the following questions?

- What evidence do I have that my parents care more about me than their jobs or hobbies?

- I think my parents love me, but do they like me?

- Are my parents interested in me as much as their own plans and goals?

- How come my parents spend more time doing their own thing, than they do with me?

- How can I think of my parents as my heroes, mentors or role models when I see them do things they have told me not to do?

- What is more important to my parents, my feelings or my behavior?

The best thing we can do to prepare our children for the world outside our home is to grow our relationship with them. The environmental shield we build around them is meaningless if it is constructed at the expense of their respect and love for us. If our children do not *know* they are ground zero for us, they will inevitably seek out other role models or relationships to give their loyalty and affection to. Our own actions will drive them beyond our care and control. This happens with monotonous regularity, as surely as the sun rises and sets. It is happening right now, with your friends and neighbors. It may be happening to you without your knowledge. Or, it's happening to you right now and you're devouring this book because you feel compelled to do something to reverse this alarming trend.

As parents, our priorities must be the three R's: relationship, relationship, relationship. If we want to succeed in transitioning our children from potential victim to hard target, we are going to have to re-arrange our priorities. We are going to have to accept the *fact* that we cannot have it all *at the same time*. We must be willing to post-pone some of the things that are important to us personally, so we can focus on the prime directive: becoming the single greatest positive influence in our children's lives. If we don't do it, they will certainly find others who will, because children need and desire a mentor or role model as much or more than healthy food. By allowing our children to adopt role models other than ourselves, we are relinquishing control to an unknown source. Are we going to leave that decision up to them, trusting to luck and hoping they will make wise choices, or are we going to exercise some intestinal fortitude, take the reins of control into our own hands and *become what they need us to be for them?*

Our primary objective as parents is to prepare our children to succeed in what we know can be a very unfriendly world. This can only happen as children are gradually made familiar with and conditioned to the hazards that exist there. It will *never* be accomplished with shelter and protection alone. Animal parents in the wild protect their young by continually training and preparing them to be self-sufficient. *This is a one-on-one endeavor*, involving regular, supervised exposure to hazard—identical to the dangerous situations their young will someday face alone. Failure to do this will result in the eventual death of their offspring.

As a society we are failing our children in this arena, because we have bought into the "Village Concept," which spreads the responsibility for raising our children in ever-widening circles. This allows us more personal freedom to achieve our own objectives and goals. The problem is that the so-called "village" no longer exists in urban America. Where is this closely bound community? We barely speak in passing to those who live right next to us; we are insulated from each other by cars, cubicles, cell phones and the internet. Our lives have become so complex and busy that the close-knit, supportive community of yester-year has been squeezed out. We are on our own. I am telling you directly and with all the power and passion I am capable of: *It does not take a village to raise a child.* The parameters that govern parenting are similar in every environment: A minimum of one parent with the resolve and determination to make wise, powerful choices based on good information; a parent who is willing to put that child's welfare at the forefront of every single decision—even if it means risking the parent's life.

Denial

When confronted by unpleasantness, we have two initial choices: acceptance or denial. We dread the unpleasant truth that we or our children could be victimized by a predator at any moment and we try to keep this thought as far from us as possible by resisting acceptance of it. To accept or deny a thing requires that we first be aware of it. Therefore, denial becomes a fundamental rejection of reality.

This is such an unnatural act that it upsets our emotional equilibrium and requires grotesque mental gymnastics to maintain for any length of time. As a result, those who reside in denial are nervous, unhappy and irritable—pre-occupied with maintaining what can only be described as willful blindness. Their crankiness comes from the subconscious knowledge that their effort is doomed to fail. It is an exercise in futility, because sooner or later reality confronts us in a way that cannot be ignored, usually when it is too late to apply the solutions that might have made a difference in the outcome. Consider for a moment the sinuous path our minds follow to justify denial and free us from involvement. When confronted by an unpleasant reality we:

1. Don't want to know too much because knowledge imparts responsibility and responsibility requires decision-making that might necessitate action.

2. We are not familiar with our gifts, nor how we are designed to function under severe stress, therefore,

3. We feel inadequate—unequal to the task before us. We fear failure.

4. We shun the feeling of fear, yet it is right there all the time, waiting for an opportunity to influence us.

5. We fear taking action, and we fear remaining passive, but since taking action requires an expenditure of energy, it is *easier* to remain passive.

6. We are not given to taking the path of least resistance, *we are addicted to it.*

7. By remaining in denial of reality, we insulate ourselves from it, gambling that it won't catch up with us. We become part of the problem rather than part of the solution—enablers of the cycle of victimization and violence.

For our children's sake and for our own, it is imperative that we respond to an unpleasant reality with *acceptance*. A parent in denial is a child's most potent vulnerability. Denial does not solve the problem. Denial does not make the problem go away. Denial does not give us peace of mind, which is what we are really seeking when we engage in it. Denial is a liar. It compounds the problem, because it keeps us from seeing a solution, and taking action to resolve it. Denial tries to tell us that if we accept reality, then we will have to worry ceaselessly about the feared outcome. There is only one time when denial is actually an asset: It becomes a very useful short-term psychological tool when the objective is to manage panic in an attempt to maintain sanity and with it, survival.[11] However, this caveat only applies when *everything* else has collapsed.

Worrying about the future is in reality a distraction from paying attention to what is happening in the present. It is because of this effect on the intended victim that denial is so valuable to predators. It is such a powerful mechanism that they rely on it heavily in the victimization process.

Denial is a state of willful ignorance used to justify inaction at the precise time when our senses are clearly warning us to make a decisive move in our own best interest. No wonder predators love it so much. If denial is emotional arsenic, then acceptance of reality is the elixir of life. We want peace of mind regarding our own personal safety and that of our children and are rewarded with the genuine article by accepting reality. To accept that we live in a world where terrible things can and do happen to children, perhaps *our* children, and to prepare ourselves and them to have the best chance of avoiding and overcoming threat, is a thousand times more empowering than suffering the quiet agony of denial. Those in denial often consider themselves to be hopeful people, but this is the same as standing on the railroad tracks with our hands over our eyes, hearing the approaching train. We want to avoid the problem, and our way of dealing with it is to hope it won't happen, when what we really need to do is *step off the tracks*.

Unfortunately, habitual denial dies a slow and painful death for most of us. Even when we get to the point where we are ready to admit it's time to confront the problem, many of us are waylaid by procrastination. We tell ourselves, "I'll do it, just not right now. I'll do it tomorrow, next week, when it's more convenient," etc. If enough time passes, so does the opportunity to take the action that will make a difference. Whether we stay in denial or acknowledge reality but procrastinate, the common denominator is failure to *act* in a timely manner. When we combine the influences of denial and procrastination, the result is apathy, or the belief that our effort won't make a difference in the outcome anyway.

This whole process is deadly to the habits and practices of safety, both individually and as a society. Denial is the most dangerous and pervasive influence our culture faces in regard to safety. I beg you not to be a part of the problem. You absolutely, positively *must* change this dynamic in your life, or you will surely hand it off to your children. Even if you manage to keep them safe to adulthood, it won't end there. As a grandparent, you will agonize over your grandchildren, only this time you really will be helpless, since you are not directly responsible for their care.

The way out of this mess is to recognize how little denial does to give you peace of mind. The simple truth is that you struggle so hard to maintain denial that acceptance of reality, when it comes, is a relief. Once you see this clearly, begin to accept what is real, and act accordingly, you will find the serenity you seek. You will discover that taking action when and where you are able is tremendously empowering, so much so that even worry about what you cannot change is reduced. Remember that worry is always about something that may or may not happen in the future, so it is twice removed from where you are in the present. That is a powerful thought. Worry distracts you from what you should be doing *right now*. You need to be so busy dealing with reality that when a worrisome thought intrudes, it engages you only long enough for you to check your horizon.

Complacency

Now that I've beaten up on denial and worry, it's time to discuss their upside because as bad as they are, complacency is far worse. At times, worry can motivate us to take action. When people worry, they are at least aware that there is a possible problem. Complacent individuals are highly vulnerable to threat, especially in the arena of personal safety. They are the ones who are least prepared, and therefore, are the most easily surprised. Complacency is one of the reasons it is so easy to be in denial. Some of the common justifications and excuses for complacency are:

- Not in my family!
- It happens to others but not to me (so far).
- The odds of that happening are a million to one.
- I am protected by a higher power.
- It's never happened to me before.
- When your time is up, it's up.
- Those things only happen to stupid people.

Interestingly enough, most of these reasons can be true to one degree or another. The problem is, we use these justifications as *excuses to do nothing* to make ourselves more aware, nothing to improve our odds, and nothing to prepare ourselves to avoid or overcome what we dread. This is living in a state of disempowerment. What is truly frightening is the fact that this is accepted as normal for vast numbers of our population. Worse, we transmit this emotional lethargy to our children and others within our sphere of influence. Then, when disaster finally strikes, our last thought is, "I never thought it would happen to me!"— and we are overcome with a feeling of how *unfair* this all is.

Webster's Encyclopedic Unabridged Dictionary 1996 edition defines complacency as: *"a feeling of quiet pleasure or security, often while unaware of some potential danger, defect or the like; self-satisfaction or smug satisfaction with an existing situation, condition etc."*

The thing that makes complacency so dangerous is, in contrast to denial, complacency feels good. It is the state of feeling untouchable—by ignoring the fact that we are vulnerable. It occurs when denial has become our default state of mind. Human beings have a strong attraction to taking the path of least resistance. Crime is on the rise because we make it easy for the predators among us to take advantage of us. This is not really about what we do; rather it is the result of how we think and what we have become: nuts, bolts and brackets in the victim factory.

The opposite of complacency is anxiety: worry on steroids. It is the state of being fixated on a problem for which we see no immediate solution. Anxiety is a distraction: a broken record, a closed loop that uses up energy reserves without productive gain. We hate being in this state of mind, because it produces stress in levels that will literally shorten our lives and destroy the quality of what is left. Yet, like a ping pong ball, most of us bounce between these two extremes and only with great difficulty achieve a healthy balance.

The elusive middle ground between being complacent and anxious is the state of being *aware*. To commit to an acceptance of reality is our first concrete objective in becoming a counterpredator. The problem is that becoming aware of a threat and feeling vulnerable to it leads most of us straight into anxiety, just the place we don't want to go. It's easy to see why we choose denial instead: it leads us right back to the comfort of complacency. This continual smacking back and forth over the net of awareness is beating us to death emotionally. For many of us, this results in apathy, not because we are lazy, but because we are emotionally exhausted.

The secret is to combine awareness with preparation. When we know that a possible threat or danger exists and are prepared to deal with it, we can stop devoting so much emotional energy to anxiety. Therein lays the balance. Confidence in our ability to overcome an obstacle or a hazard allows us to focus on the details necessary to secure success. Ergo, in the moment of truth, we have the full complement of our abilities, skill and energy. This was my experience in the aftermath of my ordeal with the riptide. Once awareness is linked to preparation, the choice is between complacency and confidence. Put in this light, any reasonable person would agree that this choice is a no-brainer.

Pro-Passive Bias

There is a direct link between a child's vulnerability to predators, abusers and bullies, and the will to be assertive in their relationships with others. In turn, assertiveness is a product of healthy self-image, or identity and value. How do children know that they are valuable? Regardless of culture, the clearest proof of self-worth children will ever receive is when others come to their aid. It is the currency of care. This positive re-enforcement of self-image is vitally important to every young child. Its absence is significant because the only other layer of protection in their possession is how they view themselves.

Left to our own devices, all of us have this built-in failsafe that is designed to engage the moment we feel threat. When we have a healthy self-image, when we know our value, we come to our own aid because we defend what we love. The more we love, the greater our efforts. *Self-defense is at core self-care*. Yet countless times I have heard parents, teachers and counselors tell children that fighting is wrong. I have heard them equate fighting with violence, and that violence never solves problems. I have heard them talk among themselves about using conflict-resolution techniques and the value of just sitting down and talking about it. I have heard them advise the children under their care to turn the other cheek, walk away, avoid confrontation, ignore predatory behavior in their peers—and repeatedly, that getting involved in a physical confrontation will get them in all kinds of trouble. Any assertive physical defense is treated with automatic suspicion and often the person who takes action in response to physical provocation is punished more harshly than the one who initiated it.

It is time to take a critical look at this pro-passive bias, because I am absolutely convinced it is dangerously imbalanced and exposes all of us to significantly increased levels of threat. When we stack the deck in favor of passive response to threat, what we are really telling ourselves is that we are not worth defending. We are saying that it is wrong to engage in a vigorous defense of what is most precious to us: ourselves. Nature's most-sacred and ancient principle is that *we protect what we love*. Self-defense is an inalienable right. The net result of passivity is this: Our children come to dread and fear confrontation in general and physical confrontation in particular. Fighting is not automatically wrong. In truth, not being willing to fight for what you believe in, what you value and hold dear is a terrible weakness, and a society that promotes this imbalance is doomed.

We have all witnessed the spectacle of predator versus prey on television. A large, savage animal has cornered a much smaller one, intent on devouring it. The smaller animal, in a desperate effort to save its own life, responds with a vicious and determined onslaught. Often the predator gives up because the little meal was not worth the big fight. Under those circumstances, no one could credibly argue that because "fighting is wrong," the smaller animal should try the non-violent approach or that it should be punished for resorting to unnecessary violence.

I am reminded of an incident that occurred in the aftermath of the Randy Weaver trial. This was the infamous Ruby Ridge case during which federal officers surrounded Weaver's home and opened fire, killing the family's dog and his teenage son. During the ensuing gun battle a U.S. marshal was killed, Weaver's wife was shot and killed while she was holding their baby, and Weaver himself was shot. A family friend, Kevin Harris, was also gravely wounded. After an 11-day standoff, Weaver, exhausted and wounded, finally surrendered. Gerry Spence, arguably America's finest trial attorney, decided to defend Weaver pro bono. Spence, who has never lost a jury case in over 50 years of active practice, succeeded once again. Weaver was acquitted. Immediately following the trial, on the lawn outside the courthouse, Tom Brokaw, NBC News anchor, made the mistake of trying to pressure Spence by asking him how it felt to be responsible for setting a "dangerous" man free. Spence responded by asking him, "You see that hole in the ground over there?" Brokaw nodded yes. "What kind of animal do you think lives in that hole?" Brokaw didn't know. Spence said, "Well I'll tell ya. It's a rabbit: a cute, cuddly little rabbit. Now, is a rabbit a dangerous animal?" "No", Brokaw said with a smile. Spence continued, "You're right, he's not. But you stick your hand down that hole and try to harm that rabbit or his family and what do you think is going to happen?" Brokaw answered, "Well, he'll bite me!" Spence replied, "That's right. He'll bite you. And *my client is just like that cute, cuddly little rabbit.*"[12]

Pro-passive bias arises from a three-way combination: dread of conflict, ignorance of environment and smug moral superiority. It is an attempt to drive a square peg through a round hole, and it has devastating consequences for us and our children. Young or old, we are more easily victimized if we add this heavy sack of rubbish to the normal and natural fear of threat. Those with predatory intent are drawn with magnetic regularity to those who are least likely to put up a strong defense. Because of the ideology of pro-passive bias, our society is fostering three classes of children: spineless voyeurs, weaklings and those who prey on them. Since nothing is being done to arrest this Darwinian process, countless thousands of our children are gaining a double major in Group Think 101: indifference and apathy. Thus, we continue to remodel the victim factory, and it is increasing its production with each generation.

Broad-brushing self-defense as "*resorting* to violence" implies that the intended victim has the option of thoughtfully selecting from a smorgasbord of choices. Since personal combat normally involves high levels of fear or anger, most people engage in it only under the most severe circumstances. This is especially true of children. Intended victims, who normally avoid conflict, are often driven to it *because their survival instinct gave them no choice.* In these cases, the result is that a successful defense actually does solve a problem—it stops the attack.

There is even a benefit to the attacker: He receives a learning experience in cause and effect. If he changes his behavior because of it, his intended victim's actions have saved others who would have suffered at his hands. If you are an administrator in our public education system, I want to urge you to stop uselessly wringing your hands and broad-brushing the problem by automatically expelling both participants. It doesn't take a rocket scientist to see the difference between the abuser, who is pursuing conflict, and the intended victim, who is forced to respond to it. Yet the system continues to punish the one who hits back.

Often educators, eminently qualified in the academic arena, are unwitting participants in the disempowerment cycle, because they attempt to apply methods they are familiar with in situations where those methods are not effective. Using conflict resolution skills in attempting to mediate between a bully and his victim is a prime example. Sometimes teachers and parents do not take these incidents seriously, and their attitude reflects a "kids will be kids" mentality, when in truth a crime has been committed. Imagine suggesting that a rapist and his victim engage in "conflict resolution". Ridiculous, but that is exactly what happens all the time between bullies who viciously and maliciously engage in crimes of power against vulnerable human targets.

Presented with this perspective, inquiring minds are driven to ask, "Why? What is the benefit to society in pro-passive bias and other, similar social trends?"

The culturally scripted, politically correct narrative that engenders victim mindset in the populace is not a conspiracy—far from it. A conspiracy would be easy to expose and refute. This societal ill is much more deeply entrenched. What I am referring to is the natural outworking of the intentions of those with a vested interest in reducing fellow human beings into compliant, easily manipulated *consumers*. Whether they are actively or peripherally involved, corporate leaders, politicians who support big government, the media, lobbyists, social engineers, thought influencers and many intellectuals support the subtle disempowerment of those they propose to lead.

The established power brokers in *every* society have an investment in the dependence of the masses. This is basic social physics. People who feel vulnerable are *always* more receptive to authority figures who seem to have their best interest at heart. This is because rescuers are inherently more powerful than those they rescue. Those who are self-reliant do not need rescue and they resent attempts to stifle their self-determination but these individuals are only a small minority.

To get the general public as a whole to accept its own disempowerment does not involve coercion in any form. The most effective means to accomplish this objective is to disguise it by the adoption of a set of ideals and beliefs that claim to involve the "higher moral ground," appear good or at least benign, yet which ultimately lead to disengagement and passivity. This is the object of political correctness, a control mechanism that is in direct, willful opposition to constitutionally protected freedom of expression. As such, it should be rejected by every freedom-loving American citizen.

Here is an example of how this relates to pro-passive bias. One evening during the writing of this book, I was watching Anderson Cooper on CNN facilitating a program on bullying. On the set were three young people who had been relentlessly bullied. Dr Phillip McGraw was there, as well as the parents and two bullying experts. They had video footage of a young boy being severely harassed on a school bus, with other students cheering the bullies on. They also interviewed bullies who expressed little or no remorse. At the same time, on another channel, the program "Bully Beat-down" was being aired. On this program, bullies are challenged by the host to climb into the cage and engage a professional MMA fighter for a monetary reward. If the bully loses, he has to pay the money to his victims who are watching. Almost without exception the humiliated bully, after having to wear the shoes of his victim, apologizes and publicly promises to cease and desist from bullying.

As I channel-flipped between these two shows, I was struck by the contrast between what was transpiring on each program. On CNN, the politically correct dialoging, counseling and "all violence is wrong" hand wringing, was on full display but no viable solutions were arrived at and there was no apparent behavioral shift in any of the participants. This conflict resolution model was talk, talk, talk, blame, point the finger and make excuses for the status quo. No change.

This was the result of the politically correct, so called "higher moral ground" approach.

On "Bully Beat-down," the time-tested, cause and effect model resulted in true conflict resolution: The bully decided to change his behavior, the victims were compensated emotionally and monetarily, and the viewers received an object lesson in pure justice. Real, measurable change was achieved by fighting fire with fire. Whether or not people agree with the methodology, the results cannot be argued with. In spite of this, leadership on every level, whether or not they agree with the real world solution privately, show overwhelming public support for *an anti-solution that institutionalizes victimization in our youth.*

To portray this process the way I have, might seem to indicate a well-thought-out plan on the part of those who are responsible for it but this is not the case. It is self-deception, which happens subconsciously, as those in leadership positions come to believe that they know what is best for the rest of us, while protecting both their self-image and their public persona.

The current social engineering succeeds because both those who lead and those who are led, believe the others are their servants. We elect officials to positions of public trust and service and we believe that they will represent us honestly and fairly. However, entrenched leadership, especially at the higher levels, often loses sight of the public service mandate and in many cases they reverse it. We are living in the eye of a hurricane, blind to the surrounding storm because *our individual spheres of interaction* seem pleasant and harmless. We are unaware of the subliminal power contest that is being played out just beyond our horizon. By degrees, our society has grown into an economic organism that feeds off its own cells, while convincing them that this is the healthy, natural order of things.

The pro-passive bias lobbyists are at war with the concept of self–defense and have waged an effective campaign against it. Over the last three decades, the philosophy of pro-passive bias has become institutionalized. Perhaps you too, have been adversely impacted, and it has affected your ability to see the issues clearly. We will explore the subject of bullying at length in Chapter 20. For now, consider that a balanced approach to the problem begins with acknowledging that, from time immemorial, human beings have engaged in physically protecting themselves and their children from harm. It is a God-given and inalienable right. Social engineers and thought police should not be allowed to tamper with it, just because it doesn't fit the politically correct narrative.

Your children have the moral and legal right to *assertive self-care*. Learning to exercise it is not only healthy, but normal. Without this component, it is impossible for them to feel and experience the full measure of their value. Denying our children's right to self-protection is a direct attack on their self-worth, so much so that even if they are never the victim of a predator or a bully, they learn to live their life in victim mode. They become a victim of the ideology of disempowerment and a life half lived is no life at all. Never forget that self-defense is never about violence; it is always about value.

Protection without Preparation

Our first concern—the whole focus of our world—is the safety of our children. It is precisely because young children are so vulnerable, especially as infants and toddlers, that the hedge of protection parents provide is essential. Like walls around an ancient city, we stand between the protected and the threat. Every society in history is built around the core concept of the survival of its young. It is our duty to make the environment in our home as safe as possible. It is our duty to do all in our power to insulate them from a myriad of dangers outside of it. *It is up to us to transition them from the innocence of childhood to fully aware, self-sufficient, powerful adults.* Because of this, most of the expert advice commonly available through books, videos, classes and seminars is focused on what parents, teachers, counselors and coaches can do to protect the children under their care. Almost nothing is said about training the children themselves.

Sadly, we have become so concerned with protecting our children that we have neglected to *prepare* them for the environment they are entering, day by day with less and less of our supervision. We have failed to realize that preparation is part and parcel of protection; it is the older and wiser sister of the pair. This is especially noteworthy because parents are rarely capable of being with their child twenty-four-seven. We shield our children from the world *while they are young*, hoping that as they mature and gain more freedom, reason and common sense will take hold. Yet this skips a crucial step. Sooner or later, our children must engage the threat environment on their own and because of our protectiveness, they may lack the behavioral templates that exposure and immersion would have forged.

This situation exists primarily because so many of us are not fully aware, self-sufficient, powerful adults ourselves. We have the maternal/paternal instinct that drives our will to protect them, but because we are not conditioned by experience in the predatory environment, we are not equipped to prepare them. Unlike wild animals, we are not the example that is needed to become their role models. Our children compare us with examples of the street survivors the media presents to them. Measured against that yardstick, we are cautious, soft and sadly lacking in that elusive "right stuff." I personally reject the media version of the predatory environment as being inaccurate and unreliable and so should you, but at the base-line, this is about our children's perception and they need us to meet them where they are.

We must increase our knowledge of what preparation actually is. More importantly, we need to become aware, self-sufficient and powerful ourselves so we can hand those essential advantages off to our children. This is the greatest gift of love we can give them. Protection without preparation must be replaced with the emotional and physical conditioning at least equal to, and hopefully better than, what is common in the predator's world.

*   *   *

In our quest to develop a safe house that shelters and protects all of us, we have unintentionally eroded our connection to nature's gifts. For many of us, these advantages have ceased to function as originally intended. Instinct, intuition and the survival impulse, in combination with experience that conditions us to its use, are no longer common learning formats. We have unwittingly traded these essential resources for logic and reason, placing nearly all our dependence on them.

Then, when disaster strikes and we need to access our full array of weaponry, it is rusty with disuse. We discover we are weak, vulnerable and open to approach by predatory humans. We are unfamiliar with hostile environments and fear what we do not understand. We have lost touch with our capacity to be tough, tenacious survivors who think on their feet and act decisively under pressure. We are missing a crucial facet of ourselves, of what it means to be a *whole human being*, with the plethora of benefits and assets this entails.

THE VICTIM FACTORY FORMULA

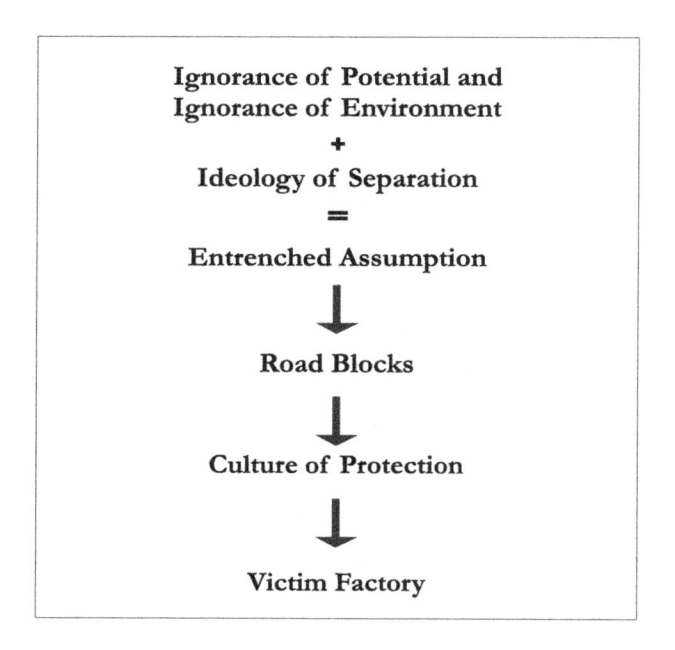

Ignorance of Potential and
Ignorance of Environment

+

Ideology of Separation

=

Entrenched Assumption

↓

Road Blocks

↓

Culture of Protection

↓

Victim Factory

Fig. 1

Individually and collectively, we need to reacquire this missing piece of ourselves. The rewards are enormous. It is the key to a safer existence, as well as a vast improvement in quality of life. No matter how great the gulf appears between our existing self-concept and who we would like to become, there is hope. Our potential is hard-wired into us. *It's all there*; the only issue is access. Every person who has suffered this disconnect has the potential to re-engage, re-connect and reclaim their birthright as formidable, powerful, vibrant, sentient beings.

To jump-start this process, let's examine courageous behavior.

Chapter 4

Ordinary People—and Heroes

"Courage is reckoned the greatest of all virtues, because unless a man has that virtue, he has no security for preserving any other."

–Samuel Johnson

On the morning of January 11, 1992, John Wayne Thompson, of Hurdsfield, North Dakota, slipped on the icy ground of his family's farm and got caught in the power takeoff of the grooved shaft-and-auger he was using to transfer barley sacks from a truck to a grain bin. The powerful machine ripped off both his arms just below the shoulder and flung his body twenty feet, knocking him unconscious. He was eighteen years old and nobody was home, his parents having left for Bismarck earlier that morning. The nearest farm was two miles away.

Regaining consciousness, he attempted to get to his feet, and discovered that both his arms were missing. *"I was lying on my left side…I looked at my right and couldn't see my arm and thought it was broken. Then I tried to use my left arm to lift myself up. That's when I saw it was off, that both of them were off. … I was against a tractor tire, so I put my head against it and just stood up. I looked again for my arms. It was pretty red where they'd been. …I went berserk, screaming for a few seconds."*[13]

Already, John's survival mechanisms were engaging. After the emotional dump of the screaming bout, his brain began to process with absolute clarity on one objective: He needed to get help. Automatically, his blood pressure was dropping to reduce blood loss and shock was suppressing his pain level. The house was 400 feet away, and it was uphill. As best he could, John covered the distance, but then he was confronted with a new problem: opening the sliding glass door at the rear of the house. Using the stub of the humerus bone protruding from his left shoulder as a lever against the door handle, he attempted to crack it open, but could not exert enough pressure to succeed. He circled the house and tried to kick the front door open, but without his arms to maintain his balance, it was impossible to produce enough impact. He fell to his knees and turned the brass knob with his teeth.

Once inside, John used the same method to open a second door leading to a small office where the phone was. The town of Hurdsfield had a population of 72. There was no 911 service available. Using his nose and then a pen clamped between his teeth, he called a girlfriend but got a busy signal. Next, he dialed his cousin. At last, help was on the way. Noticing that his blood was making a mess, John headed for the bathroom and climbed into the tub. The ambulance was coming from Bowden, eleven miles away.

John's Aunt Renee and Cousin Tammy Thompson arrived first. The ambulance crew found his missing arms and packed them in ice. In a five hour relay, he was transported by land and air to Minneapolis, where after hours of surgery, his arms were reattached. After many years of rehab and countless operations, he is functional but has limited dexterity and range of motion.

John Wayne Thompson views himself as a normal person. He has never been comfortable with the publicity and attention his story has generated, and considers it a burden. He believes his actions were a natural, normal human response in a survival situation. *"What was I supposed to do, just lie there? C'mon, I mean, what would you do?"*ibid. *"Some people expect me to be a hero, but I can't do it,"* he says. *"I just want to get on with my life."*[14] *"Anyone would have done what I did..."*[15]

And that is really the issue, isn't it? What would you do? I am willing to bet you would do just about what he did, or certainly make a valiant attempt. The survival instinct is one of the most powerful compulsions human beings can experience. It would be unnatural to give up without a fight. Our capacity to endure and overcome is far, far greater than the limitations we impose upon ourselves, especially those produced by unreasoning fear.

As human beings, we crave examples of heroism, perseverance in the face of adversity, overcoming the odds, raw courage. Through the media, many of us have learned to experience these things vicariously. It is common to consider these qualities as something rare and special, and those blessed with true grit obtain a mantle of greatness in the public eye. The average person today feels no real connection to these individuals. We try to imagine what we would do in their place and feel only fear and uncertainty. Since we automatically equate fear and uncertainty with inaction, it is easy to convince ourselves that only a relative few of us have the elusive "right stuff."

In reality, nothing could be farther from the truth. Almost without exception, those among us who become heroes are ordinary, everyday people who suddenly find themselves in harm's way and do what is necessary to survive the situation. Like John Wayne Thompson, they don't feel like heroes. Their conduct under pressure is a natural function of their survival instinct. This also holds true for those who risk themselves to rescue others. Contrary to popular belief, the urge to help others in need, especially desperate need, is natural; it is hardwired into us and only fear out of balance is able to cancel it out. Without this most basic instinct, we never could have survived as a species. It is not my purpose here to lessen the accomplishments of those society honors with hero status, rather, I wish to highlight the astounding capacity for dealing with hazard and adversity that *all* human beings possess inside them. It is nature's gift to humanity.

Imagine receiving a car in a shipping crate. The crate itself has been stenciled "Toyota Corolla" and you assume that is what it contains. You take a crowbar, pull the nails, open the crate and there it is—a beige Toyota Corolla. You take it out for a test drive and think "Yep, it drives just as dependably as all the other Toyota Corollas out there!" As you scan the dash, you see an unfamiliar button marked 'Panic,' but you're too busy with destinations and errands to open the owner's manual right now. After a time, you don't even see it anymore.

Then, one day, sitting at a traffic light, you have a strange premonition of danger. Suddenly, there is a man with a gun motioning you to get out of the car. At the same time, that button, the one marked 'Panic' lights up. Without thinking you push it. Instantly, you feel the Toyota sink down and flatten out. You sense the vehicle is lower and longer. The color of the interior changes from brown to black and sophisticated computer displays blossom from the dash. The windows seem to have thickened and grown darker. Through them, you glimpse the shocked expression of the gunman as the Corolla becomes a sleek, powerful, candy-apple red Ferrari right before his eyes. It radiates subtle menace. This is a car that could turn on a dime and run him over. Your foot begins to shake a little, and you inadvertently graze the gas pedal. Your ears are filled with an unfamiliar and savage growl as 460 horsepower shoves you back into the seat. The gunman becomes a tiny dot in the rear-view mirror. *There is so much power!* It's actually a little scary. You pull over to the side of the street and stop.

You're very, very tired now, and so you close your eyes and take a couple of deep breaths. When you open them, you are in your dependable little Toyota again. You wonder just what it is you've been given. Do you accept the gift? Do you climb back behind the wheel and learn by experience what it is capable of, or do you send it back because you are intimidated by its power and potential for risk? Would you rather own the familiar, ordinary Corolla?

On investigation, you discover that this is no ordinary Ferrari, either. It almost thinks for itself. Instead of a radar detector, it has a bona-fide radar system designed to detect incoming objects. It has advanced road–hazard warning indicators that operate through its state-of-the-art GPS system. In other words, this car can warn you of the road ahead and what is approaching you. But that's not all. What really sets this Ferrari apart is that as soon as the panic button is activated, all of the sensory functions and operations of the vehicle itself are transmitted into you. Your will is fused into the Ferrari, and the Ferrari's power and sensitivity are fused into you. You become one entity. Realizing this, you become uneasy. There is so much you don't know about yourself when you enter a new environment.

There is only one experience as prevalent as fear in human beings—the desire to overcome it; to be free of its negative effects. Ironically, it is a surprisingly elusive goal, given its universal attraction. To understand this, consider that we often attempt to convince ourselves that freedom from fear's negative effects is impossible. We've tried many times before and failed. We have accepted our failure and achieved a level of comfort from this acceptance. We associate comfort with security, so we invest considerable time and energy in actually maintaining fear, disguised as caution. We congratulate ourselves on our wisdom and prudence, yet often, we are haunted by the faint feeling that somehow, in a secret place, hidden from the view of others, we are cowards. We do not challenge ourselves, and subconsciously, we recognize that a life devoid of challenge is not worth living. Then, when suddenly confronted with a life threatening situation, we flash back to the long list of our failures. This has become our experience.

Take action to save a mediocre life? Why? We won't be successful anyway. This is the downward spiral of disempowerment.

As you examine your life in light of all this, you may discover that to one degree or another you, too, have been adversely affected by this process. If so, it is time to *wake up!!* You have the power to choose how you will live! When was the last time you truly challenged your fear? Do you remember what it felt like? Did you emerge from the experience feeling more powerful, more in control of yourself, more confident? What would it be like to feel that way most of the time? How would your life change?

I believe clearly and passionately that it is possible to break free of these little mind games we play so incessantly. I believe that our limits for both happiness and success are defined by our honesty in confronting our fears. I know with certainty that seeking out experiences that challenge us and acquaint us with our gifts, with the function of our machinery, will produce confidence in ourselves and project an aura of personal power to others. Taking calculated risks to gain experience and other benefits is how we grow. All of us have different comfort levels for the risks we take. Wherever these limits are, expanding our personal comfort envelope is vitally important, even if it is by small degrees. We grow into disempowerment, and can grow out of it, as well.

The way out of this morass we face as adults is identical to the method of learning we all experienced as small children. Children learn by playing, and they play by taking risks—small ones—each a little test to build knowledge by experience. You did this yourself not so long ago, and you can do it again, if you choose to. The difference between adults and children in acquiring knowledge is that young children do it unconsciously, with very little awareness of the *process* of learning. They are not self-conscious or critical of themselves; they don't normally attempt to measure progress at all. Children just accept where they are and go forward from there, having as much fun as possible while they do it.

As adults, we waste so much time measuring where we are, who we compare to and how far we have to go, as well as wasting energy on the emotional content of those calculations, that we are easily discouraged. We think we know so much, that our supposed knowledge gets in the way of our learning. This reminds me of an ancient Persian proverb:

He who knows not
And knows not that he knows not
He is a fool, shun him.

He who knows not
And knows he knows not
He is worthy, teach him.

He who knows
And knows not he knows
He is asleep, wake him.

He who knows
And knows that he knows
He is wise, follow him.[16]

My personal quest for comfort and security has led me through a number of stages of understanding, encompassing many experiences in the mental, physical and emotional arenas of human experience. My work in Survival Response Conditioning has taught me a series of vital truths. The most important of them all is this:

> *Inside every human being there exists unlimited potential for courageous, heroic action, for overcoming incredible odds and surviving unthinkable hardship.*

Confidence and courage flow from recognizing we can deal with a situation because we have experienced this situation or something similar to it previously. Believing we can achieve a goal or overcome an obstacle is a powerful force. Yet, with belief, there is always a measure of uncertainty, because we are entering uncharted water. *The difference between believing and knowing is experience.* When it comes to taking action, knowledge based on experience is almost always a better platform to launch from, because the confidence it inspires is genuine, solid and decisive. Experience gives us superior odds in any risky endeavor. Furthermore, this type of confidence is highly contagious—a gravitational force field that draws others within our sphere of influence. It is one of the most significant qualities of an inspirational leader.

"Ok," you say, "so how do I get there? How do I begin to make the change from denial, apathy and acceptance of the status quo, to recognition, self-determination and action?" By asking that question, you are already on the path. To continue your progress, these four things need to happen within you, in the following order:

1. **A**wareness and acceptance of your true self and the environment you inhabit
2. **D**esire to change of proportional intensity to the change
3. **A**ction (preferably pre-emptive action when possible
4. **M**emory

In order to memorize how the experiential approach to learning works, I nicknamed the process "ADAM's waterwheel." Our will, or water, comes off the chute, dropping into the bucket called "awareness." Its weight and momentum spin the wheel forward, propelling the "desire" bucket under the falling water. As desire is filled with will, "action" is spun into play. In due course, "memory" is filled, completing the circuit, and so awareness and memory are constantly growing, as long as desire and action prompt them. In the subconscious mind, memory and awareness combine to produce intuition, a topic we shall explore at length in later chapters.

ADAM'S WATER WHEEL

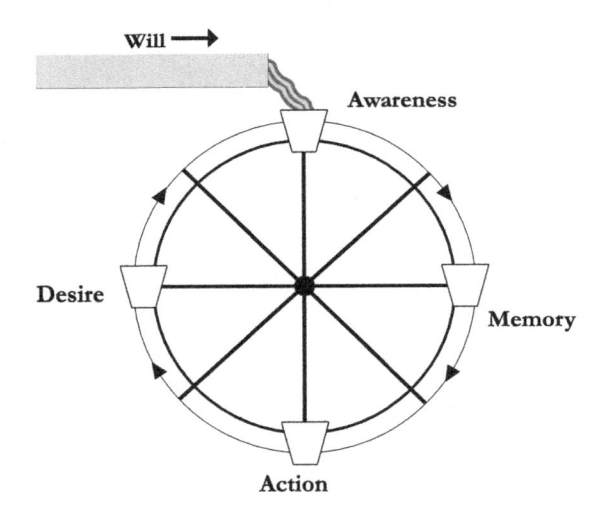

Fig. 2

I have purposefully saved the best and most compelling argument for last. As our children transition from the innocence of childhood into early adolescence, nature intends that they necessarily begin to grow apart from us. The difficulty of letting them go is often compounded by the loss of their concept of us as heroes, mentors and role models. While they are very young, our children often view us as powerful and wise. As children are given more freedom and exercise greater independence, their perception of us—and everything else—changes. Unless given in carefully measured doses, the gift of freedom can be misinterpreted *subconsciously* as inconsistency on our part in regard to their personal safety. Feeling abandoned, they seek to attach to another older, wiser substitute who is appealing to their self-concept.

As parents, it is nearly impossible to compete with the role models the media showcases for our children every day, and they reach the point where they no longer believe we are capable of protecting them. Subconsciously they are left to assume a level of control for their safety that their experience cannot deliver. This is the real reason why gang membership attracts many inner-city youths. The gang is viewed as a new family, better suited to protect them in the new world they are entering and more capable than their parents.

In order to interrupt this unhealthy dynamic, their concept of us has to change. And they are not responsible—we are. This "facelift" can only happen as parents personally experience a real and dramatic increase in confidence and personal power. We must become something entirely different than what we have been if we are to regain our rightful status as heroes, mentors and role models to our children. Whatever form this transformation takes, it better be genuine because it is not possible to fool your children for long; they know you too well and spend too much time with you. Failure is not an option. The stakes are too high.

Confronted by this seemingly overwhelming obstacle, many parents simply throw up their hands, bow out and in effect say, "I've done my best, it's just a stage they're going through—let nature take its course." They give up, and their children see and feel them give up. They are deprived of crucial guidance and experience at a time when they most need it. Yet, there is a way to begin reconstruction of the bridge between parents and children caught in this quagmire of conflicting emotions; a way that is simple, effective and entirely under the control of the parent. It involves a change of both heart and image on the part of the parent; a shift so profound and remarkable their children cannot help but notice it. A changed life always produces a ripple effect; those closest to the change feel and see the effects most strongly, and are in turn altered by it.

There are two basic ways to accomplish this change. The first is to habitually challenge your comfort envelope. It is time consuming but gradual and can be achieved entirely on your own. It works like this: You begin to challenge your everyday comfort level. Ask yourself what you fear and then attempt to stretch the borders that define your comfort zone. If you fear heights, take a chair lift up a ski-slope in the off season. If you fear water, take swimming lessons at the "Y." If public speaking gives you the willies, join Toastmasters. Know that you are a work in progress and chip away at your self-image baggage until you begin to *relish* challenge. You work at it every day. Each time you succeed, your emotional freedom expands. The marvelous thing about this process is that growth occurs geometrically. In other words, success in one arena positively affects all the others. A small success yields much larger results.

The problem with this first method is that there is a distinct challenge ceiling. There are certain situations in which it is nearly impossible to achieve powerful results safely, particularly in regard to human conflict. For instance, using this method, you would never purposefully engage another person in real physical combat just to enlarge your fear envelope. Yet, in the arena of personal protection, the *effect* of this type of hypothetical exercise would be exceptionally valuable.

The second method is called **Survival Response Conditioning**. It begins at the upper limit of the first method. This is a process that relies on duplicating the emotional intensity, fear and trauma of the predatory environment. Survival Response Conditioning produces fast, instinctive responses that are calculated to give individuals the best chance of survival when they find themselves in like circumstances in the real world. Many who experience this first-hand find it to be a life-changing event. It is the Ferrari experience we touched on earlier. *This program is for the faint-hearted who don't want to be that way anymore.* In my opinion, it is the fastest way to reconnect with your primal skill set. In fact, if you are ready and willing to expand your personal comfort envelope, you can achieve incredibly powerful results in a single day.

We have covered the problems that are an integral part of our society and that adversely affect us as individuals. By now I hope you can see that continuing to live your life as you have in the past means you must settle for the same results. I invite you to step across the fear line and reclaim who you were meant to be; that part of yourself that has been *missing in action*. Are you ready to experience true self-determination?

Are you ready to change your life?

Part I Endnotes

What is a Counterpredator?

[1] Richard Grenier, *Carrying victimization a step further—how those with social values and morals have to pay the price for other's irresponsible sexual behavior* (Washington Times essay, Monday, May 3, 1993) Note: This quote is commonly attributed to George Orwell, who expressed a similar opinion. However, Grenier, who was paraphrasing Orwell, (note the lack of quotation marks) is the author of this exact statement.

Chapter 1

[2] This is a composite character, based on the published interviews and accounts of a number of convicted serial killers. I have attempted to create a viewpoint that is representative of a mind without conscience, focused on the feeling of power that extreme violence and cruelty seems to generate in many sociopaths.

[3] Laurence Gonzales, *Deep Survival: Who Lives, Who Dies and Why.* (New York: Norton, 2003) 158

Chapter 2

[4] Mary Pipher, *Reviving Ophelia: Saving the Selves of Adolescent Girls.* (New York: Penguin, 1994) 37-39

[5] Helen Keller, *The Open Door.* (New York: Doubleday and Company, 1957) 17

[6] Laurence Gonzales, *Everyday Survival: Why Smart People Do Stupid Things.* (New York: Norton, 2008) 47

Chapter 3

[7] Theodore Roosevelt - *address, Washington, D.C., April 14, 1906*

[8] Norman Doidge, *The Brain that Changes Itself: Stories of Personal Triumph from the Frontiers of Brain Science.* (London: Penguin Group, 2007) 42

[9] Gene Weingarten, *Pearls Before Breakfast* (Washington Post article, Sunday, April 8, 2007)

[10] Gavin DeBecker, *The Gift of Fear: Survival Signals that Protect Us from Violence*. (Boston: Little, Brown, 1997) 8, 44

[11] For more details on this point, see the chapter on denial in Amanda Ripley's *The Unthinkable: Who Survives When Disaster strikes and Why*. (New York: Crown, 2008) 3-21

[12] Used with permission. (I had heard several versions of this story around the time it happened, but I was unable to track and verify the news accounts. I finally made contact with Mr. Spence and confirmed the details via e-mail.)

Chapter 4

[13] Barry Bearak, *Reluctant Hero Longs for His Past* (Los Angeles Times article, Sunday, September 26, 1993)

[14] Compiled and condensed from numerous new articles circa 1992 and on, referenced by John Thompson's book "Home in One Piece" (Fargo, ND: McCleery & Sons Publishing, 2001)

[15] Margaret Nelson, *Too Tough to Die* (People Weekly article, February 3, 1992 - Vol. 37 No. 4)

[16] English translation from Sanskrit-attributed to Omar Khayam, 13th century philosopher

II

The Adrenal Advantage

Chapter 5

Welcome to My World

"To be prepared for war is one of the most effectual means of preserving peace."

–George Washington

You are about to read six unsolicited testimonials from people whose lives have been supercharged in a way they might never have imagined. These individuals and hundreds of others who have shared this experience are the reason I am involved in the work I do, and why I decided to write this book:

"I was only invited to come to this Friday and had no idea what we were going to be doing. I am a community advocate, working downtown...with DV victims, almost all women. I do most of the 911 DV callbacks for (my) county and a lot of safety planning. I can promise you that what you and the others have taught me today will help hundreds of women—maybe even save a life. I was scared, but also found that I have strength to draw on. I didn't know it was there, having never been in a situation to test it. Just Thursday after I escorted a DV victim to Protection Order Court, a batterer came looking for me in the building, trying to find out my name. It occurred to me that I could end up a victim too, if I wasn't careful. I learned some skills today. I hope I never have to use them, but I will if I must—and I will pass on the new found sense of empowerment to as many as I can. Thank you, God bless you all." –JK, Community Advocate

"Thank you for the gift you gave me today—empowerment! I *so* appreciate that you *get it* and are willing to help us find what we need inside of us: to know that we can do what we need to protect us and the world around us! I know your job isn't easy either, thank you again! My life is different today, for the better! I won't forget you." –JH

"Thank you so much! 'Thank you' seems like so little to say for how much you gave—not only of yourselves but what you gave me. I came in here, a woman full of fear from past experiences and am leaving here with the confidence that I can take care of myself, and that my friend, is a miracle. I am amazed at how different I feel about me and what I can do to protect myself and save my life." –CG

"I was so afraid of you and the rest of them. I was starting to wonder if you all came straight from the street. I am in awe that you are a real person just like me. You are an amazing person to be part of the Safety First team. The time, energy, and commitment you put into the program showed, to be admired by all. Because of you and the rest of the team, I feel like I am ready to put my attacker in his place. You also empowered me to feel like I can protect my precious children. I appreciate not that it's over but what you did! Thank you!" –BM

"What an experience—and so empowering. You have made me face my deepest fears. I know now that I have nothing to fear but fear itself. I have grown richer by this experience and event into the core of my being. What an opportunity, challenge and experience. I'll never forget it. This may save my life one day or someone I love. Thank you, thank you." –CK

"I've been afraid to be alone so long; I don't remember what it feels like to feel safe. Now, with your help, I know I have the strength to protect myself. This was the hardest and the best thing I have ever done for myself. Thank you for giving me the opportunity to know my own strength—I'll never forget it!" –S

The focus of Part 2: The Adrenal Advantage is to give you a guided tour of the Survival Response Conditioning program itself. First, we will explore the underlying principles and methodology that make this experience so effective. Next, we will take a look at the class and exercises that the students go through. Then, in Part 3: Body Chess, we will examine the Passive-Aggressive Strategy, a threat management game plan that will help define the parameters for using the skills acquired in the Adrenal Response program. What follows in the remaining sections of the book will focus on how you can use this reservoir of power to transfer the experience you have gained to your children.

As human beings, we are motivated to take action for two reasons: the fear of punishment/loss or, the need to gain a perceived reward. Remember the carrot and the stick? Usually we make decisions and act on them because one or the other is the stronger motivator. Powerful motivation, the kind that gets solid results quickly, happens when both influences are urging us forward. We have explored the stick method in the previous chapters; now I want to offer you the carrot. Effective marketers know this basic truth: People make decisions and take action based on emotion far more often than on logic and reason. We want to *feel* confidence and peace of mind. We want to *feel* competent and powerful. Most of all, we want to *feel* secure.

Insecurity comes from two sources. First and most obvious, is negative feelings about ourselves, our future or our situation. The second source is more potent: the inability to trust the good feelings that we have. We wonder if we deserve them. We wonder if these feelings are based on reality or if we are fooling ourselves. I am reminded of a large wooden paper-weight that I have on my desk. The brass plaque on it reads: "CONFIDENCE: The feeling you have before you understand the situation." Like Dr. Doolittle's "Push Me-Pull You," we are conflicted by bouts of hope and doubt, and our progress forward is agonizingly slow.

What we need is an infusion of good feelings that we can trust with certainty; feelings based on positive experiences. We need to feel because we believe, believe because we know, know because we have experienced. This process gives birth to the feeling that supports all the other positive feelings we need to have: confidence. This is your introduction to a remarkable experience that will weed out anxiety and replace it with genuine confidence. I am going to show you how to embrace what you have obtained, until you have an excess that you will be able to impart to your children and others. The best news is that it may not be as hard as you may think.

When considering a new course of action, it is natural to experience some reluctance to commit at the start. We want to "test the water" to guard our comfort envelope. Often people voice objections, not because they are opposed, but because they are not quite sure, and they want to be convinced or persuaded that it is OK to proceed. I will start by listing five initial objections I hear from people who eventually become grads:

1. I'm not physically fit. I won't be able to keep up.

You do not have to be physically fit to defend yourself on the street, for two reasons. First, the average altercation on the street lasts four seconds. You do not need cardio–vascular physical fitness to last for that brief span of time. Second, when you are in fear for your life, adrenaline gives you super-human power right at the instant you need it. Regardless of physical condition, *we have always been able to bring students all the way through this program.* To be physically fit is an important goal and being in good condition makes the process easier, but it is not a prerequisite for success here. We have helped people with physical disabilities to have this experience. We have successfully trained many overweight students. Remember that survival conditioning is ninety percent mental/spiritual and ten percent physical. If you have the desire to change your life and need the courage to act on that desire, than Survival Response Conditioning is for you. I urge you to take advantage of this opportunity to gain the experience and empowerment you lack. When you are in possession of these assets, it will be easier to resolve the issue of poor physical fitness.

2. I'm not an assertive person. I don't think I have what it takes to resist an aggressor.

All human beings have a complete array of survival mechanisms embedded in their DNA. *You have what you need right now.* You lack only the experience to use these assets effectively. This program provides you with an environment where you can discover the amazing qualities you didn't realize you had. It is an opportunity to gain confidence based on real experience. The statement you just made about yourself is a *perception* based on untested assumptions. It is not a fact, and we can prove this to you. In twelve years, we have never experienced a single instance of a student failing to improve his or her skill set. When you decide to invest in yourself, you always get a good return on investment.

3. I don't have the time it would take to make such a large change in whom I am, or to maintain it.

A Survival Response Conditioning course is not like joining a health club or a martial arts school where you must make a long-term commitment in order to achieve small changes gradually. Most of these courses are four to five days in length. We have discovered *a way to do it in less than ten hours*. When compared with traditional martial arts training, which involves thousands of hours of practice, this seems to be an incredibly short period of time. This superficial comparison could lead to the misconception that Survival Response Conditioning is somehow inferior. Why is there such a difference between these two methods with regard to length of time? There are several reasons, the most basic of which is simplicity. The physical skills required in survival response are so easily acquired, that children can and do learn them in less than half an hour—versus a martial arts skill set, which is the work of many months and years. A much more detailed answer to this question will be presented when we examine the principles and methodology that make all this possible in the sections that follow.

4. I don't have confidence. I never manage to finish what I start.

What you need is a new experience with yourself. This program produces life-changing confidence, as you can see from reading the testimonials at the beginning of the chapter. If you want to read more, visit the Safety First website at www.safetyfirstpps.org and click on the testimonials link. Better yet, *enroll in the course and change your life.* Think about how this will make you feel. Remember, every good and great accomplishment, every advance, every discovery, absolutely and without exception began as a single thought in the mind of one individual. The knowledge that you took action and changed who you are will utterly rearrange your horizons. Later, others just like you, perhaps with your same issues, will read your "thank you" and make a powerful choice for themselves, like you did.

The experience of confronting their worst nightmares and coming out on top is so powerful that many describe it as life-altering. Our students walk out the door knowing by experience that should someone attempt to harm them, they would have a completely different response to the threat than what they may have envisioned before they took the class, and a much better chance of emerging from the incident unscathed.

5. I have a terrible time staying motivated.

There are many reasons why people fail in their endeavors when motivation is a critical factor. What I have discovered is that when you give people information, it does not help them at all unless they act on it. Even when you add motivation to the information, it is still up to them to act. Since we are such procrastinators, a speaker or facilitator's ability to motivate must have some staying power, or all is lost. Unfortunately, the moment we step out from under the influence of the motivator, the motivation begins to degrade. This dynamic is par for the course when *information* is the primary learning format. The intellectual format of learning gives you information, concepts and theories and then leaves you on your own to apply them in the real world. What makes Survival Response Conditioning different is the use of an additional learning format: *the experience of making decisions and taking action under extremely high emotional stress, until you perform well naturally when exposed to the same conditions in the real world.* Give people facts and they will be soon forgotten. Give them an experience, especially an intensely emotional one, and it will be hard-wired into them forever.

*   *   *

There are four benefits that result from participating in a program like this. All of them are directly related to you and your children's safety:

- You will become intimately acquainted with the full array of your natural abilities and assets.

- You will be familiar with the predatory environment by experience and be able to navigate it successfully.

- You will have confidence in your threat–management game plan.

- You will be conditioned to respond to threat effectively and without hesitation.

None of this knowledge will be theoretical. All of it will be based on experiences that you personally have had under very high levels of stress in a predatory environment. You will not doubt your abilities, because they have been tested in a milieu where the subconscious mind is unable to differentiate between the program and the street. Psychologically, the experiences were real. Physically, they were real. Emotionally, they were real. Intellectually, you can debate the reality of the exercises all day, but in a live environment, when you are suddenly and shockingly exposed to threat, the conscious, rational brain (where intellectual processing occurs) shuts down. Psychological and emotional physics—the very same parameters that were effectively conditioned in the program—take over because the rational, conscious brain has deserted you. This is what is so scary. Most of us are completely dependent on cognitive processing to solve our problems. We feel helpless when this processing shuts down, because we are unfamiliar with the survival mechanism that automatically replaces it.

Chapter 6

The Foundation

"Give me a place to stand and a lever long enough and I will move the world."

—Archimedes

Gaps in our understanding are like bandits waiting to ambush and kill us. It is vital that we become acquainted with the basic principles that support a new and unfamiliar process. To that end I will list and briefly comment on those that are crucial to Survival Response Conditioning. Right from the start I want to thank Bruce K. Siddle for his excellent book, "Sharpening the Warrior's Edge." I strongly urge you to obtain this book, because it contains invaluable research on the subject of training under adrenal influences.

It is important to recognize that Siddle's powerful focus on the warrior elite in combat does not eclipse the possibility of a more universal application of the training principles he so eloquently portrays in "Sharpening the Warrior's Edge." The system structure he endorses applies in many training environments, particularly the subject under discussion here.

One of the reasons I enjoyed his book so much is that when I stumbled across it, my staff and I were already involved in successfully executing major components of the system structure he outlines, so I knew his observations were spot on. We developed and fine-tuned our programs by trial and error over time, and I immediately recognized the value of his research in validating methodology we had been using co–incidentally for years. Hopefully, the window opened for you here will whet your appetite for more, as he treats the subject with great clarity and depth. You can order it from Amazon.com or contact him directly via e-mail at bsiddle@warriorsciencegroup.com.

A successful Survival Response Conditioning program is based on the following 10 principles:

1. In a predatory environment, experience trumps knowledge, theory and education.

Anything that causes you to hesitate reduces your chance of survival when approached by a person with predatory intent. Experience is defined as knowing exactly what to do because you have done it before. No time is wasted deliberating over the correct course of action. Experience not only allows you to respond immediately; it eliminates confusion and infuses you with confidence. The result is that you act decisively and with great resolve.

Siddle combines experience with observation as the basis for a confident mindset. With this approach, two steps are necessary for students to acquire skill confidence. First, they must become proficient in a specific skill and then engage in training that allows them to use that skill in a live environment. Siddle believes that experience is greatly undervalued in many training environments and I agree with him. Experience is not only the test of effective training; it is an integral part of the training process itself. Too often a student gains a rudimentary grasp of how a skill is supposed to work without ever having the opportunity to exercise that skill under real-world pressure.[1]

Example 1: As an elective in college, you sign up for a crisis intervention class and during the class you study de-escalation technique and theory. The class is interesting, and the instructor is excellent. You work hard and receive an "A." You now understand the basic principles and the steps to take in this situation. You have an intellectual understanding, based on information intake, and you have a diploma to prove your competence. Following graduation, you use this to get a job as a crisis intervention counselor. Then for the first time, you find yourself caught between two individuals who are literally at war with each other and the situation escalates into a physical confrontation. Suddenly, you realize your personal safety is at risk. Your fear for yourself is so great that you don't even think about implementing the de-escalation techniques you learned in crisis intervention!

Example 2: You decide to take a CPR class and sign up for the training. On the day of the class, you and your fellow students listen to the instructor and observe as he demonstrates how to save a life. You go through the exercises step by step, and he gives you pointers to correct your technique. Toward the end of the class, your confidence begins to build, because you need less and less help to make the right decisions in the right order, even when you have to take your turn solo. You pass the course and receive your certification. Six months later, you witness a traffic accident. Both drivers are hurt, but one is conscious and the other is not. You recognize the unconscious person as the sister of your best friend. She is not breathing, and suddenly you freeze up. You can't think. You can't remember what to do. Just then, an older man shows up and immediately takes charge, commanding that you help him. You follow his lead, swing into action and *then* it starts coming back to you.

The one thing that was missing from the training format in both these examples was emotional content. You were paralyzed by fear and couldn't think of what to do. Although you had the right *information* and had even done some role-playing, you had no experience in dealing with the effects of severe, personalized stress. You were unprepared for the live act. When things suddenly turn ugly, being seasoned by actual exposure to the specific environment is what makes an intellectual skill-set effective. You cannot be at the top of your game without it.

2. Always work in concert with nature because success in survival happens when training matches environment.

This is just common sense. When you are able to re-create the conditions in which you will be using a skill, the stimulus that activates an automatic response is programmed or embedded very deeply. Training should reflect reality as closely as possible, and include as many sensory "triggers" as possible. If the scenario can be made to smell like, sound like, taste like, look like and feel like the real thing, and if enough heat and pressure are brought to bear, then the body will respond identically in a live environment. Every effort should be made to craft responses that are similar to the body's naturally instinctive reactions. The closer a conditioned response is to a natural movement or reaction, the easier and faster it can be embedded.

3. What is learned in adrenal format is acquired quickly and permanently.

We have all heard stories of individuals who have survived an extremely hazardous incident or environment. Not only do they remember it always, but they are often changed by it. Experience molds us. In a low stress environment, the changes are so gradual that we hardly notice them, but when you add emotional heat, the process speeds up—and the hotter the fire, the faster the change. This is particularly important when training people to successfully navigate high–threat environments, where conscious memory is not enough.

What is needed for survival is the ability to transcend the cognitive processing of the rational brain—to instinctively execute the appropriate response. However we choose to react, to be effective, the action must be pre–programmed into the subconscious so that it engages without hesitation. This is best accomplished by something Siddle refers to as massed practice: the technique of using multiple repetitions of an exercise in a very brief time frame. To date, Survival Response Conditioning is the only conditioning format available to civilians that uses massed practice, adrenal influences and reality–based scenarios in combination. It is the reason this method of training is effective within such a limited time frame. Instinctive responses that are embedded in the subconscious during a highly aroused emotional state of mind are permanent.

Siddle illustrates this point beautifully by reminding us of the speed at which a new driver acquires instinctive reactions. I love this example, because we've all been there; we've all had that driver slam on his brakes in front of us, or blast through a red light just as we are entering an intersection. For the great majority of us, having this happen once or maybe twice is all it takes to cause a lightning–fast, instinctive response *ever after* when confronted with similar risk. We negotiate these hazards automatically and successfully every day.[2]

Imagine how the process is accelerated and how deeply the response is embedded when it is generated by the focused intensity of an attacker in a confined space!

4. Awareness combined with experience on a subconscious level equals intuition: nature's internal radar.

Learning to respect and trust intuition is every bit as important as looking both ways before you cross the street. It should be as reflexive as scratching an itch. Often though, we respond to an intuitive warning with automatic denial.

This reminds me of a story about the Great Hurricane of 1938. Known as the "Long Island Express," it struck Long Island and New England on September 21, 1938 with such force that the initial impact of the storm surge registered on seismographs in Sitka, Alaska. Just before landfall, one of West Hampton Beach's citizens was examining a new barometer he had received in the mail. It displayed a reading of twenty-eight, in the "hurricanes and tornados" range. A barometer is a device used to measure atmospheric pressure. The lower the reading, the more severe the impending storm. Twenty-eight is an exceedingly low reading. The daily forecast was for light rain and gusty conditions. The man shook it, but the needle didn't budge. Frustrated, he decided it was defective and drove to the post office to return it. While he was gone, his house blew away.[3]

Intuition may not always be about what we think it is, but it should never be ignored. Respect your radar and it will save your life. The moment unease rears its head, pause and ask yourself why you feel apprehensive. *Giving your intuition the credibility it deserves is an act of purpose and power*—and a crucial safeguard against the vulnerability of automatic denial.

5. Fear in proper balance is a valuable asset.

If there is one lesson that is central to the premise of this book, it is that our personal relationship with fear is of vast importance. Too much, and we are either paralyzed or act inappropriately. Too little, and we take ill-advised risks. I am not speaking of the kind of anxiety we might feel before taking a test or the emotional energy in a spousal argument, or even the fear of becoming financially destitute. I am speaking of the paralyzing fear that lurks in our darkest dreams and jerks us into sweat-soaked wakefulness—the *Thing* behind the shadow, the whirlpool in our gut that drains our vitality, confidence and will.

Whether you have self-defense training or not, you will certainly be adversely affected by the emotional content of a confrontational situation if you have neglected to prepare for it. The problem is that the preparation required is a preparation of the heart and spirit. It is an emotional conditioning rather than a physical or intellectual preparation. No amount of classroom curriculum, no wise and balanced understanding, will be sufficient to shield you from the powerful physiological effects of this kind of fear. Yet, fear in balance, doing the job that nature intended, is absolutely, positively our best friend. We need to make its acquaintance.

6. The will to retaliate is the cornerstone of survival.

In the Survival Response programs I conduct the question is frequently asked: "What is the most important thing I can do to protect myself?"

My response is often a surprise to both the questioner and the audience. There are many things you can do to better your chances of avoiding confrontation altogether. I am a huge believer in the value and importance of prevention. However, correcting your own lax habits and learning additional strategies is only half the problem. No matter how careful you are, you dare not forget the possibility of being targeted by an attacker. This may have nothing to do with your level of awareness and caution. Sometimes it is just the luck (or misfortune) of the draw.

> *The best protection you can obtain is not so much a question of what you must do. It is rather a question of what you must become.*

Again and again I have been forcefully reminded that when a confrontation or an attack happens, it usually comes as an overwhelming surprise, and surprises are responded to instinctively. You show your true colors. You need a transformational experience. You must become someone with the will to retaliate. This is non-negotiable. It is the survival baseline, the foundation upon which every other strategy depends; the prevention and the cure all rolled into one.

Kerry Sauve, director of Street Sense Safety and Security Inc., poses this question: *"What makes a good street fighter so dangerous? First, they have conditioned themselves, through repeated exposure to combat, to function while under adrenal stress. Second, they have also overcome the psychological reluctance to harm other human beings. This is an incredibly important piece to the puzzle that needs to be addressed as it is so often overlooked when people discuss and teach self-defense. We can easily teach people to learn to deal with the debilitating effects of adrenaline during combat. We can also teach them how to confront and overcome their fears. Teaching them to 'throw the switch' and physically harm another human being, even in their own defense, is much more difficult. The most devastating self-defense technique is useless if the student is reluctant to apply it during a violent encounter."*[4]

For those of you who doubt your ability to defend yourself; who cannot imagine harming another human being—I invite you to consider an alternative scenario: Imagine hearing a scream, looking out your window and seeing a strange man tugging your four-year-old daughter into a van. Would you hesitate for a moment? Would you think about consequences? Would you be intimidated by the fact that he is six feet, four inches tall and weighs 230 pounds? Of course not! You would act instantly without regard for your own safety. You would take him on and if possible, take him out! You would be unstoppable! This is the maternal instinct in action, and we can learn to direct the same focused rage and determination when we are targeted.

The truth is that if a predator is able to deprive you of your life or health, it is not only you who are the victim. Your family will suffer, as well. Who will be there to protect and provide for them if not you? You see, by protecting yourself, you are protecting them as surely as if they were the intended victims. The will to retaliate is something predators can sense a mile away, and they avoid it like the plague. Once you have this advantage, it is likely that they will not even see you as a potential victim.

7. Within limited parameters, gross motor skills are increasingly effective with higher stress levels.

Gross motor skills are simple, direct movements using the body's large muscle groups, often at full power. Under severe stress, adrenaline activates and enhances these gross motor movements, making the body capable of producing superhuman effort. Siddle posits that a normal gross motor skill can be acquired in approximately three minutes or about twenty-five repetitions.[5]

Simple, direct and powerful: These are the defining characteristics of techniques that work most efficiently under adrenal influences—and the good news is—as stress escalates, performance increases, but there is a ceiling. Siddle points to heart rate (between 115 and 145 BPM) as the key to peak performance under these conditions. Ibid. Pg 58 For all of the above reasons, effective Survival Response programs limit the use of strikes to gross motor skills.

8. Whenever possible, be proactive and preemptive.

Action beats reaction nearly every time. When you foresee that a confrontation is imminent and you cannot avoid it or de-escalate it, allowing the aggressor the advantage of acting first is a fatal error. The reason we are able to train people to be street–safe in eight hours is because we have a different approach to dealing with a physical attack.

Traditional martial arts training takes a long time to be effective because of the idea that a physical attack begins with a strike. This means that to thwart an attack you must *react*. This is a problem because as stated above, in the real world action beats reaction almost every time. Traditional martial arts focus on training the reflexes to become lightning fast, and its success depends on perfect timing. This requires long, long periods of time spent on training both the mind and body. In our fast–paced society, the vast majority of the general public does not have this kind of time.

This whole scenario is vastly altered when we redefine a physical attack in terms of intent. If you were asked at what point an attack on you began, you would probably answer, "When the assailant struck me."

Now, let's suppose you are on a hiking trail, rounding a sharp turn in the path and you come face to face with a grizzly bear. The bear rears up and charges. At what point did the attack begin?

When you detect someone moving toward you in an aggressive manner and your internal alarms begin to sound; when you clearly indicate to that person by body language and clear verbal interaction that his or her advance is alarming and unwanted; and under these circumstances that person still continues to close the distance between you, then an attack has begun. Normal people without hostile intent stop the moment they realize they are alarming you. If you cannot escape, if the threat is immediate and unavoidable and you feel at risk of great bodily harm or death; if believing you have no other options, you take physical action at this point, *you are acting in self-defense, even though you strike first. Action beats reaction nearly every time.* By following the strategy of striking first under these specific conditions, you have eliminated a large percentage of your dependence on timing.

9. Inflict maximum damage with minimum effort, as soon as possible.

It is safe to assume that, in any emergency, the resources of time and energy are at a premium. This is especially true of any circumstance involving predatory human threat. Whatever is done must be done quickly. Emergencies, by their very nature, are defined by speed: The event occurs suddenly and must be responded to in kind. The emotional content of a life-threatening situation puts a crushing drain on our energy, physically and psychologically. Actions that conserve energy: economy of motion, clarity of purpose and the intuitive decisions that support them, are the difference between life and death in emergencies.

This kind of level-headed, deft navigation of stress is embodied in E.R. Guthrie's definition of skill: the ability to bring about some end result with maximum certainty and minimum outlay of energy.[6] Athletes who practice diligently become so effective that their movements seem *effortless*. Let's return to the earlier example of driving, something most of us do daily. We don't think of this as practicing, but that is exactly what we are doing, until the actions become so automatic that we can occasionally find ourselves deeply immersed in our own inner world while driving. Then, with a start, we suddenly come to the realization that we cannot remember seeing the route we have just driven.

It is evident that we all have the capacity to respond decisively in a crisis. What is lacking is the requisite conditioning that pulls these fragmented survival skills into synergistic union. To deal successfully with an emergency, *especially* if it involves survival, there are three critical objectives:

1. Effective, successful action
2. Minimal time investment
3. Conservation of physical and mental energy

In other words, a lightning-fast response, using minimal resources, with devastating effect.

10. Hesitation equals death.

Many instructors, myself among them, believe that a half second delay in a life-threatening encounter can have potentially lethal consequences.[7] During training, anything that can be done to reduce or eliminate hesitation is essential, because it is while the intended victim hesitates, that the predator gains the advantage.

* * *

These principles form the backbone of the methodology in the Survival Response Conditioning program that my staff and I have developed. If it seems these tactics are too intense and provocative, remember that the subject matter revolves around life-or-death scenarios. The objective of saving a life necessitates creating an environment where the focus is survival by whatever means necessary. Ideology must give way to efficiency and practicality when faced with an unexpected high-stakes confrontation. What will you do when you cross paths with an individual who cannot be reasoned with, especially someone who has delusions of invincibility combined with homicidal urges?

Chapter 7

This is How We Roll

"Victorious warriors win first and then go to war, while defeated warriors go to war first and then seek to win."

–Sun Tzu, The Art of War

What happens to an individual who is suddenly and shockingly confronted by an overwhelming, frightening situation? Often, it begins with confusion, denial and a weak, sick feeling that starts in the stomach and spreads rapidly to tightness in the chest, with difficulty breathing and weakness in the knees. Hearing may be reduced and often tunnel vision is experienced. Fingers and toes may feel numb and fine motor skills are often greatly impaired, resulting in a loss of manual dexterity. "I couldn't dial the phone!"—or other similar complaints are commonly heard after the fact. It is often difficult to remember clear and concise details after the experience is over. Many individuals have reported feeling as if events were transpiring in slow, dreamlike motion, lending a surreal quality to their memory of the situation.

What I have just described to you are the results of the human body experiencing an adrenaline "rush." The intellect and higher thought processes shut down, and instinct, the function of the subconscious mind, takes over. This is why an intellectual understanding of these situations is inadequate and needs to be augmented with a physical and emotional *experience*. Studying the proper theories, understanding the relevant concepts and training the body to respond is valuable and necessary, but it is no substitute for emotional conditioning. So, the question arises, "How do we prepare students emotionally for a physical threat?" The answer is not found in teaching new information or training new physical skills alone. Effective preparation for the human threat environment requires *conditioning*.

Instead of theory, they must obtain an *experience* that programs their heart and spirit with courage, so that when the need arises, they will be able to take decisive action when confronted by overwhelming fear.

The number one obstacle students face is overcoming their own skepticism regarding the reality of the training scenarios they engage in. As we discussed in the last chapter, success in survival happens when training matches environment. A part of the brain lets students know that *a seminar is not real*, and judgment begins quietly nagging them with the question, "Would this really work on the street?"

Producing Fear in a Contrived Environment

In order to produce a genuine fear response in a contrived environment, it is necessary to trigger multiple auto-instinctive threat recognition mechanisms that lie buried in the human subconscious.

Here's why. In an artificial setting, the conscious brain is preoccupied with a constant reality check. It does this to protect itself (and its owner) from what it dreads most: making a mistake. Defensive-tactics instructors are confronted with this obstacle whenever they try to project high levels of realism into a training curriculum. Even with overwhelming pressure, the conscious brain attempts to maintain its grasp on reality. When logic goes to war with sensory perception, students in a training environment often engage in a kind of internal conversation, attempting to reassure themselves with thoughts like, "This is just a class." Yet, by questioning the authenticity of the training experience, the student unwittingly weakens its benefit. Even in the most dynamic training environment, effective skill acquisition cannot take place until the student is no longer distracted by this mindset. The real problem here is that the normal, rational brain learning format that we are most familiar with is not equipped to override its own B.S. meter.

To get around this road block, the conscious brain's programming must be over-written by a much more primal, powerful set of directives—impulses that prompt a visceral, emotional response. These mechanisms are not connected to the conscious brain and exist outside its normal function. Their purpose is to produce an automatic, lightning-fast defensive response to certain patterns of motion and sound, *before* conscious judgment and analysis begin to assert themselves. These mechanisms are most easily activated in scenarios where conditions cause feelings of vulnerability. (An example would be an individual who found himself alone in an unfamiliar low-light environment.) Without this system, we would all be terminally vulnerable to sudden threat because, by the time the conscious brain quantified the threat, chose the appropriate response and sent the signal to carry it out, we would be steam-rolled by the event itself.

What are these triggers and how can they be used to bring fear, the central ingredient in the conditioning crucible, into the training arena? Let's focus on six of them:

Fear Triggers

1. Sudden, direct, closing movement toward the subject, especially if it comes from an oblique angle—and the larger the incoming object, the more powerful the response

2. Unexpected, loud noises with threatening connotations

3. Sudden changes in visual perception—light to dark, dark to light, or whiteout

4. Any unexpected touch or voice when visually impaired

5. Abrupt, close quarter exposure to anything that bears a resemblance to snakes, spiders or aggressive poisonous insects

6. Abrupt, close quarter exposure to confined spaces, especially when immobilized

Notice that the common denominators for these triggers have to do with sudden, unexpected changes in proximity to the subject. It is the necessity of responding *suddenly* to a possibly life-threatening situation or condition that causes the rational brain to be eclipsed by these auto-instinctive threat recognition programs. For example, while walking down an unfamiliar, secluded footpath, you spot a strange, intimidating man coming directly toward you. He is approximately fifty feet away. This causes *mild unease*, which increases with his approach. Your mind produces a kaleidoscope of images and options about which action to take. It is in "What to do?" mode. You are apprehensive, worried and very mindful of your vulnerability.

Now, let's take this same scenario and adjust its parameters. You are walking down the same path when without warning, a roaring man with outspread arms lunges at you from behind a bush. You are galvanized into action. Instinctively you drop your center of gravity and your arms come up to protect yourself, your pulse is racing, you experience cold sweat and your vision narrows to the point that you can only see the threat. Instead of being in "What to do?" mode, you are *doing* automatically and instinctively while feeling high levels of fear or terror.

In a classroom or seminar environment, the scenario of the hidden man leaping from a concealed position would produce the same initial response, but then the subject would immediately revert to his/her pre-event mindset because of *the disparity between event and setting.* To prolong and authenticate an instinctive fear response in a contrived scenario, the setting must change to support the event. For instance, you are sitting in your chair listening to the facilitator speak. Suddenly a loud, explosive sound behind you causes you to turn, and you are confronted with a large man. He is less than six feet away and closing rapidly. The lights go out and his body crashes into yours, knocking you to the ground. You hear shouts of alarm and screams from those who were seated near you. Now, you are locked in a hand–to–hand struggle with a stranger in the dark. Because setting has changed to match event, the reality of the event can no longer be denied. Physiologically, contrived environment has become live experience because all the triggers for visceral, instinctive, emotional response have been pulled simultaneously.

Survival response conditioning is the missing link in modern self-defense training: emotional calisthenics via scenarios in which the subconscious mind responds as if the circumstances were real. This is the only methodology that re-programs the emotional body to act in concert with the physical body and the intellect. It is the answer to the question we posed above, "Would this really work on the street?" As a graduate, you will know because you will have *experienced* it, not once but numerous times. Massed practice in a high stress, emotionally charged environment will have conditioned you to respond to a threat without hesitation and its attendant liabilities. You will be familiar with the feeling of fear, and while it is still uncomfortable, it will not cause hesitation; rather, it will fuel your actions. The old arguments of panic and despair will no longer have the same hold on you. You will know, in your cells and in your veins, and that knowledge will give you confidence and power.

Let's go back for a moment to the subject of adrenaline and the way an individual feels when under its influence. As we respond to the warnings of intuition and real fear blossoms in our conscious minds, the brain selects one of two compounds secreted in adrenal glands and releases it into the body. These two compounds are adrenaline and nor-adrenaline. Adrenaline fuels the flight complex and directs the subconscious mind to flee at once. Nor-adrenaline prompts the fight complex and instinctively we know that we must fight for our lives. The wonderful thing about these automatic commands is that with the command comes the power to obey it. There is no lag time; it happens simultaneously.

Physiologically, the result is that powerful reserves of energy are called up almost instantaneously, and the body's preparation for supercharged action is often misinterpreted by our senses as a feeling of weakness. However, the truth is that *this seeming weakness is a signal to the conscious mind that the body is primed for action*. Feelings of fear and weakness, rightly understood, have a tremendous, positive value with regard to survival. Once again, knowledge is power. Your body has the ability to instantly prime itself for superhuman effort. Knowing that what you used to interpret as weakness is actually a signal that your body is about to unleash all its reserves, will help you to act *decisively* to save your life. Experience is what programs the body, the intellect and intuition to function in harmony for survival.

Except for risking your life on the street, there is only one way you can gain this experience—the same way the students whose testimony you read at the beginning of Chapter 4 did. It is safe, effective and inexpensive when you consider the profound and permanent changes it produces. The generic name for this method is Adrenal Response Training but after years of fine-tuning its parameters, I believe it is more accurate to refer to it as Survival Response Conditioning. I say this because an "adrenal" response can be both negative and inaccurate, depending on the circumstances, but a survival response is powerful, positive and always has a person's best interest as its objective.

There are a number of trainers around the country who offer these courses to the public on a regular basis. I happen to be one of them. We take students through a series of scenario-based exercises where they are confronted by attackers in specially designed body armor. This armor protects them against injury so that the students can respond with all their power—exactly what they would have to do to save their life in a real altercation. The strikes are all gross motor skills: very simple and designed to increase in efficiency and power as stress becomes more acute. These padded attackers are highly skilled in verbal assault and intimidating body language; it is their job to bring out an adrenaline rush in the students, and they do it very well. Since the fear is real, we are able to teach our students how to defend themselves under the same physiological conditions they would face on the street. These attackers know how to gauge the power of a blow through the armor—what would put them down or knock them out if they were not wearing it. They absolutely, positively will not stop until the student has delivered several clean blows with knockout power. The students go through eight to ten such scenarios, which increase in difficulty and intensity. With each scenario, we give them less information than before, which forces them to rely on themselves, their natural instincts and the specific techniques we teach them.

Survival response seminars are almost always coed. Men generally have no concept of the difference between a woman's level of fear and their own. Because of this, it is difficult for men to express the appropriate level of empathy. However, when they are exposed to it firsthand and witness it personally, their hearts are opened, and they become much more compassionate. Conversely, women discover that men have the same basic fears, which they might never admit in any other setting. The wonderful result is that men and women who experience this program together are more likely to see members of the opposite sex as human beings first and men or women second.

I believe that the remarkable effectiveness and success of these programs are due primarily to the profound emotional bond it produces: first, the covenant established between the students' self-worth and his/her propensity for taking action under adverse circumstances; and second, among the individual students themselves. Common experience, especially under trying circumstances, is often the mortar that cements long–lasting, positive friendships. Soldiers and policemen know firsthand that there are no friends like foxhole friends. Discovering the truth behind this powerful dynamic is our next objective.

Chapter 8

Training Day

"Pain is the best instructor, but no one wants to go to his class."

−*General Choi, Hong Hi*

I watch them enter the room, sometimes alone, more often in groups of two or three. Most are women between the ages of eighteen and forty-five, but some are younger and a few are older. The feeling of apprehension is tangible and cloying; a nervous tension revealed in averted glances and tight smiles. They are wearing masks—all of them—and this is normal. It is a protective mechanism that we all unconsciously adopt when we feel vulnerable. Cautious and reserved at first, they wonder if the others are the right people to be in "their" seminar. Tentatively they begin to reach out, attempting to establish the delicate web of support so necessary in negotiating an unfamiliar environment.

The men who come here push out the space between them, like small kingdoms. They are sensitive to the borders and tend them like gardeners. No one knows quite what to expect, although all of them are seeking their version of the same thing. I have learned to recognize their types and read them well. Today, all of them will find answers to questions that have vexed them for years. Their stories are like leaves: every one unique, yet in a certain sense all the same. The mother who has lost connection with her teenage daughter and thus feels helpless to impart her motherly wisdom, the middle aged woman recently divorced from a chronically abusive husband, the man who feels he has become too passive and wants to regain assertiveness and passion in his life. Many are parents, here in part because they are testing the water for their children. Some have been abused; some are fearful they will be. Some are not concerned with self-defense, but see the program as a way to face and overcome fear in general. The common denominator is fear and the desire to be free of its hold. They all want to fill the voids in their experience and emotional being with confidence and courage. They want assurance and assertiveness. They want to feel and experience self-reliance.

I can clearly see the question marks in their eyes. They know this day will be difficult, and they wonder if they will be able to measure up. They are wondering if they will fail again, as they have so many times before. They are questioning their own wisdom in the decision to participate in this program. They are wondering about me. It is the same every time.

I know something they do not. I know they are an elite group, a cut above the mainstream, because unlike their peers, they have freely chosen to be here, in a place where they know they will experience fear. They are here to confront the demons that have blocked their way and limited their horizons. They have come to be reconnected with nature's powerful gifts, to be reborn as protectors of themselves and their children. And they have done so in opposition to friends and family who themselves are addicted to mediocrity. They have come to realize that the status quo is not enough to satisfy them anymore, and they are willing to commit to an experience that will change them forever.

What many of them do not realize is that they have already done the hardest thing: They have decided to change their lives and they have acted on it. This decision to change direction has been a shift of monumental proportions to them. For most, it is a distinctly uncomfortable experience, yet it is not without its rewards. Like the sun rising with irresistible power over the Serengeti, the expanding certainty that they are on the right launching pad for a new journey fills them with resolve.

From beginning to end, today is actually a graduation exercise. I am filled with anticipation of the change they will soon experience. Today, I will watch them as they dismantle the barriers that have separated them from themselves and each other. I will cheer them as they erect new, healthy boundaries that actually serve them. I will feel their pain as they struggle to put their fear in proper balance and relive experiences from their past that have held them prisoner. It is my job to help them in their successful prison break, to reach inside themselves deeper than they believe they can go, and pull out victory in the face of seemingly overwhelming odds. I must play my part in creating an environment where they will find out who they really are and the limitless possibilities of what they can be. This is their day. This is their journey, and I am the one who is privileged to facilitate it. I am eager to begin to get to know them personally, but I must bide my time, knowing that the success of this process requires me to be a destabilizing influence first.

Every one of them will play the game I described in the last chapter. The name of this game is, *"I'm not scared. This is not reality. This is just a class."* As long as they engage in playing this game, I cannot help them. My first act of service to these students is to put their game in check. I will begin with something subtle and small compared to what will happen as the day progresses: breaking up the budding support cliques that started to grow among them as soon as they arrived. They will not be allowed to sit next to each other. They must first feel vulnerable, and they will feel it most acutely if they are alone in an unfamiliar setting. The expectation programs that are running in their minds must be interrupted with surprise and with events that have a sudden and unpredictable outcome.

I am the conductor; the facilitator responsible for the outcome, management, safety and in a large measure, the successful experience of the grads. Fortunately, I am not alone. For this program, I have a crew of unique individuals, all of them grads of the program themselves, who have dedicated themselves to bringing the benefits of what they have experienced to others. All of them know their jobs and do them well. Without them, none of this would be possible. All of them are volunteers who selflessly give their time, energy, money and heart.

They are divided into two groups: support staff and "ghouls." For the first two hours, while the support staff and I prep them, the students will not see the ghouls or have any evidence that they exist. After they are introduced, the ghouls will fill the students' horizons for the next six to eight hours. It is their job to welcome these students into the academy of fear and to keep them enrolled until they have a powerful new relationship with it. They are the dreadful, menacing, fully armored antagonists who bring the key ingredient that everything else in this program depends on for success: pure fear. They are human flash-bang grenades. When the ghouls step into the room, the temperature drops ten degrees. They are so successful, these bringers, that in the first few seconds of contact, many women and some men will be in tears. While the students try to slide into denial, the ghouls rip it away from them like an attorney tears up a bogus contract. As the scenarios progress, the ghouls will increase the intensity exponentially, and in doing so will they will take the students far beyond where they thought they could go. This is an absolute necessity because *it is impossible to gain courage without an up–close, personal acquaintance with fear.*

All of humanity is subject to this rule. We can talk theory for hours, and it will not increase our level of courage by as much as an ounce. If we want courage and the reward it brings, we must be willing to immerse ourselves in fear. Often, people learn to be courageous because circumstances force it upon them suddenly and they have to respond without thought. The reason I believe these people are so special is because they have taken the time to think about it and they have willingly placed themselves in an environment they dread, *with the full knowledge that they are unprepared for it.* If that is not a clear definition of hero, I don't know what is.

I am—and my staff with me—deeply honored to be a part of the transformation these students are about to go through. We hold their success to be a sacred trust and we will leave no one behind. That is why the students have been instructed to make no time commitments for the evening following the class. It ends when all have finished, no matter how long it takes, and I will not let the group be held hostage because of a football game or a Tupperware party. This is where it begins: with a commitment.

I must know that the students are determined to finish the program, no matter what. If they cannot make that commitment up front, I respect that—and ask that they respect the class by leaving now and returning when they are able to commit. If this seems harsh, consider that I know what they are about to face. I know at some point in the program they will reach a cross-road—that spot where they say to themselves, "I didn't bargain for this: it's too horrible. I feel dirty, I'm tired, and I'm scared. I want to go home!" I explain to them that I know they will reach this point, and without the iron resolve of an absolute commitment, they will have come here only to suffer another humiliating failure in their lives. I have made a commitment to them that I will not let that happen.

I explain that we are doing what amounts to psychological surgery and it can only be done with their full consent and agreement. In a medical operation, we enter into a contract with the surgeon beforehand. We agree to undergo physical trauma in order to gain the future benefit of better health or a longer life. A surgeon and his team would be held legally liable if during the operation, the patient, in great pain, demanded to be released and the surgeon acquiesced, letting him go without concluding the operation. He is obligated to fulfill his part of the contract, even if the patient begs him to stop. Disempowerment is a disease of the mind and the emotional body. It can have catastrophic, long-term and sometimes fatal results. Disempowerment denies us the right to live the life we are entitled to. This program is dedicated to its eradication. Once these issues are clear, and we have made this commitment to each other, the first part of the day can begin.

I must next construct a bridge of trust between myself and the students. I start by telling them my own story and the story of Safety First. As a young boy, I was very weak and sick for long periods of time. I was hospitalized seven times for bronchitis and eight times for pneumonia. I had a gamma-globulin deficiency and retarded bone growth. I was a poor student, mostly because of low self-image due to systematic bullying by my peers. My physical weakness made me a very easy target for anyone with a mean streak. I hated my life and wanted to escape it. I became interested in martial arts in my early teens and pestered my parents, especially my mother until she finally relented. For my fifteenth birthday present, she enrolled me in Steve Armstrong's Isshinryu Karate School. I had no natural abilities. Many students there were more talented than I was, and all of them were more skilled. I didn't care. I was happy just to be there, and though I lacked ability, I more than made up for it in desire.

I began to blossom socially, and for the first time in my life I had several friends who liked and respected me. In particular, I met a young man my own age named George Warnell, who became my best and lifelong friend, and with whom I ultimately partnered to found Safety First Personal Protection Strategies many years later. As a result of training with this wonderful group of people, my life quickly and radically changed for the better. My GPA went up, and I became an honor student. I regained my health and began to excel at the skills I loved. I became a black belt shortly after my eighteenth birthday, about the same time I graduated from high school, and became a young instructor under Sensei Armstrong. As I grew older and joined the work force, I continued my education in the combative arts and gained a working knowledge of several other martial arts to add to my Isshinryu base. Pentjak-Silat, Aikido, Arnis and Escrima –Serrada are systems I continue to find great value in.

I taught specialized classes around my community in Tacoma, Washington, including women's self-defense. As I gained experience and knowledge, I developed a program designed specifically for women called U.T.I.A. It was an acronym for "Unleashing the Inner Amazon" and focused on the eight ways that men commonly attack women. This was a very successful program. I began to get requests to put something in writing about U.T.I.A.

One morning while I was home doing research on that project, I saw Gavin DeBecker for the first time on Oprah. I was very impressed with what he had to say and subsequently purchased his book, "The Gift of Fear." His recommendation of Impact Personal Safety and the methodology of adrenal response training fascinated me. I had to know more. Eventually I was able to contact Jeff Alexander of Warrior Spirit, located in Issaquah, Washington, and I enrolled myself in his four day program, the "Leap of Faith." That program changed my life. I loved the experience and joined the Warrior Spirit staff. I stayed actively involved with their organization for two years. During that time, I was able to talk my old friend George Warnell, my son Brandon and a number of others close to me into going through the Warrior Spirit program. Right after 9-11, George, Brandon and I decided to begin our own program. We believed there was a way to teach this to people in a much shorter period of time, and we wanted to do something proactive to help others overcome their fear in the aftermath of 9-11.

Since then we have continued to grow our program through empirical research, practice, trial and error. We have been blessed with the help of many, many other dedicated and selfless individuals along the way. Together, we have discovered the meaning of true love, using the medium of extreme violence. I don't expect these students to grasp the meaning of that strange statement just yet, but by the end of this day they will and it will be one of the most powerful, insightful experiences they have ever had. Many have even called it beautiful.

By telling my story, I have connected myself more intimately with the members of the class. I can sense that they are identifying themselves with me and now have a stronger basis for trust. It is time to put them squarely on task. There are four goals that we are aiming for today.

The first and most obvious is to train our students to be street-safe in eight hours. What this means is that if they become the intended victim of a predator, they will possess a much greater than normal chance to succeed in resisting the aggressor with little or no injury to themselves or their children, should they happen to be present. They will have a new set of behavioral templates that direct their actions in ways that are wholly unexpected to those who intend them harm.

The second goal is for our students to experience the reality of their power consciously and even more importantly, in the subconscious. When experience imprints specific knowledge, and the student has established subconscious skill confidence, little time is spent focusing on executing the skill. It is as automatic as breathing, keeping your balance or steering your car. This subconscious confidence is the definition of empowerment.

Third, as the students progress through the exercises and repeatedly witness examples of heroism under stress, they come to realize that this is the way human beings were meant to function. They will internalize the beautiful observation of Albert Camus: *"In the depths of winter, I finally learned that within me, there lay an invincible summer."*[8] This understanding has a powerful ripple effect and touches every human being we come in contact with whether we choose to recognize it or not.

The fourth and last goal of the program is a natural result of the other three: a strong and lasting group bond. A mutually beneficial shared experience is the foundation of a lasting friendship and the tougher the circumstances, the stronger the attachment. Soldiers who have defended each other's lives on the battle-field never forget the honor of having served together, and though they may be separated for years in their civilian lives, the friendship remains over time and distance. Students in this program develop a room full of new friends, a powerful support group bound together by a common experience.

I can see and feel that the group is beginning to loosen up a little with each other, although their personal stress levels are high. Like Cape Buffalo on the African Savannah, they are beginning to press together to confront threat. I cover the topics we need to discuss in an open discussion format: the will to retaliate, intuition, fear, empowerment, the predator's mindset and proactive boundaries.

To keep their attention, I break up the presentation and discussion every ten minutes or so by having them stand and do strike-drills as calisthenics. I want them focused on the learning process, not comfortable in their chairs. I tell them to take advantage of the rest they are getting now, because once we start interacting with the ghouls, we won't be taking rest breaks except between the exercises.

We move on to the subjects of distance or range and positioning. Support staff and I demonstrate different approaches that predators use in different circumstances. I really have their attention now; they are on the edge of their chairs because they sense that the moment of confrontation is not far away. Hard, soft and blind approaches are demonstrated at full power and speed.

A "hard" approach is a frightening situation in which the assailant physically closes range with the intended victim while initiating a verbal assault. Predators use this tactic to test a target's level of resistance and to determine if an attempt to intimidate and to break the will to resist will succeed. It is a type of *interview* designed to answer the question, "Will the intended victim be easy prey?" Surprisingly, the benefit here is that there is no ambiguity about the situation. The intended victim understands that they are in a very threatening position immediately.

A "soft" approach is more dangerous than a "hard" approach because the intent is disguised. Using a prop, like asking for the time or directions, allows the predator to close range and be within striking range before the target realizes a threat is present. The "blind" approach is the most dreaded of all. In this scenario, the intended victim is assaulted from behind, tackled and taken to the ground before he or she realizes what hit them.

I can see from the look on their faces that the students are now seriously in doubt they will be able to perform well under these circumstances. This is exactly what I want. I need them to feel their powerlessness for two reasons: First, fear is necessary to the success of this process and second, the greater their fear, the more pronounced their freedom from its control will feel. Right now all of them are wondering how on earth they could deal with the speed and power of the blind approach. I can see it on the faces of most of the men as well as the women.

Once in a while, we get a man who is so full of machismo that nothing I say makes an impression with him. Men like this are very valuable to the class because they allow me the opportunity to give them and the whole group something the support staff calls a "learning experience." These men are judging the situation by what they have seen and what they think they are capable of. The problem for them is they have absolutely no idea of how quickly our staff can escalate a situation to horrific proportions. The minute they present a challenge, I change the circumstances, so that the odds are many times more than they bargained for.

Remember, I am not at all concerned about what is "fair." My goal is that every student in the class will meet their worst nightmare, not once, but many times over, so that they can experience the power of *determined effort in the face of overwhelming odds*. This is the defining characteristic in any measure of raw courage.

These students are now ready to adopt the will to retaliate and this always starts with finding their voice. In the program, we call it "voice power." Overcoming this challenge can be surprisingly difficult, especially for women in the group. Normal, decent people are not prepared for the verbal intensity of a street confrontation—they are not accustomed to speaking that way. Police officers know this very well, and they freely use the language of the street to gain "shock advantage" in controlling a volatile situation. Words are like sharp tools. Predators use them to carve up potential victims before they ever lay a hand on them. One of the first and most important things we must accomplish in this program is to take the edges off the predator's verbal blades. There is an important lesson here. Simply put, *"If you can't say it, it has power over you."*

One of the exercises in voice power that is very difficult for students involves identifying the words and phrases that deeply disturb them. In this exercise, a staff member shouts those vile expressions at the students, who shout them back in turn. Many times as a facilitator I have been confronted with students who for moral or ethical reasons at first refuse to engage in this exercise. I have found that the most helpful way to deal with this particular problem is to empathize with them and explain that this is a self-contained environment; sacred ground, so to speak. These words, like a growl or a roar, are just sounds that are calculated to provoke a fear response. I invite them to *give themselves permission to learn how to protect themselves against the effects of these weapons*, using the only proven way that actually works: de-sensitization. We are not advocating that they add them to their vocabulary; on the contrary, they are a criminal waste of energy and may escalate a situation unnecessarily. There is a powerful word that we want them to learn instead. They need to discover the power of verbal resistance; the "know of No." We conclude the voice power drills, and the students all have it: they are able to verbally check someone who is invading their space with a forceful and loud command, "NO!"

Now it is time to test their abilities under real pressure and stress. At this moment, the door bangs open and six ghouls enter the room. They are large, powerful and covered from head to toe in black armor. The students cannot see their faces because their huge helmets with netted eye sockets make identification impossible. From the second they enter the room, the ghouls own the space they occupy. Staff arranges the students into six lines. A ghoul faces each line, radiating menace and rage. They are like bulls straining against the gates waiting to trample and gore the matador.

In this exercise, the students are instructed to clasp their hands behind their back and stand their ground. They are not to back away or to respond verbally. They are to be silent. The purpose of this drill is to connect them to the rage of the aggressor, to accept the verbal and physical intimidation as real, to receive its full impact and to do nothing. This is stage one. I release the ghouls, and they explode into the student's personal space. They make Marine Corp drill sergeants look like Sunday School teachers. The students are pale, shaken; some are weeping openly, others are simply shell-shocked. I put the ghouls in check—and ask the students how they felt. Anger, fear, helplessness, powerlessness, terror and shock are all at the top of the list. Now I know they are really feeling it; this is beginning to become emotionally real to them.

Stage two is a repeat of stage one except this time I want the students to assume a launch position, otherwise known as the submissive guard, where the right foot is usually eighteen inches behind the left foot and the hands are raised with the palms pointing outward. The upper body is leaning slightly back, so that the general impression is one of revulsion or strong denial. This is universal body language for "Stop! I don't want any trouble!" I want them to assume this position as soon as they see the ghoul begin to move toward them, and I want them to use the voice power skills they acquired in the previous exercise. I want them to resist the ghoul verbally with all their power.

Again the ghouls crash into the line of students like a wave overwhelming a beach–head, but this time the students respond with power. The ghouls press the issue because I have instructed them not to stop their intimidation until the student's response is powerful enough that the ghoul is convinced they really mean it. After stage two is complete, I ask the students to compare the way they felt in both stages. Most if not all feel that verbal resistance makes them feel more powerful and less vulnerable to the physical crowding and verbal assault of the ghoul.

What the students have just experienced is an exercise we call *verbal break-down*. Their pulse is up; their adrenaline is beginning to flow and they are beginning to enter the "acquisition zone" where skills are permanently imprinted in the subconscious mind. Quickly, before the effect begins to degrade, we will take them into their first combat experience. In the center of the mat, a ten–foot square has been taped off. This is the "ring." On each of the four sides are staff members holding an air shield, a device martial artists use to practice full contact strikes. This ring is where the altercations between students and ghouls will take place. The "shields," as they are called, are there to keep the fight indexed in the ring. Their job is to guard the line they are positioned on and use the air shields to keep the participants within the ring. As the students become acclimated to the ring and how the scenarios are conducted, they will take over the "shield" positions themselves.

This first combat scenario is called a Front Fight, because the approach is from the front and the ghoul will be using either a hard or a soft approach. This fight will be demonstrated with a staff member playing the part of the intended victim, so that the students can see what they will be engaging in momentarily. The staff member steps into the ring. She is wearing shin protectors and elbow pads but no other protective gear. The ghoul approaches and stands outside the corner of the ring. I ask the staff member if she has any body parts at risk (weak ankles, a bad back etc.) The ghoul has to know this and give a signal that he understands in order to keep the student safe. She confirms that she has no body parts at risk. I ask if the shields are in place and ready and they "green-light" me. "Ghoul is free!" I shout.

Instantly the ghoul launches himself at the staffer, hurling verbal obscenities at her at the top of his lungs. He has chosen a "hard" approach. With all her power and a loud, focused "No!" she strikes him with both hands in the eye sockets. He is roaring with pain and anger, as his hands fly up to his eyes, exposing his groin. Her soccer-style kick, fueled by the fury of her "NO!" catches him there squarely and with sickening power, doubling him over. She is short, no more than five feet, and he is well over six feet tall, but doubled over, he is in proper range for a devastating right elbow to the temple, which she executes with full body rotation. This snaps his head and torso upright, and she closes, grabbing the front of his armor with both hands and kneeing him a second shot to the groin. Every time she strikes, she yells. The knee drops him to all fours. Another knee to the front of his helmet actually drives him over onto his back. At this point, the fight is over because he is off his feet and stunned, leaving her the opportunity to escape with a reasonable chance of success. She runs out of the ring, turns and shouts "NO!" one last time. This entire scenario takes less than five seconds from start to finish.

I watch the students' faces. They are truly frightened now. No one is playing The Game anymore. It has become real to them, and now they feel intense fear. They are about to fight for their lives, with all their power, and they will experience all the effects of adrenaline: tunnel vision, auditory exclusion, loss of fine motor skills, and inability to recall clear details in the immediate aftermath.

One by one, they take their places in the ring and to their amazement; all of them get the job done. It's not real pretty this first time, but *all that* is going to change very quickly. Immediately upon realizing they have actually faced what they feared and succeeded, they begin to change, and it is visible. Like the Vikings, they discover that what doesn't kill them makes them stronger. As the day progresses and one experience is pasted into the next, they are transforming. As individuals and as a group, they are adopting the warrior mindset. They are evolving into something they never thought possible, at a pace that before today was unimaginable. They are becoming counterpredators.

Facilitating this program and working on staff is like being a photographer recording the growth of a plant in time-lapse photography. When you watch the process on television, you know the effect is artificial. Imagine the wonder and joy you might feel if what you saw on the screen was real. That is what we experience and why grads want to volunteer their time freely. It is magical and addictive; it is powerful, and most of all, it is deeply fulfilling.

As the day progresses, the different exercises are completed. The more pressure they are put under, the better they perform. The group functions smoothly as a unit. The individual students are not the same people they were just a few hours ago. Now, it is time for the ultimate and final exercise, and for this, they will not have each other. They will go into the darkness alone. This pushes new fear buttons, but they now have a record of successes and without exception, they commit to facing the unknown with determination and resolve. I will not describe that exercise. If you want to know about it, you must drink from the same Elysian spring. You must do what they did, walk the same path and cover the same ground.

A story I heard as a young man makes the point eloquently. Back in the 1800's a religious revival swept England. Many of the preachers in that movement were children. They would stand on boxes on street corners or on carts in the public squares and speak to any who would listen. Often they were ridiculed and mocked. On this particular occasion, two young boys were taking turns and the crowd was particularly hateful. The older boy was nearly reduced to tears when the younger one tugged at his sleeve. He wanted to take his turn and willingly the older boy let him. The younger boy stood facing the crowd and said nothing. The spectators began to shift nervously, and at that moment, the boy reached in his pocket and pulled out an orange. Without a word, he began to peel it. When he was done peeling, he split it apart, pulled off a wedge and popped it into his mouth. Slowly, he chewed and swallowed. When he was done, he addressed the man who had taken the lead in heckling them about their religious experience. Holding the orange up, the boy asked, "How did it taste?" "How should I know?" the man asked. The young boy smiled and said, "That's right. You can't know until you've tasted."

This program works on surprise, on facing the unexpected, on exploring the unknown. The grads pledge on their honor that they will not reveal more about the individual exercises than I have here, because it would rob future students of the full measure of the experience. Also, no matter how powerful the results are, there are those who will have strong objections to the methods we use because they are focused on the liability, fear and negativity associated with risk taking in our society. Since they were not there to see the excellent results in the students, one can hardly blame them for an adverse reaction. Silence is golden. Let them discover the merits for themselves when the time is right for them. In this case, as in life, it is the journey that makes the destination possible.

By the end of the day, these students have literally been forged into very mentally tough, physically skilled protectors of themselves and their families, and because of the passive-aggressive strategy they have learned to use in conjunction with their physical skills, they will be more than a match for a predator who makes the mistake of choosing them, because he thinks they are weak. Their motivation is stronger, their physical skill set is unexpectedly effective and their ability to outmaneuver the predator is superior. The deck is stacked in favor of their survival, *and they know it*. The game plan they now possess is surprisingly effective. In the following chapters, as I focus on the game plan, you will learn how it works and why it is such a powerful strategy. Personally, outwitting a predator is my favorite part of this program.

Frequently asked questions

1. What are the age limits?

The program we have been talking about is an adult program. By that, I mean eighteen and older. The oldest person to have graduated this class is seventy-six years old. Young people from fourteen to seventeen years of age can do the program with what we call *informed parental consent*. By definition, this means the parent must either be a grad or be willing to go through the program with them. Maturity level is everything here, and we are not qualified to make that judgment; only the parents are. There are exceptions to every rule, but under normal circumstances, children under the age of fourteen are not suited to the process and should enroll in an age-appropriate Survival Response program.

2. What is the risk of injury?

Obviously injuries occur in this type of training environment and participation is utterly at your own risk. What I can tell you is that, in nearly twelve years of conducting these programs on a monthly basis, we have yet to experience an accident during the exercises that required hospitalization. It is nearly unheard of to have an accident complicated by roughness on the part of the ghouls. Normally the injuries that may occur happen because the students' bodies are used to "regular unleaded" and suddenly they are being propelled by rocket fuel. The body pushes itself hard in adrenal mode. Staying adequately hydrated and performing warm-up exercises just prior to a scenario significantly reduces the risk of injury. It is also very important that the student be thorough in completing the medical portion of the registration form, so that the staff can make allowances for special circumstances. It is strongly recommended that a person with a heart or respiratory complication see a physician prior to enrollment. Everybody gets a little bruised, tired and scraped up. That is the nature of the beast in any Survival Response program. We have never had a student complain about these minor injuries. Most of the time, the grads are proud of themselves and happy with what they accomplished. Occasionally they show these "war wounds" off to co-workers and friends with comments like, "See this bruise? Ask me how I got this bruise!"

3. Is it better to go solo when I take this course, or should I invite friends and family to attend with me?

The answer to this question depends on you, and why you want another's company. Husbands and wives who go through together often find that they have a closer bond and a husband who sees with his own eyes what his wife is capable of will have a little less anxiety over her safety. It is the same for parents who go through with their teenage or adult children. If you feel you need another's support, ask yourself whether it is necessary and if not, push your envelope. If it is necessary, then by all means invite them. They may need you just as much as you need them!

4. Just how far will the attacker go to produce fear in the students?

This is an excellent question that we touched on briefly at the end of the last section. A very good friend of mine, who is an extremely gifted martial artist, sent his wife through our program because he trusted me. He had never been through himself and was not familiar with how intense the scenarios can be. She had an awesome experience and went happily home to her husband. He saw a huge change in her and asked her about the program. She answered that he would have to go through it and find out for himself. This answer did not satisfy him, and he pestered her until she finally broke down and told him the details of the program. He became enraged and called me immediately. I spent the better part of two hours calming him down, as he wanted to beat the hell out of all my ghouls for some of the things they had said to his wife. He asked me what the limits were. He wanted to know if we allowed the ghouls to grope the female students in an attempt to bring on a fear response. He asked the same question posed above, "Just how far will you let them go?" I told him, "Just this side of breaking the law." Then I asked him a question or two of my own. "Do you love your wife?" "Of course I do," he responded heatedly. "Would you break the law to save her life?" I asked him. "Without a second thought," he said. "I wouldn't have expected any less," I replied. "So how come you're angry at me for doing considerably less for exactly the same reason, because we love her?" He chewed on that one for a while and a couple of months later he let it go. Since that time, he has sent us students on several occasions and will continue to do so in the future.

5. How often is a refresher course necessary?

Because the instinctive response templates are so deeply imbedded, you don't really need to do this program again, especially as it would not have the same impact without the surprise factor. Some students, however, like to brush up on the physical skills and are always welcome to come back on staff to demo fights or for staff training.

6. What would appropriate attire be for a program?

Wear loose, old clothing that can be destroyed and lace-up tennis shoes. No shorts, tank tops or leg wear with side buttons or zippers. Sweats with button-down sides have been torn off students to everyone's great embarrassment, and since we spend a lot of time on the ground, the buttons can be quite painful to roll on. Dressing in layers is recommended so you can control your temperature.

Part II Endnotes

Chapter 6

[1] Bruce Siddle, *Sharpening the Warrior's Edge: the Psychology & Science of Training.* (Belleville, IL: PPCT Research Publications, 1995) 92, 93

[2] Siddle, *Sharpening the Warrior's Edge*, 99

[3] While this may be an apocryphal account, it appears consistently in the volume of literature describing the event and the details dovetail remarkably well with documented eyewitness accounts of the 1938 hurricane.

[4] Posted on The Adrenalin Factor and used with permission. Contact Kerry Sauve at http://www.streetsensesafety.ca, for full article.

[5] Siddle, *Sharpening the Warrior's Edge*, 21, 43, 46

[6] Edwin R. Guthrie, *The Psychology of Learning.* (Oxford, England: Harper, 1952) 136

[7] Siddle, *Sharpening the Warrior's Edge*, 83

Chapter 8

[8] Albert Camus, *Return to Tipasa*, (lyrical and critical essays) 167-168 variant translation.

III

Body Chess

Chapter 9

The Passive/Aggressive Strategy

"Never interrupt your enemy while he is making a mistake."

–Napoleon Bonaparte

Having gained some insight into the fascinating way that nature has prepared human beings to overcome hazards, survive and even flourish in a dangerous environment— we now pose the question: "Is it possible to augment the powerful and effective subconscious mind with strategies designed to *enhance* its survival mechanisms?

In a threat environment, the adrenal effect over-rides the thinking brain because the conscious mind is too slow under extreme stress. Nothing can stop the over-ride process. It is simply too strong. However, the subconscious mind, like the body, can be conditioned. To condition the body, we exercise regularly and often with specific goals in mind. To condition the subconscious mind, we expose it to intense, emotional stressors, repeatedly. We provide it with an environment where instinct can be molded to produce responses with a predictable, planned outcome. The exercises in Survival Response Conditioning are scenarios that expose students to common threat, based on the methodology predators use to turn a human being into a victim.

Let's begin by exploring the anatomy of a predatory physical attack. First, what is an attack? It is an attempt to impose the will of the aggressor on and over the wishes of his chosen target, by whatever means necessary. Seen in this light, *no attack is a senseless one from the viewpoint of the attacker.* There is always a reason and an objective. Perhaps he wants to humiliate you. Perhaps he wants you to give him money. Maybe he wants you to acknowledge his power and superiority, to feel his pain or to change your mind about something. The list of motives is limited only by the scope of human emotion. He wants to get his way and will use whatever tools, props or stratagems necessary to accomplish his goal.

Physical attacks are usually sudden, unexpected and violent, and *the attacker is expecting and depending upon your acting in a certain predictable manner.* He has motive; he has selected a victim, and a setting in which to act. He will use surprise, threat, intimidation and domination in order to achieve his objective: power over you. He wants to shock you into a state of confusion and fear, and while you hesitate—wondering what to do—he will tighten his control over you until it is absolute. Every successful predatory attack is composed of the following eight parts:

Predatory Attack Components

1. Motive
2. Selection
3. Setting
4. Surprise
5. Threat
6. Intimidation
7. Domination
8. Conquest

Since you have little or no control over the first three parts, let's begin with surprise. This is the pivotal step for both the attacker and the intended victim. If you knew beforehand that you would be the victim of an attack at a certain time and place, you would take steps of your own to avoid it or thwart it. The problem is you don't know, and when the attack comes, you may count on being surprised. It is unavoidable. So far, in the attacker's mind all is well. He has a motive, a target, and a time and place to spring his surprise. In order for his continued success, you must respond to surprise with shock and hesitation, to threat with fear, to intimidation with retreat and to domination with capitulation. It is a process, like rolling a snowball down a hill.

The way to thwart an attack is to interrupt this process and once again, surprise is the key. When you roll a snowball down a hill, you expect it to continue to the bottom, especially when there are no visible obstructions. This expectation is the weak link. The attacker knows you will be surprised, and he will expect your confusion and hesitation. What would *your* response be, if halfway down the hill, the snowball you just pushed over the edge stopped dead and then began rolling back up the hill toward you, getting larger by the moment? Would you be surprised? Would that surprise prompt hesitation or action? If action, what would you do? Personally, I would run in the opposite direction as fast as my legs could carry me, screaming for the nightmare to end.

As we analyze the motivation and methods that predators use, it becomes apparent that a series of options are available to us, which can be used to successfully navigate threat. I call this collection of options the Passive-Aggressive Strategy. Using this method in survival response scenarios, we are able to pre-program the natural responses of the subconscious mind to threat stimuli. The Passive-Aggressive Strategy allows us to bring reason and logic to bear on these situations. I am not speaking of the conscious mind *regaining* a measure of control. Introducing conflict between the subconscious and conscious mind is highly counter-productive, and it is often this very conflict that can cause us to "freeze" or "choke" at the moment we need to act. Instead, we can preprogram the subconscious mind, leaving it in perfect control as nature designed it to be, when the situation requires it.

In effect, we can rewrite existing programs, or create new programs designed to eliminate confusion and hesitation. We can improve response time. We can become a predator's worst nightmare: someone with the means and the will to retaliate, someone whom he has misjudged. Aleksandr I. Solzhenitsyn, author of "The Gulag Archipelago," pointed out that individuals who lacked internal preparation for violent acts against their person would always be vulnerable to the perpetrators.[1]

It is interesting to note what takes place when we invert this statement:

> *People who obtain an inward preparation for targeted violence become more powerful than those who would use violence against them.*

This reminds me of the story of the Zen Master, The Fox and the Rabbit. One morning, a famous Zen master was taking a walk with his disciple. They were strolling on a winding path through a beautiful glade, when suddenly a rabbit darted across the path in front of them. A split second later, a red tailed fox burst out of the bushes in hot pursuit. The disciple, being a pacifist, was upset by this. "Master," he exclaimed, "that rabbit will be torn to bits by the fox! Shouldn't we do something?"

The Zen master kept his silence and walked on. "My," thought the disciple, "the Master is not as compassionate as I thought." They continued walking and upon rounding a bend in the path were treated to a view of an open meadow. There, right in front of them, they again saw the fox in pursuit of the rabbit. The disciple quickly became overwrought. "Master!" he cried, grabbing his sleeve, "The rabbit will be killed! Don't you care?" The Zen master replied calmly, "The rabbit will escape."

Just at that moment the rabbit jumped straight upward, turned a back somersault, landed and took off at an oblique angle. The fox, momentarily confused, tried to recover sight of the rabbit and discovered immediately that it was out of reach. After a last look, he trotted off. The disciple, amazed at the Master's accurate and timely prediction, asked him, "Master, how did you know?" The Master replied, "The rabbit was running for his life. The fox was only running for his dinner."

Clearly, the threat of losing your life is an incredibly powerful motivator, so much so that even predators are cautious of activating it. It is the reason they interview potential victims and it also the reason they use deceit so often in their approach.

The Passive-Aggressive Strategy is an extremely flexible, adaptable game plan for threat management. It is a five tiered process that starts with a wide array of options. Each level completed either resolves the situation or narrows the field of choices, until the incident is concluded. The Passive-Aggressive Strategy puts intuition and logic in harmony using proactive boundaries while in adrenal mode. It sets us up to win in all three arenas of conflict: emotional, physical and legal. This is learned only by experience within a very special set of circumstances. Once the Passive-Aggressive Strategy is programmed into the subconscious mind, it cannot be reversed or undone, any more than resisting the impulse to blink when someone pokes a stick toward your eye. It becomes a part of who you are and how you function, permanently.

Students of the Passive-Aggressive Strategy who have had occasion to use this method are fairly uniform in their opinion: Once the templates have been created in the subconscious mind, it feels completely natural when those options are exercised in the real world. "I had no sensation of making a decision," said Angela, a student. "I just *knew* what to do." She had been threatened by her boyfriend, who then tried to throw her down a stairwell. She was able to defend herself easily, because she responded without hesitation. This put the element of surprise back on her side. It was enough to neutralize his attack and give her the opportunity to escape.

There are five components to the Passive-Aggressive Strategy:

Passive-Aggressive Strategy Breakdown

1. Perception of threat
2. Response to warning
3. Use of proactive boundaries
4. Disguise of resolve
5. Initiation of pre-emptive strikes

In the following chapters, we will explore these components thoroughly and at length. They are the heart of the Passive-Aggressive Strategy and the key to out-maneuvering a predator who is bent on your destruction. Your survival—and your children's—may one day depend on how clearly you grasp them.

Chapter 10

Alarms and Triggers: Your Internal Radar

"It is through science that we prove, but through intuition that we discover."

—Henri Poincaré

Perception of threat is the most vital and yet the most underrated natural gift we possess. Perhaps this is because, as human beings, we are drawn to the bold, the imposing, the beautiful and the *visible*. For example, when we see a river, our eyes automatically focus on the turbulent white water, rather than its clarity and depth, or the way it magnifies and enhances the color of the stones beneath it. Motion draws the eye, and for a brief moment, our attention is focused there—to the exclusion of everything else.

To perceive threat, we must first be aware. Do we take the time to cultivate sensitivity to our surroundings? Do we validate our own feelings? At core, do we trust ourselves? Are we comfortable with whom we are? Many of us so lightly regard our inner promptings that we are barely aware of their existence. With a little thought, it's easy to see how this has happened. Our warning and defense mechanisms, which were designed to keep us safe in high-risk environments, are rarely used. It is not because they are ineffective, but because they have worked so well! Because we live a relatively safe life, we are not connected to our internal radar with the vibrancy that animals, which depend on it every day, possess. Then, when the need arises, we sabotage our own passport to safety because we no longer recognize its authenticity. As Gonzales puts it,

> "...we just don't understand the forces we engage. We don't understand the energy because we no longer have to live with it. Even when we're told, even if we understand it at an intellectual level, most of us don't embrace the facts in that emotional way that controls behavior."[2]

We need to recognize and accept what has happened to us socially and culturally with regard to our self-preservation instincts and how intuition has been repressed and replaced with analysis. This has led us to distrust and reject the fastest and most efficient threat detection system in nature: the adaptive unconscious. Science is revealing more every day about how complex and accurate these "snap judgments" can be when we are receptive, aware and have confidence in this mental radar. Malcolm Gladwell, who wrote "The Tipping Point," does a superb job of covering this fascinating subject in "Blink: The Power of Thinking Without Thinking." We need to reacquaint ourselves with the resources available to us on demand. We need to reclaim the wonder of whom and what we are, to give value and credence to the internal mechanisms that make perception of threat so vitally accurate.

The following examples are indicative of just how powerful and awe-inspiring the human brain actually is. Until recently, scientists believed that the brain operated somewhat like a Cray supercomputer. But in reality, each individual *cell* is like a very powerful personal computer, and these cells are connected. The adult brain has approximately 100 billion cells. To better grasp the immensity of this figure, consider that world population recently passed the seven billion mark. To keep the math simple, imagine that we are at five billion, each of us has one of these powerful computers, and they are all connected. Now imagine twenty worlds just like this one and you might begin to have some concept of the power and capacity of the human brain. Hans Moravec, Ray Kurzweil and many other scientists agree that the brain is capable of computing *ten* trillion calculations per second.[3] When suddenly threatened, we can react very quickly, over a minimal range of between one–tenth and one–fifteenth of a second.[4] The evidence is overwhelming that human beings are capable of responding to threat with blinding speed.

However, to internalize this awareness of our potential in a way that will benefit and protect us in real-world situations, requires us to assume a different mindset—what amounts to a prison break mentality, because that is what it is. Remember porthole perspective? For some, this prison feels like a very safe place. It is comfortable and familiar. There is a real resistance to opening the door and stepping outside, because suddenly you are forced to accept responsibility. To become aware, "self-aware," it is necessary to be open and accept *what is*.

Our conscious mind is continually inventing interpretations of the data received by our senses. *Our mind tells us what reality is.* We view a situation, and our mind says, "This is what is happening," based on the simpler information package, "This is what I see." The interpretation is a program that has been run countless times and we are so comfortable with it that it is seldom questioned. Often the program is accurate and serves us well, but it is still *just a program* and the program may not fit the facts every time.

We need to check these programs often, by going to the source information and asking the *original* questions with the conscious self–aware brain: "What do I see? What do I hear? What do I feel? What do I smell?" We need to accept the answers without judgment, *before* we automatically accept the interpretation that worked yesterday. Again, Gonzales advises: *"Be here now."*[5] It is his first rule of survival. Being in the present, accepting it fully; being alert, aware and open to new possibilities gives our internal alarm system the support it needs to carry out its prime directive.

Mike Gomez was just about to pull out of his driveway. He was on his way to the airport for his first trip to Las Vegas. He had been bothered all day by the nagging feeling that something *just wasn't right*. It had to be the money. He was leaving $2,200 in cash in a safe in the house he shared with his brother, who was riding with him in order to drive the car back from the airport. On impulse, he dashed back inside, removed the cash from the safe and hid it elsewhere in the house. When his brother returned from the airport, the safe was gone.

"At the time," he said, "I had no satisfying explanation as to why I moved the money. All I knew was that I felt better the moment I had done it. Yet, I actually argued with myself, because it seemed like such a foolish thing to do. Take the money out of a safe, because it didn't feel safe? It didn't make sense, but I just had this *feeling*, you know?"

This is a great example of a program that was interrupted by perception of threat on a subconscious level. Reason and intellect said the money was secure. It had been before and should be now.

But, looking back, there had been burglaries in the neighborhood recently, and because of the timing and nature of some of the items taken, the burglar was probably someone with more than a casual knowledge of the environment. As it turned out, the thief was later caught and identified as a distant relation.

A closer look at this scenario reveals that all the facts were available to make the decision Mike did. Like points on a "connect-the-dots" child's coloring book, all the information was there. However, the picture it contained was invisible to reason and logic. Intuition was required to draw the lines of inference and an open, aware and receptive mind to act on the shape those lines revealed.

Perception of threat very often involves patterns: patterns of movement, sound, light and shadow. We see or sense the pattern, and once the whole of it is grasped, we become sensitive to its symmetry. We visit a neighbor; washing up for dinner, we notice the tiled tub surround. To what are our eyes drawn? The one cracked tile that interrupts the mosaic. Even our language reflects this passion for the symmetrical. Words such as odd, irregular, twisted, etc. are used to describe behavior or circumstances that give pause or prompt unease.

The subconscious ceaselessly engages in pattern recognition to warn us of possible danger. A piece out of alignment, a sound that doesn't fit, a shadow that should not be there—each gives us a sense of unease, often before we become aware of the reason why. Because uneasy feelings are not comfortable, people commonly allow denial, complacency and apathy to dull their instincts and lull them into a passive lethargy. Additionally, feelings of unease, nervousness or worry are quite often interpreted as signals of weakness and fear. Yet these feelings, when granted the favor of examination, are the very edge that separates those who survive from those who do not.

Must we live in a continual state of unease? That would be as poor a choice as habitual apathy. After a time, the constant tension born of hyper-vigilance would blunt our ability to perceive genuine threat because it would be so well disguised among its shadows. The balance, like most profound truths, is actually quite simple. When confronted by an internal prompt, or alarm, pause for a moment and *respect your radar enough to ask why.* Why am I feeling this way? What is the source? What should I do about it? Then, make a decision, based on the answers to those questions, with a sense of gratitude for a warning system that will not fail you, provided you are willing to take advantage of it.

The idea is to recognize the sound and feel of a genuine alarm as opposed to constant worry. We already live in a fairly secure environment. You will gain an additional advantage for yourself, just by pausing to give some thought to your feelings, rather than immediately pushing them aside for the sake of comfort. As this becomes habit, it provides a real and valid sense of security, based on acceptance of reality. It is a great way to begin to "be here now."

Before we leave this lesson for the next one, I want to touch briefly on the fascinating subject of the seven senses. (No, it's not a typo.) We are all familiar with the five senses: sight, hearing, touch, taste and smell. I believe there are, in reality, at least two more. Dr. Norman Doidge, in "The Brain That Changes Itself," argues convincingly that balance is the sixth sense.[6] He is addressing possession of our physical ability to spatially orient ourselves, without which effective movement of any kind is doomed to embarrassing failure. I believe physical **balance** has its counterpart in the realm of pattern recognition with regard to the events that unfold around us. For example, have you ever walked into a room (or any new environment for that matter) and felt either a very strong sense of ease, comfort and *harmony*, or... the opposite?

I remember an experience I had when I was eighteen that illustrates this perfectly. I was on a long weekend hike in the Olympic Mountains of Washington State. It was one of those perfect midmornings: fresh, quiet but charged with exhilarating energy, as if the molecules in the air around me were vibrating like Mexican jumping beans. I rounded a bend in the trail and found myself captivated by a stunningly beautiful view—a glade encompassed with vine maples. Fingers of the sun were filtering down through leaves of living, spring green. Tiny dust motes were dancing on the breeze coming from behind me, and the wild flowers were everywhere: purple and yellow and blue. It was breathtaking... a vision of paradise.

As I stepped into the glade, thinking to rest and have a snack, I suddenly had a strong sense of unease. I remember how remarkable that felt, in contrast to everything else that my senses were picking up, but I could not shake the vibe. I returned to the trail, but that feeling followed me all day at the back of my mind. On the way back, I decided to try to find the source of what troubled me earlier.

Entering the glade, I felt no recurrence of the unease I had sensed that morning. On the far side of the glade, about forty yards from where I had stood earlier, I discovered the fresh carcass of an elk. Its throat had been torn out but otherwise it seemed to be untouched. I didn't waste any time getting back to my car, let me tell you.

How were my senses able to detect the discordant note in an otherwise supremely benign scene? It could not have been the sense of smell. The breeze was blowing from behind me, and the elk appeared to be a fairly fresh kill. I will never know for sure, but looking back, I now believe that whatever had killed it was still there, just out of sight, and somehow I sensed its presence. For years, the "how" of this troubled me. Some years ago, I came across a fascinating book, "Love Scents" by Michelle Kodis.[7] The author's treatment of the subject of pheromones opened a whole new world for me: how the subconscious mind receives signals from these chemical messengers.

I now believe that what people have long referred to as the elusive "sixth sense" is, in reality, the seventh sense—a subconscious awareness of the information these very tiny molecules silently carry from one mammal to another. This is the only credible physiological explanation for the surprising accuracy of the premonitions that numerous people experience. I want to urge you to read that book because the author makes her case beautifully, and while it is very helpful, it is beyond the scope of this book.

Still, let's take just a moment to see how this hypothesis might work out in a more familiar setting. Have you ever found yourself in proximity to someone who seemed harmless and yet you felt repelled by him? You step into an elevator and here is this well-dressed man who greets you politely, avoids excessive eye-contact and is outwardly a perfect gentleman. He even smells good. Yet instantly you feel uncomfortable around him, so much so, that you move into the opposite corner of the compartment. This is strange. You are not normally a paranoid person, yet you feel a strong urge to get off the elevator immediately, even if it is the wrong floor. You restrain your urges, but when you do get off, and he does not follow you, you feel immense relief. What happened?

As the elevator door closed, you came into contact with this man's pheromones and at least one—but possibly more—got sucked into your nostrils as you drew breath. These pheromones were captured by your Vomeronasal organ (VNO): a tiny pheromone receptor inside your nasal passage. From there it was transported directly to your hypothalamus—the brain's seat of subconscious judgment. There, its message was decoded and given negative marks. Perhaps the message indicated latent aggression or nervousness caused by dishonesty—whatever the case—the hypothalamus didn't like what was there and triggered an instinctive reaction. As instinct glimmered on the edge of the conscious brain, intuition, (the combination of your awareness and your experience), sent a text message to the emotion of discomfort, and *now* your fully aware, conscious brain makes the decision to move away from this person.

I hope this rather simplistic interpretation gives you some inkling of the wonder, complexity and accuracy of human sensory perception. Recognizing the value of this detection system can be the springboard that launches life-saving survival decisions.

Chapter 11

The Power of a Decisive Choice

"Nothing is more difficult, and therefore more precious, than to be able to decide."

–Napoleon I

The second component of the Passive-Aggressive Strategy, *Response to Warning* is the act of turning confusion and helplessness into wise and powerful choices. Before we explore this in depth, we should review the six ways in which human beings intuitively respond to threat. Often these responses seem automatic as we reflect on what passed through our mind when faced with threat or danger. That *"Do This Now"* urge can seem overwhelming in its power, especially when compared to the rational brain's indecision and confusion when under severe stress.

Why is there such a disparity between the function of the intuitive brain and the rational thinking processes? I believe the rational brain operates under a handicap—or a series of handicaps—that the intuitive brain is utterly free from.

When we are confronted by a threat, our intuition will direct action according to three basic options: submit, resist or avoid. Each option is supported by two choices. We can submit directly by surrendering or indirectly by negotiating. We can resist directly by fighting or indirectly by posturing (counter-threatening). We can avoid directly by fleeing the threat or again, indirectly, by hiding or using some form of concealment.

THE INTUITIVE RESPONSE TO THREAT

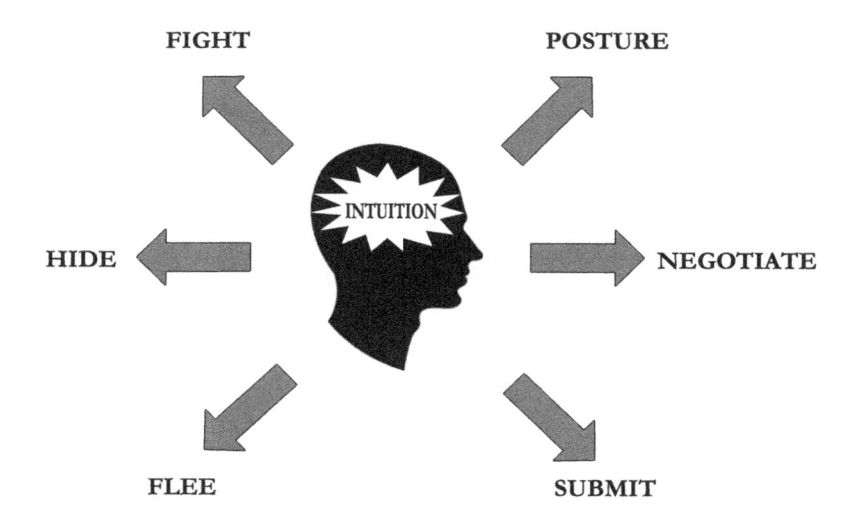

FIGHT POSTURE

HIDE NEGOTIATE

FLEE SUBMIT

Fig. 3

    Remember, the subconscious mind is ceaselessly engaged in sifting through reams of data provided by the senses and comparing it to the template for that environment. When data and template fail to match, a warning is triggered, often felt by us as a premonition—and immediately intuition selects one of these six options. When the threat is overwhelming, the prompt to act quickly and decisively comes straight from instinct, that is, it bypasses the rational brain. When the threat is not so intense, we feel a pull or a tug in a specific direction, but the rational brain is included in the route this time because there *is* time. The moment that the rational brain is consulted, the decision-making process bogs down because the rational brain attaches labels, tags and programs to each one of these six options.

    A **label** is a judgment call on a specific action that society enforces or promotes. We have a very natural and powerful desire to be accepted and honored by our peers. What others think is deeply meaningful to us, so much so that the most basic decisions related to our life are often made in reference to those around us. The judgment of our peers carries weight—a psychological backpack we carry wherever we go.

A **tag** is the emotional response we attach to the label. We may not agree at all with what the popular judgment is regarding a specific action, but more often than not we do agree and we have a list of reasons why or why not. Those reasons originate from **programs**: patterns of thought so familiar, we simply accept them as fact. We rarely question them, and when we do, it usually happens because of some traumatic event or incident.

For example, Jim is walking from a restaurant to his car. It is 10 p.m. and dark. Suddenly, he is accosted by three teenage hoodlums demanding his money. He feels a strong urge (intuition) to give it to them, to submit. However, the thought of being considered a coward (label) repulses him (tag). After all, he is a take-charge type of guy and not someone to mess with (program). So Jim decides to defend himself and his wallet, and is shot dead because his rational mind literally could not escape the box constructed by his labels, tags and programs.

All this thinking, judgment, questioning, indecision, confusion and drama enter into the mix and must be cleared away *prior* to making a choice. Constant multi-tasking under stress produces an anxiety of its own, draining our vitality away. The result is that in a true emergency, we often experience a melt-down rather than clear, cool, level-headed decision making followed by immediate action. Statistics tell us that up to 90 percent of the populace is unable to keep a clear head and respond decisively in a crisis[8]. Those individuals who do, command respect and have great potential to become leaders, if they are not leaders already.

The labels, tags and programs that are such a large part of the rational mind all have to do with *identity*. Self-awareness is what defines us as human beings. However, as important as our identity is, it is worthless without our life force. Physical survival supersedes identity. For example, certain individuals who have been subjected to horrific conditions develop amnesia as a result of the ordeal. Memory that would mentally cripple them is suppressed to keep intact the faculties necessary to survival. They bury their identity to protect their sanity.

Once we understand how our mind operates under stress and become familiar with the relationship between the intuitive and rational mind, once we recognize how advanced our radar actually is and begin to heed it and to trust it; our instinct becomes free and powerful, like an animal in the wild. Have you ever tried to surprise a squirrel or a bird? It sensed your approach and was out of range long before you became a real threat. What would it be like to possess that kind of sensitivity in our own environment?

The intuitive mind is actually the stronger sibling because it is free of ego. When a life–threatening situation is encountered, the intuitive mind shuts all these diversions down because survival is king. When security is achieved, the rational brain can run all the programs it wants to. Intuition simply says, "I'm taking charge here; shut up 'til I'm done!"

THE INTUITIVE RESPONSE TO THREAT vs. THE RATIONAL BRAIN

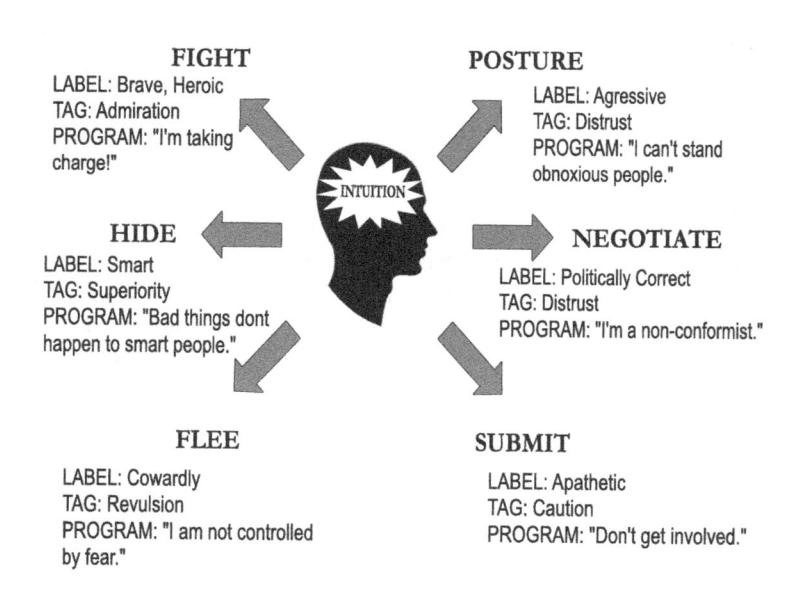

FIGHT
LABEL: Brave, Heroic
TAG: Admiration
PROGRAM: "I'm taking charge!"

POSTURE
LABEL: Agressive
TAG: Distrust
PROGRAM: "I can't stand obnoxious people."

HIDE
LABEL: Smart
TAG: Superiority
PROGRAM: "Bad things dont happen to smart people."

NEGOTIATE
LABEL: Politically Correct
TAG: Distrust
PROGRAM: "I'm a non-conformist."

FLEE
LABEL: Cowardly
TAG: Revulsion
PROGRAM: "I am not controlled by fear."

SUBMIT
LABEL: Apathetic
TAG: Caution
PROGRAM: "Don't get involved."

Fig. 4

The rational mind wants to be in control and causes us to feel very uncomfortable when it is not. It tells us not to trust intuition and that whatever it cannot immediately grasp should be distrusted and feared. It is almost as if a sibling rivalry exists between the rational mind and its intuitive counterpart. When suddenly and shockingly confronted with threat, the intuitive brain deals with the threat. The rational brain cannot deal with the threat in an expedient manner and *disguises* this fact with labels, tags and programs, all of which have nothing to do with survival— while casting doubt on intuition, which has everything to do with it.

These six choices operate on the principle of escalating risk. Accordingly, perceiving threat allows us to avoid it, reducing our exposure to the law of unintended consequences. The man who is confronted by a bully doesn't consider that his wife, whom he dearly loves, might marry another man while he is in prison for manslaughter. All he knew *in the moment* was that he would not back down. To avoid a threat is to overcome it. Confronting threat doesn't always work out the way we hope it will.

> *"The law of unintended consequences teaches that the result of our actions is almost never what we intend...Whenever we act, especially when the stakes are high—surprising things go wrong. And surprising things go right. We can have our way and later regret it, or not have our way and later be thankful we didn't...You may prefer calculating cause and effect... but the same paradox holds true. Life doesn't check. Rational actions can trigger irrational results."* —Forrest Church[9]

Brandon's Story

In late September 2010, my adult children, Brandon and Alana, decided to take a road trip from Washington state to Southern California. Brandon wanted to drive straight through, so they agreed to make pit stops every two to three hours for either a power nap or a little exercise.

Somewhere between Grant's Pass and Roseburg, Oregon, they entered a rest stop to take a short break. It was a particularly lonely stretch of Interstate 5. There was only one other vehicle in the parking lot and Brandon parked three spaces over from this car. A young man was seated inside. Both the driver's side door and the passenger doors were open, as well as the trunk lid.

Something about this situation made Brandon feel mildly uneasy. He was unable to identify the source of his discomfort readily and put it to the back of his mind. Alana didn't need to use the facilities. Brandon left the keys in the ignition and told her to lock the car door after him. It was the first time during the trip that he had said this to her.

As he approached the restroom blockhouse, he could see that the entrance to the men's room was on the left. Rounding the corner of the blockhouse, he noticed the near restroom's interior was dark. Brandon knew that the lights are required to be lit around the clock, and the fact that they were out added to the unease he had felt earlier. He moved toward the lighted entrance instead. Just before stepping across the threshold, he paused. What if someone had fixed the lights in the first bathroom to funnel unsuspecting and oblivious people into the second one? He had never had such a strange and suspicious thought before. Where was it coming from? Slowly and carefully, he sneaked a look around the door. The restroom seemed to be empty. He crouched down and scanned the stalls for tell-tale feet and legs. The stalls appeared to be unoccupied, yet for some reason, Brandon's radar was telling him someone was there.

My son is one of the bravest and toughest people I know. He is an experienced martial artist and a pit fighter. Backing away from a challenge, especially from a human source is unlike him. He considered going in anyway, thinking to himself that whoever was in there had probably never met someone quite like him. Then he thought, "What if I lose?" He pictured Alana, alone in the car and the young man killing time, three spaces over.

Suddenly Brandon lost the urge to use the restroom. He turned abruptly and made a beeline for the car. As he approached, he saw the man in the car talking on a cell phone and shaking his head in the negative. He appeared frustrated and angry. Upon re-entering the car, Brandon told his sister he had a weird feeling and wondered whether she felt it also. Whatever it was, she seemed not to have picked up on it. As he accelerated away, Brandon looked in the rear-view mirror. What he saw sent chills down his spine. A large, burly man had exited the lighted restroom and was walking toward his buddy in the parked car.

When my son related this story to me, I asked him what he thought gave him the uneasy feeling in the first place. After thinking carefully, he said that he still wasn't one hundred percent sure but it seemed that the man in the car was *trying* to look busy. Brandon's radar somehow picked up on this small attempt at deception and transposed it over the watermark of a remote location. This combination triggered unease.

I couldn't help thinking how fortunate my children had been. Those two men had chosen the setting for a perfect crime. After subduing and incapacitating the unsuspecting man entering the lighted restroom, the assailant would call his partner in the vehicle. That man would lean across the front seat and loudly slam the passenger door shut to draw Alana's attention to his next move: to exit his vehicle and move toward the back using the pretext of shutting the trunk. Once she had quantified his movement and dismissed it as harmless, she would return her attention forward. This would leave him free to make a lightning–fast approach from an oblique angle, smash out her window, unlock her door and drag her into his still–open trunk. His buddy could jump into her car and follow him onto the interstate. Inside of ten seconds, she would disappear without a trace.

Do we confront threat because we truly have no other options, or does the rational mind badger us into it? Are we afraid to be afraid, or is fear actually working for us? As we view the diagram of the six intuitive responses to threat, we can all envision scenarios where each of those responses would be wise choices, or perhaps poor ones.

Pause for a moment and consider the labels, tags and programs that you personally associate with these responses to threat. Do this exercise often because it will help to free your mind of the tendency to automatically assume these qualifiers fit the situation correctly. Ask yourself, "How does this conclusion serve my safety?" When confronted by an individual who intends to harm you, these six options are reduced by most experts to a choice between fight and flight.

It's almost never that simple. What you choose to do depends on the situation and what your intuition tells you about it. Some experts will tell you that under certain circumstances, submission is wiser and others fall on the side of resistance. Do not listen to any of them. This kind of advice is worthless to you as an individual because it is statistical and minute differences in each and every situation can and will vastly alter the outcome. It is impossible to second-guess these situations before they occur. Only in the moment can the best choice be made.

Jackie's Story

My friend Jackie grew up in Trinidad & Tobago. One Saturday morning when she was thirteen, Jackie's older sister gave her an errand to run. She was told to walk several blocks over to a restaurant/club and collect a sum of money the proprietor owed her sister. Jackie had met this man on several previous occasions. He had always been kind and polite to her so she had no qualms about going to meet him.

She arrived at the front of the restaurant at about 10 a.m. At the entrance, she slipped off her shoes and made her way inside. Boswell, the owner (who was in his late fifties), greeted Jackie and invited her to the back of the restaurant. He was alone. Jackie returned his greeting and told him why she was there. Boswell gave her the money but said he wanted to talk to her about something else before she left. He turned toward her and took a step forward, backing her into a corner. He was very close. Then he propositioned her. Jackie was terrified. Seeing her discomfort, Boswell said he would give her money for herself and that they would keep it a secret. Thinking quickly, Jackie agreed but said she had left her shoes at the entrance and needed to get them so that no one would know they were there together. Boswell stepped back, and Jackie hurried to the front entrance where she put on her shoes and ran toward home as fast as she could go. Nothing was ever done to Boswell because Jackie never told anyone, including her sister. From that day on, she avoided Boswell completely.

What I kept coming back to in this story was the shoes. It was not the custom there (as it is in some countries) to remove your shoes before entering a public building, and she had never done so before. Jackie herself does not know why she did it. She did not feel uneasy at the prospect of visiting Boswell, nor was she uneasy in his presence—until he violated her personal space.

Sometimes a warning signal is buried so deeply in the subconscious mind that our cognitive processing does not discover its origin. I am convinced that this was the case in Jackie's situation because the action she took (taking off her shoes) was so unusual, and there seemed no obvious reason for it. Whatever the rationale behind that action, it saved Jackie from a terrible experience and an uncertain conclusion. That fact cannot be debated.

You must learn to listen to your own inner voice, to respond to intuition because it is the only expert that is utterly committed to you. Which of the six intuitive responses your intuition selects, depends on the unique circumstances in the moment. The best advice I have is to give yourself the freedom to *respond to intuition by trusting first and judging later*. It is not wrong to examine your intuitive promptings thoroughly, but do so after your safety is no longer at risk. There is no guarantee that intuition will always be right. In fact, I can say with certainty that it will not. But make no mistake: intuition should always be taken seriously because it is a mechanism fundamentally dedicated to self–preservation.

In reality, avoiding threat often has more to do with our self-concept or image and level of perceived security, than with what is happening in the world around us. Secure people with nothing to prove normally seek to avoid unnecessary danger or threat, especially when the threat comes from human aggression. There are exceptions to this statement, of course. There comes a time for all of us, sooner or later, when we feel obligated to stand up for what we believe in; for what is right, good and noble. Occasionally a situation arises where our personal integrity and honor is at stake. We are compelled to take action because we cannot live and continue to be who we are if we don't.

I am not suggesting that avoiding threat is always the best choice. What I am saying is that when the choice to confront threat is made, it is done so with full awareness of the unpredictability of the outcome and the best available knowledge of the environment. Then, *when we engage, we are free to do so with absolute commitment.* In a worst-case scenario, that perfect commitment may be the only edge you possess. Your life will depend on a clear and focused mind.

Chapter 12

A Line in the Sand

"Fortune sides with him who dares."

−Virgil

In adopting and following the Passive-Aggressive Strategy, we have opened our senses to perceive threat. We have become aware and sensitive to our surroundings. Our internal radar picks up an anomaly that we recognize and identify as a signal of danger. We take action to avoid the threat and this time, in spite of our best efforts, threat remains. Since it cannot be avoided, we must now take its measure. The third step of the Passive-Aggressive Strategy uses a technique called a *proactive boundary*. Its purpose is three-fold: to reduce hesitation, to de-escalate the situation or, failing that, to define the threat clearly so that it can be neutralized.

The best way to reduce hesitation is to limit the decision-making process to a minimum. In other words, we can decide now, in the present, how to respond in the future. We can decide what we will and will not put up with, what situations we will instantly respond to and what that response will be. When these decisions have been programmed into our conscious mind and acted upon in an adrenal format, they form what I call proactive boundaries. When engaged, they will protect us by flipping the surprise advantage over to our side.

Proactive boundaries are the counterpart to a predator's interview. In the case of an unwanted approach in an isolated area, protecting your personal space becomes a vital issue. You don't know this person, and you sense a possibly hostile intent. Remember, this person does not know you either. If he is bent on doing harm to you, he is taking a risk himself, and he is very aware of this. He would like to be able to gauge your level of resistance before he commits to an attack. His method of approach, the words he uses (if he uses words at all), the way he looks at you and the gestures he may make are all calculated to test you.

If you show resolve—and if the level of resistance the aggressor senses indicates you will be more work than he bargained for—he may decide to break off his approach, and find an easier mark. In this way, the incident may be de-escalated. If you tell this person in no uncertain terms to stop, he is too close to you and you don't know him, you have verbally put him in check. What he chooses to do next is the defining moment in the encounter. How would a normal person without malevolent intent respond?

If you are walking through a parking lot and a stranger begins an approach by asking directions to the nearest service station, how can you tell if this is an innocent question or the beginning of a predator's interview? He may be testing you to see how close you will allow a stranger to approach you. You must now, in the interest of safety, test him. The way to do it in this situation is to put both your hands up in the universally accepted way that says, "Back off!" In addition to this clear visual cue, you must tell him forcefully, "Stop! You're too close to me! I don't know you! I can give you directions from right here!" An innocent person without ulterior motive will always respond in two ways, and *both* must be present for him to pass your test.

Remember, if he is honestly representing himself, he wants your co-operation and would not purposefully alarm you. He should immediately express respect for your request by physically stepping back and apologizing profusely. He must acknowledge your level of discomfort both physically and verbally, and then leave, whether you grant his request for directions, the time, etcetera, or not.

A predator who is put in verbal check may continue the interview by either stopping his physical approach while arguing the point ("Aw, c'mon, Lady, I'm just asking for directions, what are you afraid of?") and then beginning a second approach—or simply continue moving forward while apologizing.

Either way, your request is not being honored, and that is the point. At best, this is a rude individual, a jerk with whom you want nothing to do. At worst, he is a predator, bent on turning you into another statistic. Using a proactive boundary this way is extremely helpful, because it removes confusion over misinterpreting a possibly hostile approach. It either de-escalates the situation or defines the intent. Do you see how valuable this is?

Never worry about appearing abrupt in defining your personal space on the street. If you are a woman, know that decent men will understand your unease and respect it. Who cares about the rest? If you are a man, take care that you are polite and respectful, but firm. If possible, give the other person a way to save face or your words may be taken as a challenge, especially in a public setting. However, failure to set and maintain your boundaries is almost always a grave mistake. It is better to risk offending someone than to announce vulnerability to a stranger when there is a question of hostile intent.

Up to this point, we have made the assumption that the individual confronting us is a stranger. There are two basic categories of predators: those who are strangers and those who are not. Each category can be further sub-divided into two additional types as illustrated in the breakdown below:

COMMON PREDATOR TYPES

Type A: Casual and Opportunistic **Target**: Anyone Vulnerable	**Type C**: Familiar Face, Friend, Acquaintance **Target**: You
Type B: Personal Fixation **Target**: You alone or you and those connected to you	**Type D**: Family Member, Spouse, Relative **Target**: You

Fig. 5

There is a fifth category of predators, but they are rare in spite of the fact that they get a disproportionately large amount of press. A type "E" predator is motivated by his or her ideals and is willing to use extreme violence to get a point across. Terrorists are type "E" predators. As an American, your chance of personal interaction with them is statistically unlikely within the borders of this country, but rises geometrically if you are operating in their territory or environment. Since these individuals believe the end justifies the means, they cannot be negotiated with or dissuaded from their objective. They must be avoided utterly or engaged and defeated, because human life, whether their own or another's, is meaningless to them except as leverage.

A physical confrontation with a terrorist is almost always fatal to one or both of the parties involved. *Violent fatalities are their objective.* As awful as that sounds, the good news is that this knowledge provides clarity in our choice of options. We won't waste valuable time on decisions that do not directly contribute to the solution. I mention this type of predator in passing, solely to cover the subject thoroughly. The likelihood that you will meet a person like this in your lifetime is small, provided you are not a soldier, a policeman or someone whose profession requires you to travel or reside in a high-risk region.

The media have done us a huge disservice by blowing this issue out of proportion for the average citizen. Before you allow yourself to be adversely affected by the obsessive attention the press devotes to this subject, ask yourself how many terrorists have been arrested and convicted of their crimes, especially when compared to something that is a common threat like domestic violence. Then relax a little, and you will be better for it.

Proactive boundaries are most valuable with a Type "A" or Type "B" predator because they define intent. You have no idea who this is or what the person really wants, and you need to find out. A proactive boundary is designed to do this. A Type "B" predator, especially one who has stalked you and may have some knowledge or familiarity with your personality and habits, will be well prepared—or shall we say, less surprised by your response to him. With Types "C" and "D," you are much more likely to know and understand their motives. There are noteworthy characteristics for each of these predator types. Let's explore the high points.

Type "A" Predator

The Opportunist

This is the easiest predator to thwart. What attracts him most often is the level of vulnerability of his mark. This situation can be very frightening because of the lack of information. Not knowing what this person is capable of can be unsettling in the extreme. The good news is that if you can survive the encounter, it will end there, because unlike types "B," "C," and "D," this individual has no personal relationship with you. Usually he will disengage when he senses a strong measure of resistance to his approach. He is also the predator type most subject to unpredictability in the behavior of his intended victim. He is taking on more risk than even he is aware of, because the moment he begins his approach, and you spot it, he knows less about you than you do about him.

Consider this: by initiating an attack against you, he is telling you that he thinks you are an easy mark, and he can subdue you. However, he does not realize that you understand this. He is blind to the fact that *he* is behind on the learning curve. Knowledge is power! You will know that he has chosen you. You will know that he is betting that you will be intimidated, and then capitulate. But this predator is going to receive an unpleasant surprise. You are not what you seem. By the end of this chapter, you will understand how to use the knowledge he just gave you to shut him down—and he will never see it coming.

Type "B" Predator

The Stalker

A type "B" predator has a relationship with you, but it is in his own mind. You may have never met him until now, and if you did, you probably had no idea that he had any interest in you at all. Because of his fixation with you, he is very difficult to dissuade. He is persistent and usually resourceful. Avoiding this threat is difficult because it keeps trying to attach like a nail to a magnet. He may approach you in the most benign and unobtrusive manner or in a violent and reckless rage, depending on his warped perception of reality.

While rage is frightening, it is transparent: obviously a threat. The stalker mentality is one reason why it is so important to be open and receptive to instinct, to be sensitive to the presence of balance (or the lack thereof) in our interaction with those we meet. The earlier you pick up on strange behavior, the sooner you can take steps to protect yourself. A proactive boundary in this instance may involve complete nonresponsiveness to the advances of this person, while being fully aware of him.

You must accept the unsettling truth that a person with a fixation or an obsession does not think like you. For him, any response, even a negative one, is better than no response. The moment you respond, you acknowledge that he exists, and you are aware of him. From his point of view, this is progress forward. It feeds his twisted belief that he has a relationship with you. The only time you should acknowledge his existence (to him) is if he attacks you physically, and then the rules of engagement are the same as any other physical assault. You verbally check him and take action according to how he responds.

Type "C" Predator

The Angry Acquaintance

A type "C" predator is someone you know: a co-worker, a casual friend—a face you recognize. Somehow, the relationship between you has changed, something has happened, and this person has become angry enough to trigger your alarm system. Usually the best short-term solution is to be humble, apologetic and to negotiate your way out. This person is in your life and difficult to ignore or avoid. In the longer term, you should give serious thought as to whether or not you wish to maintain the relationship.

Once an aggressor escalates unpleasantness to physical threat, a precedent has been set. If this invasion of your rights is not rebuffed or deflected, the odds of a recurrence are significantly increased. Passive behavior can be an effective, low risk way to handle an angry acquaintance *initially*, because the flare-up is almost always short-lived. There is, however, a vulnerability unique to this scenario. Because you know this person, you may be shocked by his or her behavior and find it very easy to slip into a state of denial. If that happens, you will be unprepared for an assault if the acquaintance snaps.

Many, many times I have listened to victims of this situation say, "There was no warning; it took me totally by surprise!" No, not completely true! They had warnings and in nearly every case, simply refused to believe the evidence of their senses. Again, when in doubt, establish a boundary. If this person is a friend, you are granting an opportunity to respect your space. Always listen to the inner voice, no matter how well you think you understand the situation.

Type "D" Predator

The Family Member

Surprisingly, this is the most dangerous predator type, both in terms of real threat and frequency of attack nationwide. In addition, it often requires a lengthy, super-human struggle to escape an individual who has ownership issues concerning you, who knows all your habits and your friends, who may have access to your bank account, and most disturbing, is intimately familiar with your thought processes. It is like being locked in a cell with an unpredictable psychopath. How to escape? Your only hope is to create and then execute a well-thought-out plan involving very severe and drastic measures.

Further complicating this nightmare is the haunting specter of disempowerment. Remember Crystal. Long-term abuse destroys self-image and with it, the capacity to initiate proactive decision-making. Under these conditions, it can be terribly difficult to sever the relationship because the victim no longer believes he or she can. A type "D" predator knows this, and capitalizes on it in numerous ways. The moment the victim makes an attempt to assert freedom, the predator tightens his hold.

It is crucial to give no hint of what you are planning if your objective is to effect a permanent and successful escape. Also, recognize from the start that you may be unable to physically sever the connection on your own. It is essential that you develop a support system to aid you in your exit strategy. There are numerous groups around the country with chapters in every city whose sole purpose is to provide support to individuals in this situation. They can be found through friends, the phone book or the internet.

The real problem here is not that help is not available or that funding is insufficient. Politicians love to bang those drums because it makes them appear as concerned and trustworthy leaders. The problem is that we often fail in accurately perceiving threat. Then, we do not act with sufficient vigor and resolve in the interest of self-preservation. Both failures stem from denial. This is the root of the problem in two branches: denial on the part of society and denial on the part of the individual, but the lion's share of responsibility rests with individuals. We absolutely *must* wake up and accept what *is* rather than surrendering to the momentum of denial. This is the silent killer among us, more lethal by far than all the serial killers of the world lumped together.

We must face the fact that predators live among us, not just at a comfortable arm's length (society), not even close to home (our communities), but right next to us, sometimes in our own homes and certainly among our friends and acquaintances. This is our darkest social secret. According to the 1991 Federal Bureau of Investigation Uniform Crime Reports, a woman is beaten every 15 seconds in this country and legal advocate Sheryl Burns of the Battered Women's Support Services in Vancouver, B.C. reports that the average abused woman goes through *nine violent incidents* before she calls the police.

The point of all this relative to our discussion is this: *Long-term* victimization by a type "D" predator usually results from either a failure to set proactive boundaries in the first place, or a failure to use them effectively once they have been established. For example, a woman whose husband becomes verbally abusive very often fails to respond in a manner that is calculated to end the abusive behavior *the first time it happens*. What she does at that point often becomes the template for future victimization, which unchecked, is all too likely to escalate into physical abuse. Let me be crystal clear: I am not blaming the victim for the abuser's actions—far from it. Instead, I am suggesting that as soon as the abusive partner attempts to rob her of her own power, that she checks him and takes it back, by physical force if necessary.

The key to establishing a proper response pattern is to respond with great power and resolve the moment a threat or other abusive behavior first occurs. In this scenario, one solution is to leave him without a word right then and stay away, with no communication what-so-ever for a protracted period of time. Then, when the result of his actions have sunk in and led the aggressor to consider cause and effect, the victim should respond in writing, stating that she will not come back until he has completed counseling. If there is ever, under any circumstances, a repetition of this behavior, permanent separation is a foregone conclusion.

In most domestic conflicts, what I have described constitutes an effective, proactive boundary, especially if she had set it with him before marriage. The vast majority of people do not discuss these things with their partners prior to entering into a committed relationship with them. They just assume that everything is going to be wonderful and that they will live happily ever after. The effect of this woman taking the action I have described would have been many times more powerful, had she told him previously what she would do if he behaved in an abusive manner. It would establish her credibility while limiting his envelope–stretching. This is a simple and effective strategy, proven many times over. Yet, how many people—men or women—have the forethought and resolve to carry it out, *the first time it happens?*

Developing your own proactive boundaries requires some in-depth soul searching. Ask yourself:

- How much am I worth?

- What parts of me are worthy of defense? My body? My spirit? My pride? My integrity? My honor?

- Under what circumstances would I defend myself physically and mentally?

- How close would I allow a threatening person to come without warning? After having been warned?

- What kind of punishment do I think I could survive?

- How badly would I be willing to hurt another to preserve my life? The life of a family member? Or a friend? What about a stranger?

- Would I kill to live? Under what circumstances?

Be specific in your answers to these questions and any others you can think of. Remember, there are no right or wrong answers, only your answers. Write down these proactive boundaries and post them on your vanity or bathroom mirror and review them daily.

Spend some time everyday visualizing these scenarios and your responses. Remember also that survival and victory occur twice, first in the mind and then in the action, and the mind controls the body.

Proactive boundaries are always specific, never general in nature. They are like fences that separate two fields: the one you stand in right now—passive—and the one in which you are galvanized into action. Proactive boundaries reduce hesitation and confusion, acting as catalysts for morphing fear into outrage—which fuels action. They prepare the way for you to catapult your attacker into what he is most unprepared for: an overwhelming surprise.

Another advantage of proactive boundaries is one that begins to benefit you immediately. Once you have decided these issues and reinforced them with mental practice, once you know what you will do, you will begin to achieve a whole new level of confidence and peace. Eliminating indecision is naturally empowering.

KNOWLEDGE IS POWER

SELF KNOWLEDGE

+

POSITIVE ATTITUDE

=

EMPOWERMENT

Confidence radiates from an individual who knows what to do and knows he or she is capable of doing it, because knowledge is power! When you walk down the street, this aura of personal power will surround you and in a very real sense protect you because it sends a clear message: "This is a person to be reckoned with—take care!" If you want peace, then claim the power that is your birthright: the power of self–determination. Notice that all of this is in the mind, which is the *authentic* you. What you look like on the outside, your present physical circumstances, and your financial situation, none of these things can ever define who you are or what your potential is. The act of deciding and the strength of will to make it so—these make the difference between success and failure.

Proactive boundaries are a declaration of freedom and downpayment on self–worth. That is why I stress their importance. How you see yourself will ultimately determine how others see you. While this might not be true in the present, it will eventually come to pass because your self-image, hopes, dreams and direction in life are all bound together by invisible but unbreakable cords. If your self-image is low, you will achieve little because little is attempted. If you see yourself achieving great things and if you believe with a passion that leads to action, you will surely succeed. Again, we are dealing with the mind, with the will, the root of all action.

In our society, we are often reminded to plan for our financial future, to make sacrifices now in order to experience comfort tomorrow. Doesn't it make sense to invest some effort in defining our self-worth at present to secure our emotional health and physical safety as we continue to grow? A good friend of mine told me about a psychologist who made the reference of looking at ourselves as a bank. We need to proactively and consistently make investments over time so that if an event comes along that requires a large withdrawal we will have something to draw from.

Proactive boundaries shift and change to meet various situations, threatening circumstances and predator types, but the underlying principle remains constant. Predators depend on surprise and other *predictable response patterns* in their intended victims. Preplanning your limits and responses can give you the edge over a predator, propelling an *unexpected* sequence of events, like falling dominos.

Chapter 13

The Art of Misdirection

"Have an open face, but conceal your thoughts."

–Italian Proverb

In threat management, the Passive-Aggressive Strategy functions like a giant funnel. We start out with a broad array of options and as circumstances unfold, intuition kicks in, helping to guide our choices. This happens automatically and naturally. The trick is to become consciously aware of, and familiar with, our innate abilities so we can have enough confidence to give them free reign in the appropriate situation. Additionally, the Passive-Aggressive Strategy welds the powers of reason and judgment—conscious brain functions—to intuition, establishing harmony between processes often discordant in high-stress situations. The result is improved awareness, superior response time, greater confidence and most important, a proven game plan: vital assets when faced with surviving a violent confrontation.

The Passive-Aggressive Strategy is named after what occurs in step four, *Disguise of Resolve*. In step one, we perceived a possible threat. In step two, we attempted to avoid the threat. The threat persisted, so in step three, we used a proactive boundary to either de-escalate it or define it.

Often, situations arise where it is possible to calm the aggressor by appealing to reason, expressing humility or using the language of appeasement. This is commonly referred to as de-escalation. However, viewing it this way limits its usefulness. It is much more. Fundamentally, de-escalation is *negotiation*, one of the six intuitive responses to threat. It is *the creative process of affecting the outcome of a potentially violent encounter in a way that benefits you and diffuses the situation.*

Some years ago, I witnessed a brilliant demonstration of de-escalation tactics that perfectly illustrates the above statement. I was sitting with a friend in a cocktail lounge. Our table provided an unobstructed view of the bar. A well-dressed, older gentleman was purchasing a drink when an acquaintance called his name. As he turned toward his friend, he inadvertently bumped into a very large, heavily muscled young man standing behind him, sloshing his drink onto the man's shirtfront and losing his grasp on his tumbler. The young man became instantly enraged, drawing himself up and fixing the older man with a savage glare. His bad intentions were obvious, and I thought, "This is going to get ugly!"

Then, things took a different turn. Apologizing profusely, the older man averted his eyes by shielding them with his right hand while simultaneously touching the other man's elbow with his left. With a combination of body language and verbal finesse, he was able to communicate embarrassment, humility and goodwill. He then shifted his position to the man's side, moved his hand from elbow to shoulder and directed the man's attention to the array of bottles on the shelves behind the bar. "Let me buy you a drink," he said. "Anything you want—what will it be?" The young man thought for a moment and made a selection. Things went back to normal.

What made this interesting was the series of subtle adjustments the older man made that changed the negative energy, diverted it and eventually caused it to dissipate entirely. First, he averted his gaze. Direct eye contact would have been confrontational in this situation. Second, he made gentle physical contact as he apologized, establishing a very human and *non-threatening* connection with the offended man. Third, he moved beside his adversary, facing in the same direction. By doing this, he demonstrated not just the absence of conflict—he was *literally on this man's side*. Last, he directed this man's attention away from the offense by asking him to make a choice between attractive options. As soon as this offering was accepted, the threat was neutralized.

Failure to dissuade the aggressor by reason or appeasement leaves us with two options. We must **enroll them** in an alternate scenario or we must **engage them** physically. I want to focus on this more "active" interpretation of de-escalation and explore it thoroughly before we turn our attention to the physical realm. Surprisingly, this extremely effective strategy is rarely discussed as a viable option.

Enrollment

First, following this path is subject to certain common denominators. For instance, women seek non–violent solutions to threat much more often than men do. This is a statistical fact.[10] Because victimization is not gender-specific, I try to avoid referring to gender issues unnecessarily. I want to be very clear: I am not excluding men in the pages to follow; these strategies can be used effectively regardless of gender. However, predators tend to be male and their victims are often female.

It is abundantly clear that women, for a variety of reasons (common sense being at the top of the list), tend to avoid physical violence more often than men do. Certain Passive-Aggressive Strategy components will seem natural to them, as well as easy to implement and vice versa. We must take into account the differences between men and women regarding physiology; emotional make up, intuitive power and approach to problem solving. It follows that the Passive-Aggressive Strategy should have alternatives within its structure to accommodate these natural differences, some of which are distinct advantages.

At this point, I want to focus on the use of misdirection and deception, rather than confrontation in the practice of personal protection. This is fundamentally an exercise of intuition. I call it the Primrose Path. It consists of six basic steps that form a separate and non-violent set of tactics within the Passive-Aggressive Strategy framework. At times, the order in which they fall is slightly different, but commonly they are as follows:

The Primrose Path

1. **Sensing the Path:** The growing awareness of clear and present danger

2. **Seeing the Path:** Sizing up the situation to determine the attacker's expectations

3. **Pointing to the Path:** Setting up a scenario or situation you are able to influence and control; that he is willing and even eager to participate in

4. **Entering the Path:** Leading the attacker down the path with a combination of yielding, luring and hinting

5. **Exiting the Path:** Once the attacker is fully committed, exerting your control—which manifests itself as an overwhelming surprise

6. **Closing the Gate:** Making good your escape, leaving him trapped, neutralized or defeated

The following true story happened to a young woman I have known all my life. It is an excellent example of the Primrose Path, even though Maria didn't understand where her intuition was leading her at the time. This clearly illustrates that the Primrose Path is a natural process. Allowing the intuitive process free rein, unshackled by conscious judgment, is often the response that best serves safety.

Maria's Story in Her Own Words

"I was a petite twenty-year-old, single woman, new to the area and unfamiliar with my surroundings. I had just accepted a position in an investment firm and I wanted to share an apartment, close to my employment in Irvine, California.

On a Saturday, I answered an ad for sharing a beach home in Newport Beach. When I met the owner at the rental house, I found if I chose to live there, I would have three male roommates. I had never had a male roommate before and wasn't comfortable with the idea. The owner's name was Gary Faber. He was forty years old, tall and stoutly built. He expressed disappointment that I did not want to live at this beach house and told me he was in the real estate industry and had several other homes for rent that did not involve male roommates. He was very friendly and very pushy. He asked for my number and promised to call me with a time when I could see the other places.

Sunday morning at 12: 30 a.m. Mr. Faber telephoned me. I was surprised and uneasy that he called in the middle of the night. He wanted to show me two houses the following evening. I hesitated and said I'd get back to him. He pressured me that he'd gone to a lot of trouble to set up appointments for me. I agreed to go. Since I was unfamiliar with the area, I agreed to let him pick me up at my aunt's house that evening to show me the rentals. I remember feeling a bit uneasy about the situation, but he was twenty years my senior and I assured myself he was just being particularly kind, maybe even fatherly.

I believe it was around 6 p.m. when Faber picked me up. I planned to return later that evening, and my aunt said she'd be home or would leave the door unlocked for me. I climbed into Faber's convertible and he began driving toward Newport Beach. He asked where I worked and when I told him "Irvine," he volunteered that both places he was showing me were in Newport Beach, a short drive from Irvine. He said he needed to make a quick stop on the way to pick up some wine. This made me uneasy, but I forced my unease to the back of my mind, rationalizing that Faber was doing me a favor. If he needed to make a stop, it would seem rude of me to complain.

I began talking to Faber about my boyfriend and our plans for the coming week. I did this to make absolutely sure he understood I was unavailable. He seemed very interested in my personal life, and while I can no longer remember the gist of our conversation, I do remember that he talked down my boyfriend (whom he'd never met). I remember being angered by our conversation. I remember thinking that it was odd.

Next, he stopped at the house in Newport Beach where I had met him the previous day. He explained he had to drop off the wine there, before we went on our way and I told him I'd wait in the car. He suggested that I not wait alone, but accompany him inside. He said he needed to talk to one of the renters and he'd be a few minutes. I felt uneasy with this situation, but did not want to appear rude and so I acquiesced.

As we neared the house, I could hear music playing. He used his own key to open the front door. I remember thinking it was odd that he would just enter the home of a renter without knocking first, but I concluded that perhaps he was just that trusted. As I stood in the entry way, I heard the door close behind me and the dead bolt click shut. My unease became real. Faber told me to have a seat and motioned toward the couch. I told him that I was comfortable where I was and preferred to wait there. He again told me to sit. I responded, "No, thank you. I'll stand here."

"I said sit!" Faber commanded. He grabbed my arm and led me to the couch. In front of me was a big-screen TV. He turned it on and with a laugh said, "We're gonna watch TV and get to know each other better." He entered the kitchen just a few feet away and, still watching me, poured two glasses of wine. As he came back in the room, he handed me a glass of wine and smiled. "Cheers," he said.

I told him that, no, I didn't want the wine and preferred to leave. He laughed at me and said I didn't have a choice; we were just gonna relax and watch a show together. I remember getting angry, standing up and saying something to the effect that he was a jerk, and I was leaving. As I stood, he grabbed my arm and yanked me back on the couch next to him. "Now, drink the wine!" He was commanding me and for the first time, I felt fear—and also the need to keep a clear head. I pretended to sip the wine. I told him my boyfriend was expecting me home before long and would be worried. He leaned his head back on the couch and let out a loud laugh, almost like a roar. He said I should just relax, because I was going to stay and watch the movie with him and I wouldn't be going home soon.

He went back into the kitchen, continuing to watch me and talk to me. He reached on top of the refrigerator and pulled down a large bag of ready-made popcorn. I remember feeling desperate. Looking out the window, I saw a 7-11 store kitty-corner from me. I wondered if I could make it to the door, unlatch the dead bolt and get outside before Faber would be able to reach me (as I was sure he would try). Could I get away? Would anyone help me if they heard me scream, or would I be able to run fast enough to escape to the 7-11? I didn't think I could make it.

Faber came back with a large bowl of popcorn and sat down next to me. All of a sudden, he grabbed me and pushed me back on the couch, pressing his lips against mine. I struggled and yelled at him, and began crying. He seemed to take immense pleasure in my reaction and roared with laughter.

Something inside me clicked. I remember thinking, 'This man is not normal, he doesn't think as I do; he is turned on by my reactions of anger and fear.' I knew then I was in terrible danger, and if I were to survive that night, I could not show any signs of anger or fear.

I don't know how I did it, but I managed to start laughing myself. He stopped laughing and with a look of surprise, turned his attention toward me. I said something to the effect of, "Look Gary—I really like you and want to get to know you better, too. But I'm kind of old-fashioned and think a gentleman should at least take a lady out to dinner first—give us a little romantic time together and I'm really hungry. So why don't you take me to dinner, and after, we'll come back and watch this movie of yours, and I'll show you a really good time."

"Well that's a thought," he said, watching me intently. Then he suddenly put his hands on my breasts and began kissing me. I pushed away against him and, in as nice a voice as I could muster, I said something like, 'Oooohhhh, you're fun, but you're supposed to take me to dinner first. No kisses until you do.' I remember my voice shaking with fear and I didn't think he'd believe me.

To my astonishment, he agreed and pulled me to my feet. My mind was spinning, and I wondered if he were really going to take me to dinner. He took my arm and walked me through the kitchen, toward the back yard. Suddenly, he slammed me up against the refrigerator, pushing his body against mine. I was terrified, but managed to say, "Now, now, you can hold my hand, but no hanky-panky till you feed me."

I was surprised when he backed away and pulled me toward the back door. Would he really take me to dinner or was I just trading one empty house for an even worse destination? As we left, he had a firm hold of my arm. I glanced around the neighborhood, but it was dark, the noise from Pacific Coast Highway was loud and I saw no one.

As Faber drove, I kept praying he really would take me to a restaurant where I could get help. From behind the wheel, he sang loudly and off key. Sometimes, he'd just laugh. I felt immense relief when he pulled into the parking lot of a Newport Beach restaurant. As soon as we were seated, I told him that I had to use the ladies' room. Faber followed me. Once inside, I waited. Finally, another woman entered, and I sent her to get the Maitre D'. I told him I was being held against my will and was frightened. (I did not know or think that a crime had been committed). At this point, restaurant staff escorted Faber off the premises.

I called a cab with instructions to take me to my aunt's home. I was still terrified. I had tricked Faber and I was afraid he would want to hurt me. He had picked me up and knew where my aunt lived. I was afraid for both of us. Upon arriving at my aunt's home, I asked the taxi driver to wait until I informed him I was safe.

The house was dark, and I knocked repeatedly, but no one answered. Since my aunt's car was outside the house, I was very afraid. I knew she often left her front door unlocked, and the thought crossed my mind that maybe Faber had arrived before me and was inside with her. I asked the taxi driver to take me to a phone booth. From there, I tried calling my aunt, but received no answer. I then called the police.

The police picked me up and took me to my aunt's home. They knocked loudly and then used their bullhorn to call her. Finally, my aunt opened the door. She was fine and had no unwanted visitors. Angered that I had not returned at an early hour, she had locked the door, gone to bed and unplugged her phone. After I told the police why I had been concerned for my aunt's safety, they encouraged me to go to the police department in the morning and file a report.

I really didn't think anything would come of my visit to the police station. When I related what had happened and the house location, I was asked to look at some mug shots. I was shocked to see Faber's picture and positively identified a face I would never forget. It was then I learned that several crimes had been committed against me—kidnapping, false imprisonment and assault. The police told me Faber was under suspicion for several other crimes and they had been trying to pick him up for some time.

Faber was arrested the following day and a news story with his picture was printed in the Orange County Register. I later learned that, in response to this article, seventeen women called in, claiming Faber raped, sodomized, tortured or held them against their will. One of his intended victims, I learned, escaped from him in just the method I considered—she ran from the same house to the safety of the 7-11 store.

Faber later went to trial for crimes he committed against six different women (I was not among them and considered myself as very, very fortunate). He was found guilty on many charges including kidnapping, rape, sodomy, false imprisonment, assault and battery. His prison term was six years and he was released after serving only two. Years later, I learned that shortly after Faber's release from prison, he again raped, brutalized and threatened at knife point another young woman. He was convicted and returned to prison. I believe he is today, again, a free man.

I was very fortunate to have escaped without harm. In hindsight, however, I recognize I had many, many warnings. Had I heeded any of them, I might never have had the frightening experience I did. From the first time I met him, I intuitively felt uneasy and intimidated. I was not secure enough with myself to listen and take heed of my intuition. I hope I have since learned."

*   *   *

Several things in this account of Maria's ordeal become readily apparent. First, from the beginning, she intuitively sensed a potentially dangerous situation but denied the record of her senses. Her intuition warned her, not once but *nine separate times*, and in each case, reason and judgment overrode the danger flag. Second, under the leadership of reason and judgment, Maria did everything wrong, but from the moment she gave credence to the warnings of intuition, and decided her survival was at stake, she did everything right. In "The Gift of Fear," Gavin De Becker writes that an intuitive warning should be trusted rather than ignored because *"it is always in response to something"* and *"it always has your best interest at heart."*[11]

Third, the first clear directive, the first command of intuition in Maria's case, was to use deception. *"I pretended to sip the wine."* And last, Maria had described to me how summoning the courage to act deceptively felt like an out-of-body experience. She said she felt as if she were on auto-pilot. Again, De Becker says it best:

> *"She... described a fear so complete that it replaced every feeling in her body. Like an animal hiding inside her, it opened to its full size and stood up using the muscles in her legs."*[12]

I bring this up because intuition doesn't only warn—it sparks fear. Not the kind of fear that paralyzes us like a rabbit caught in the headlights, but the fear that fuels life-preserving action. It says, "Do this right now!" and compels us to follow its instruction. Let's spend a moment comparing the six steps on the Primrose Path with Maria's story to see how intuition applied them:

Step 1 - Sensing the path

On a subconscious level, our brain has a pattern for what is normal in any given situation and is constantly doing a running comparison between what should be and what is. This continues even while we sleep, which explains why a sudden noise or even a scent can wake us from a sound sleep, instantly aware that all is not well.

Aside from the fact that Gary Faber was pushy, the first signal that something was amiss was his 12:30 a.m. phone call. In the very best light, it was a strikingly unprofessional thing to do, and Maria's radar picked it up, instantly signaling unease. At worse, it was a sign of an unbalanced mind, with sinister intentions. Coupled with this, he pressured her to comply with his wishes, attempting to make her feel guilty even though his efforts on her behalf were unsolicited. This is one of many tactics predators frequently use to manipulate their victims.

It is enough to say that even though Maria felt pressure, even though she felt unease, which grew steadily stronger, she not only denied it, but attempted to stamp it out— *"I forced my unease to the back of my mind, rationalizing.."* A whole litany of signals, which viewed separately might not seem convincing, assume a radically different cast when we step back and survey the whole. First, he seemed pushy. Then, the late phone call and pressure, the stop for wine, the overt interest in her personal life and the undermining of her boyfriend. A second stop, the use of his own key without knocking and finally, the sinister sound of the locking deadbolt—with each signal ignored, his control over her grew, and with it, her unease.

Step 2 - Seeing the path

It was that sound—the slide of the deadbolt—that finally broke through Maria's wall of denial. In that moment, she began verbally resisting Faber. As soon as she did, he escalated the situation by resorting to physical control over her. This resulted in two things: It confirmed all the previous intuitive warnings and it removed all her doubts, clearing the way for her to search for an avenue to escape. She states, *"For the first time, I felt real fear and also the need to keep a clear head."* Immediately, the domino of intuition fell into the domino of fear, and the domino of fear propelled a sequence of action. She appeared to acquiesce. This was to buy time to think clearly, to see the way out.

In this scenario, you may have one and only one chance to survive. It must not be wasted. Faber had physical control over her at that moment, and resisting physically would have been playing into this predator's hands. Her intuition sensed this and signaled deception. She looked out the window, saw the 7-11, assessed this escape option, and rejected it as unlikely to succeed. Fear now manifested itself as desperation.

When Faber renewed his physical assault, Maria "struggled and cried" and Faber's reaction was one of "immense pleasure." Maria says, *"Something inside me clicked."* This is the pivotal point in her ordeal. Realizing what turned him on was the door to her escape route. *"I knew then, that I was in terrible danger and if I were to survive that night, I could not show any anger or fear."* Like the cross hairs of a hunter's scope, Maria's survival instinct homed in on the one aspect of her attacker's psyche he didn't consider vulnerable—his ego. Instinct acquired the target and fear opened her eyes, enabling her to see and then choose a course steering him right onto the Primrose Path.

Step 3 - Pointing to the path

What is the "hook" Maria used to divert Faber from the immediacy of his assault? What unexpected thing made him open to other possibilities? It was the most surprising behavior (under the circumstances) possible: laughter. First, laughter is not a response people commonly associate with fear because normally it signals the opposite! Coupled with Maria's slightly condescending and playful rejoinder (*"Look Gary, I really do like you and want to get to know you better too"*), which was an appeal to his vanity, he could suddenly see the evening taking an entirely different turn or, possibly, he was just playing along with her—either way, he changed his behavior, signaling that a measure of control had passed back to Maria. The suggestion of a romantic dinner at a restaurant, the linchpin of her escape plan, was cleverly disguised and glossed over with the possibility of a sexcapade to follow. This was the succulent carrot he would soon be hippety-hopping down the path to reach.

In a situation like this, the power of suggestion, especially subtle suggestion, cannot be overemphasized. There is an extensive list of things a woman can appeal to with a predator of this kind. Adventure, curiosity, discovery, vanity and even generosity can be exploited, but to do this successfully and believably, the attacker must be seen in a new light. Yes, Faber was a predator, *but he was first a man*, and most likely saw himself this way. Men enjoy discovery and adventure in amorous relationships. It's one of the reasons we pursue women under normal circumstances. For the same reason, most men love sexy lingerie—not for the fineness of the fabric but because of the mystery of discovering and revealing what lies beneath.

Faber considered himself, in a twisted way, a Casanova. His props (the convertible, the wine and the movie with popcorn) reveal this. By not responding to fear and suggesting a romantic evening together, Maria may have caused Faber to think, "This is not working." But instead of allowing him to become frustrated, she immediately filled his mind with visions of his own charm. As the proverbial saying goes, *"The silliest woman can manage a clever man, but it takes a very clever woman to manage a fool!"*[13]

Step 4 - Entering the path

"Well, that's a thought." With this statement, Gary Faber entered the path Maria had pointed out. As soon as his mind entertained the idea of an alternative, curiosity and vanity tugged him irresistibly toward it. Yet, he was not completely convinced and tested her resolve twice, but she passed his tests because her subsequent actions were in harmony with her original suggestions. *Maria created an alternate scenario and she **enrolled** him in her vision.* Notice how she teased and lured him with promises of intimacy later. As he became convinced of her sincerity, his eagerness to follow her lead grew.

You might be wondering, as Maria did, whether she risked a bad situation for a worse. It is difficult if not impossible to judge, but one thing is certain—it was imperative for Maria to get out of that house, where he was in complete control. She needed to be out in public, where she would have a greater chance of success if forced to resort to desperate tactics. Always remember that *a public struggle with a predator is preferable to a private one*, for the simple reason that he does not want to be seen, to risk being thwarted or captured.

Step 5 - Exiting the path

Maria notes that Faber, still worried she might bolt, kept a tight hold of her arm while leaving the house. Since no feasible opening appeared, she made no attempt and they were soon in his car, arriving shortly at the restaurant. She states, *"As soon as we were seated, I told him I had to use the ladies' room."* This was a natural request and for Faber to object in that public setting would not have been in his best interest. At this point, he had lost all tactical advantage. From the moment they entered the restaurant, Maria held the winning hand. Too late, Faber sensed his control beginning to slip and insisted on accompanying her to the ladies room, where he waited outside.

Maria waited for another woman to enter, beside herself with fear and anxiety. When one did, Maria rapidly explained the situation, begging her to summon help. Maria's leaving Faber and entering the restroom constituted exiting the path.

Step 6 - Closing the gate

Restaurant staff confronted Faber and expelled him from the premises. The next day, he was arrested. In this case, the gate that closed happened to be the slammer. In breaking down and comparing Maria's story with the Primrose Path, we must be careful not to lose sight of reality. Maria's conscious mind did not analyze and carefully plan out her responses, as I have done. She didn't have time. Remember, logic is much slower than intuition. As De Becker says,

> *"Intuition is the journey from A to Z without stopping at any other letter along the way. It is knowing without knowing why."*[14]

Maria didn't hesitate—intuition spoke, and she acted.

As you can see from this example, the process I call the Primrose Path is the natural result of intuition combined with deception when under severe threat. It is a defense mechanism that already exists inside you. Some might object, "But I'm just not an intuitive person." Yes, you are! And we all have an equal share; the problem lies in clearing the obstacles away that block ready access to this wonderful gift.

In Maria's case, intuition signaled the use of deception. Had circumstances been different, intuition may have directed her to respond otherwise. Often what we most fear is physical confrontation because the immediate consequences seem so much more drastic and we are less *familiar* with that dynamic. Predators know this and to maximize our fear and hesitation, they often confront us first with what we fear most.

Engagement

We have covered what I referred to earlier as "enrollment" using the Primrose Path strategy. Now let's turn our attention to "engagement," the physical option. Assuming that flight is not an option and de-escalation and negotiation have failed, we are left with the remaining option: To physically defend ourselves. We are faced with a determined assailant and we need an edge to survive, right now! That edge is granted us when we disguise—with *apparent submission*—our resolve to resist forcefully.

The objective here is to get the assailant to lower his guard as he advances, making him vulnerable. Remember, he is taking a risk, too, and is well aware of it. As soon as he sees *evidence* that you are intimidated by his approach, language, gestures etcetera, he will anticipate success. Laurence Gonzales, in "Deep Survival," has this to say:

> *"It is part of the natural cycle of human emotion to let down your guard once you feel you've reached a goal."*[15]

The power of this strategy is in its disguise. The predator has, in his mind, set you up. While he expects you to respond in a certain way, he does not immediately become a believer. It is up to you to convince him he has chosen wisely. This is done by giving him multiple pieces of evidence. Verbal and visual submission is easy to manufacture because a part of you will feel like that anyway. Leaning back and putting up your hands in a shielding, cowering manner, backing up, widening your eyes and pleading with him not to hurt you fits the bill nicely. It is the opposite of what you just did a moment earlier, when you used a proactive boundary to measure him, but he will not be suspicious of this discrepancy. Instead, he will be contemptuous of your apparent cowardice and false front. He will congratulate himself, gratified he was right about you all along. Like a man who inadvertently steps onto an overhang, he is blissfully unaware of his vulnerability. All he can see is the beautiful view. It fills his awareness and blinds him to his real situation: extreme exposure. He believes he is on solid ground and the first warning he receives—a crumbling support system—comes too late to save him.

The balance of power changes the moment your knowledge of the reality of the situation exceeds his. *You know what **you** are going to do.* He does not. His body language reveals his expectation of success; he thinks he has already beaten you. Supremely confident and vulnerable because of it, he steps into range.

Chapter 14

"Thank You, Sir, May I Have Another?"

"Never contend with a man who has nothing to lose."

–Baltasar Gracián

As a last resort, you have the legal and moral right to strike preemptively if you are in genuine fear of receiving life-threatening injuries. By following the Passive-Aggressive Strategy, you have reviewed all the available options and exhausted every effort to avoid physical confrontation. It has become clear that this person intends to harm you and that you must defend yourself. Now you can focus all your energy with complete purity of purpose on one objective: **stopping the attack**. Under these circumstances, *it is absolutely crucial that you strike first*, the moment he comes into range—and keep on striking until the threat is ended. Here's why:

1. The element of surprise is now working for you.
2. It eliminates the timing issue.
3. It neutralizes the predator's back-up plan.

The value of surprise in this situation is self-evident, so let's take a look at the timing issue. Traditionally, self-defense has been understood and interpreted by the general public as *reactive behavior*. In other words, the victim responds with defensive tactics *only* after the attacker attempts to strike or otherwise physically harm him or her. However, this is a flawed and simplistic understanding. We must define assault the way the law does, as *threatening movement toward the intended victim*, keeping it separate from the act of striking (battery). This is an advantage for the intended victim because the law gives us the right to defend against *assault*. So, as a last resort, initiating strikes to stop an unwanted, threatening *approach* is *still* considered self-defense.

A definition of self-defense that omits preemptive action limits the intended victim to response and puts the person at a great disadvantage, because action beats reaction every time. This simple principle is the one of the main reasons why traditional martial arts training takes so long to prepare a student for actual combat. It is also the reason why predators jump from verbal to physical aggression so quickly. Defensive techniques that are designed to intercept an attack after it has begun require perfect timing to execute successfully on the mat. How much more difficult do you think it will be when the attack is unexpected, shock is eclipsing perception, and the student is facing a real world threat, perhaps for the first time in his or her life? Worse, consider the demoralizing effect that the failure of these techniques will have in a moment of real crisis.

The attacker's initial objective is to cause his victims to hesitate, to slow them down, to confuse them so they *cannot* mount a successful defense. A predator's worst nightmare is a target who suddenly and without warning goes ballistic. When you initiate action before an assailant is prepared to deal with it, the advantage shifts to you because you are *handing him your disadvantage*, forcing him to respond to your action. He will be slower. You don't have to waste time with timing.

Additionally, if you have followed the Passive-Aggressive Strategy successfully, the attacker will be experiencing an overwhelming surprise, because up to this moment, all the signals he has received have pointed to submission. He is expecting and actually depending on your co–operation because he now believes his investment in aggression has paid off. Suddenly, like a lightning bolt on a clear day, he is confronted with an elemental force of nature: the desperate rage of a cornered animal.

The next time you see a nature show on television involving predators in the wild, watch the sequence of events carefully as the predator corners the smaller and seemingly defenseless animal. Does the intended prey wait patiently to be attacked, or does it initiate its own attack with savage ruthlessness out of proportion to its much smaller body size?

Rob's Story

Rob was involved in survival response work for years and helped me develop the concept of proactive boundaries. On a Wednesday night, he went to a local Mexican restaurant, which had a nice cantina and live music. He had dinner in the cantina and spent an hour or so listening to the music.

At some point, he felt the urge to use the men's room, which was located around two corners and down a long hallway. As he dried his hands and turned to leave, the door burst open and slammed violently against the wall. Silhouetted in the door was a large, unkempt man talking over his shoulder to at least two other males in Spanish. Something about these voices, combined with the large man's body language, put Rob on instant alert. He did not make eye contact and as the large man stepped into the room, Rob moved out of the way, stepping around him toward the door.

Rob is a small man, about five feet, six inches and 135 lbs. There is nothing threatening about his appearance; at first glance, he appears frail. As the larger man stepped through the door, he threw his shoulder into Rob's chest, shouting, "Get the @!#$ out of my way!"

What took place next happened far faster than it takes to tell. Rob recalls, "Everything in my conscious mind faded out of focus except for a feeling of great danger and the need to respond right then! I acted instantly, striking him in the throat with my left hand, twice in the ribs with my right, and again with my left to his solar plexus. That put him down, and I needed him to stay down so I kicked him a good one in the ribs. I was afraid if he got back up, I'd be in serious trouble, having lost surprise."

At this point, Rob whirled to face the other men just coming through the door. The one in the lead, smaller than the first man, was shouting threats and again, without hesitation, Rob lunged forward shouting, "Bring it on, @!#@!#!@!" Suddenly, seeing his larger buddy down and destruction coming his way, the second man jumped back, his hands in the air, shouting, "It's cool, man! It's cool!" Rob pushed through them and left the premises immediately.

Rob's proactive boundary for this type of scenario was immediate and drastic action. He had decided long before, that he would respond to threatening physical contact with vigorous defense and had mentally rehearsed this type of scenario repetitively. Two things were responsible for his emerging from the situation unscathed. The first was reversing the surprise factor with an unexpected and instant response. He didn't shrink back or cower. He didn't return a threat. He didn't speak at all, he just acted, and so suddenly that the assailant never even got his hands up. As for the second attacker, Rob's decisive action left no doubt that he was more than capable of defending himself against a larger opponent. This was intimidating enough that it ended the altercation.

The second reason for victory was commitment. Once Rob engaged the assailant, he was completely merciless, hitting him with all his power and striking continuously until the attacker was no longer a threat. For those who think he over-reacted, consider this:

1. He was alone in an isolated location.
2. There was potentially more than one assailant.
3. It was an unprovoked attack by a significantly larger man.
4. His attackers were blocking the only escape route.
5. Most importantly, his intuition signaled EXTREME DANGER.

Rob's story is a beautiful illustration of the Passive-Aggressive Strategy in action. As we look at the steps he took, it becomes obvious that all five were there, in order. In this particular situation, the entire process took less than five seconds from start to finish. Will it always be this clear–cut? Of course not. Circumstances alter cases—but rest assured predators and their stratagems are quite predictable, provided you are conditioned to their methods, as Rob was.

The Passive-Aggressive Strategy Applied to Rob's Story

1. **Perception of threat:** The violent slamming of the door and the aggressive approach of a much larger man; unprovoked on Rob's part

2. **Response to warning:** The feeling of extreme threat without denial

3. **Use of proactive boundaries:** The decision and commitment to retaliate under those specific circumstances

4. **Disguise of resolve:** Immediate action without hesitation or warning

5. **Initiation of preemptive defensive strikes:** Relentless counterattack until the threat was neutralized

There is one final, conclusive argument supporting the use of preemptive defensive strikes under the circumstances we have been discussing. Human predators, especially experienced ones, often have what is referred to as a *back-up plan.* They know quite well that they may experience resistance and that the situation could go awry. Anticipating this, they will often carry a concealed weapon, which they do not initially brandish. Then, when their intended victim gets tough, the predator pulls his gun, knife or blunt instrument to either guarantee co-operation or to punish the resistor.

In the infamous Ted Bundy case, police got their first real break when, on November 8, 1974, he attempted to abduct eighteen-year-old Carol DaRonch. After posing as an undercover police officer and luring her into his car, he assaulted her, attempting to handcuff her wrists. When she verbally and physically resisted him, he drew a handgun and threatened to kill her on the spot. In abject terror, she responded instantly by kicking him in the genitals and making her escape. She was very lucky. Had he intended to kill her immediately as he claimed, he would have done so. Bundy used his back-up plan as a lever to gain compliance and if not for her instinctive response, he would have succeeded as he did with so many others.

In the interest of your safety, you must assume the person threatening you has a back-up plan, and you cannot allow him to access it. *If this were the only reason for striking first, it would be enough.* Only action that is sudden, continuous and over-whelming has any chance of preventing a predator from escalating a confrontation by introducing a weapon. The effect of being struck suddenly and powerfully produces a one to two-second window of time, during which the recipient of the blow is stunned and disoriented or is immediately rendered unconscious. This is the opportunity to strike again—repeatedly if necessary—with the goal of increasing the delay in the predator's ability to respond *until it is great enough to ensure your escape.* Any use of force beyond and in excess of that objective will turn you, in the eyes of the law, into the aggressor.

Escaping this situation has been your aim all along, as you followed the Passive-Aggressive Strategy, and the use of physical force is simply an extension of that plan, made *necessary* by the predator's refusal to cease his attempts to injure you or take your life. Ignoring the "overkill" limit can land you in the worst kind of trouble. Avoiding this danger by successfully navigating the legal mine field is the goal of the next chapter.

It's not over when you think it is.

Chapter 15

The Third Arena

"Detached reflection cannot be demanded in the presence of an upraised knife."

—Justice Oliver Wendell Holmes

The vast majority of peaceful, law-abiding citizens have never been in an altercation as adults. They have no experience, no idea of what a delicate dance on a slippery slope the immediate aftermath of an altercation can be from a legal perspective. It is my purpose to bring some clarity to those who may find themselves suddenly blindsided by a process that was designed to protect them, but occasionally does not.

As you peruse this chapter, it would be easy to misconstrue my intent. I want to state clearly and forcefully that I am supportive of law enforcement in general and police personnel in particular. Because of pro-passive bias, referred to at length earlier in this book, the entire structure of our society casts a critical spotlight on those who take action to assertively defend themselves. Often, more scrutiny is placed on the individual who is forced to respond to violence, than on the one who initiates it.

Pro-passive bias tells us that we are sheep—we should wait for the legislators to decide for us, for the police to protect us and for attorneys to defend us. In a democracy, legislators should never be given this kind of trust; it is far too great a temptation, and to place such an incredible burden on an already overtaxed police force and legal system is both ineffective and ridiculous. The police cannot be there around the clock. When seconds count, the police are only minutes away. This is not a critique of law enforcement; rather it is a sad commentary on our culture. If a majority of citizens knew the law, and were counterpredators themselves, law enforcement would be greatly simplified and officers could assume their rightful, honorable role as public servants with far greater ease and efficiency.

Although I am supportive of the law, and law enforcement, I am not coming from the perspective of the law, attorneys or police officers as I present what follows. In their own way, each of these entities attempts to stack the deck in its favor—and not necessarily with malevolent intent. The district attorney wants convictions; it is his or her job to get them. Attorneys want billable hours; they are pursuing their legitimate business objectives. Policemen sort out chaos, complete reports that begin the process of assigning blame and often risk their lives to apprehend suspects. Among these conflicting interests, humanity and common sense are sometimes lost sight of. My purpose in addressing this subject is to provide some benchmarks for those unfortunate persons caught for the first time in this legal quicksand, so that their very innocence and naivety does not work against them.

Every physical confrontation is made up of three separate conflicts: decision, action and consequence. For the sake of clarity, we will briefly touch on the first two conflict arenas so that this third arena is understood in its proper setting.

Decision

Arena number one concerns the battle we have with confusion. What are our options and how do we make the right choice? Can we talk our way out of this? Do we run? Must we defend ourselves? Should we engage in a vigorous verbal defense, hoping the assailant will back off? To have the best chance of surviving the encounter intact or with minimal injuries, it is imperative to have a set of proactive boundaries firmly in place, reinforced by either experience or scenario–based Survival Response Conditioning.

Yet, proactive boundaries by themselves are not enough. When unexpected things happen quickly, it is not the event, but the resulting confusion that becomes our greatest enemy. Defeating confusion requires us to rely on intuition, and to rely on it to a degree many of us are unfamiliar with. We need a strong trust relationship with ourselves and this only develops over time as we endure stressful circumstances with a measure of success. This is the reason full-spectrum Survival Response Conditioning is relevant, efficient and valuable. Outside of real world events, it is the only training format that provides an environment where this conditioning can happen.

Predators are unprepared for individuals who have the ability to size up a situation and instantly make an intuitive decision based on personal, proactive boundaries. I can say this with confidence because in almost every case, those with predatory intent are given to taking the path of least resistance, just like the rest of us. They will be reluctant to choose you if they have the slightest inkling that you have been conditioned to resist and thwart them.

It is crucial to note that, while even the most skillful and experienced trainer cannot guarantee your success, there are principles governing the emotional physics of each encounter, and these can be learned and adapted instinctively, just when they are most needed. Confusion leads to hesitation and hesitation can equal death. Intuition in concert with proactive boundaries reduces both confusion and its spawn, hesitation. This is the secret to gaining the advantage in the battle with confusion.

Remember, an intellectual knowledge of stressful encounters, while informative and interesting, does not always make a difference in the outcome. Only experience, the kind of knowledge that recognizes a situation and promptly directs the appropriate action is trustworthy, and the language it speaks is unfamiliar to the conscious mind. Whatever the conscious mind cannot process and control, produces anxiety which can lead to denial and rejection. Our internal alarm system is programmed to recognize this and override the conscious brain when survival is at stake. This experience is distinctively uncomfortable for the average individual, but the good news is that the goal of this process, which feels like paralysis, is really its opposite: lighting–fast, life–saving action!

Action

The second arena is where the action that was chosen in arena number one takes place. As we noted in Chapter 10, human beings intuitively respond to threat in six possible ways:

| 1. Flight | 2. Submission | 3. Concealment |
| 4. Combat | 5. Posturing | 6. Negotiation |

Each of these may be a correct response depending on the situation, if the objective of the intended victim is safety, but sometimes it isn't. Some of us are more concerned with image and how we are perceived by ourselves and others, some of us like to fight, some of us are bound by principle, and some put the safety of others first.

When threat escalates into physical assault, the choices narrow from six to five because negotiation has obviously failed. How human beings respond to threat is directly linked to self-image. The way we see ourselves either reduces or expands our options. Nowhere else is this more clearly revealed than when confronted with the possibility of being physically harmed by a fellow human being. Individuals with a very strong self–image have the advantage of choosing equally between all the options. They are not worried about what bystanders think—they know they are not cowards. They do not need to fight to prove themselves, yet they will fight if it becomes necessary to do so. They can make decisions concerning their safety unencumbered by emotional self-worth issues.

Someone with a poor self–image may regard a threat as overwhelming and not even consider self-defense or posturing (acting tough) as options. Instantly, six choices are reduced to four. First, they ignore the threat, hoping it will go away. When it doesn't, they run and when caught, they submit. Or, insecurity issues may cause these individuals to dread being called a coward so much that they choose the posturing option to avoid this label. The trouble with posturing is that sometimes it works, and other times it escalates threat into assault.

Without regard to gender, the cult of masculinity rewards adults who are willing to fight (or at least not back down) with hero status, while those who submit or flee are branded as cowards. The perspective of self-preservation is not concerned with either of these labels. However, since a strong self–image gives us more options that may serve safety, it can make the difference between life and death on the street. Survival Response Conditioning will help you in the second arena in at least two ways: it teaches you how to ward off a physical attack, and that experience will greatly improve your self–image, giving you ready access to the full array of your options.

So let's re-cap. The battle with confusion in arena number one is won by honoring intuition in concert with firmly established proactive boundaries. The resulting action in arena number two:

fight, flight, etcetera, is taken based on real world experience gained by prior encounters or participation in Survival Response Conditioning: by gaining familiarity with the adrenal state and the ability to function effectively within it.

Consequence

This brings us to the central subject of this chapter: the battle you must be prepared to face in court, in the aftermath of a physical altercation. This is the third and final arena—a minefield for the naive and unprepared, regardless of which party initiates the conflict.

Important Note:
What follows is not intended to be a definitive legal answer to specific concerns regarding self-defense; rather, it is an attempt to explore the fundamental principles on which individual jurisdictions base specific procedures and laws. For specific situations, consult a local attorney who specializes in this subject.

In order to succeed with the self-defense argument in court, six basic questions in three categories must be answered correctly. The first two concern the nature of the attack. They are qualifying questions because, unless both are answered in the affirmative, nothing else matters. The self-defense argument cannot be used.

Category One: Qualifying Questions

1. *Was the attack immediate?*

In other words, did it have to be met right then? Many battered wives and girlfriends are subjected to long-term violent physical abuse, beatings and threats on their life. Feeling helpless, disempowered, at risk of losing their life or their children's lives and unable to escape an assailant familiar with their habits, they kill the abuser in desperation and are sent to prison. To initiate an attack with the objective of neutralizing a future threat is against the law, no matter how certain you are that it will come. Our hearts cry out to these long-term victims of abuse. This is a terrible dynamic, which underscores the importance of self-image, and how it is directly linked to survival.

2. *Was the attack unavoidable?*

The relative importance of this question depends on whether or not you live in a "stand your ground" state. If not, you may have a legal duty to attempt a retreat before engaging the attacker. At the time of this writing twenty-four states have some form of the "stand your ground law," which simply interpreted means you are not obligated to retreat in the face of threatening aggressive behavior—as long as you have the right to be where you are (your home, a public place, a private residence you've been invited to, etc.). "Duty to retreat" states put the intended victim at a disadvantage because the obligation to retreat does not always serve physical safety best. Accordingly, *you absolutely must know the law in your state on this point.*

Since residence in a "duty to retreat" state presents the greater physical and legal liability, let's assume you reside in one. Could you have gotten away? Were you boxed in? Did the attack take place in a confined space like a car or an elevator? Was the attacker between you and the exit? If not, did you believe this person could and would catch you if you attempted to flee? Did you try to talk your way out? If there is any way for you to get away and you choose to stay and fight, you may run afoul of this question unless you stay to protect someone else who is unable to flee.

Category Two: Reasonable Response

3. *How extreme was the level of fear felt by the intended victim?*

Were you afraid of being insulted, of being pushed or shoved, or were you in fear of great bodily damage or loss of life? What did the attacker do that generated this level of fear? Did he have the means to carry out his threat? Did you believe him and why?

4. *Were the actions taken by the intended victim similar to those that a normal, reasonable individual would take in like circumstances?*

If this is a jury trial, then I would question how many of the twelve have actually been involved in like circumstances. From the outside looking in, you might expect jurors to understand. You think, looking at them, "What would you do in my place?" You expect them to understand how you felt, what you were thinking, how you couldn't think fast enough, how everything was a blur, that you could not hear, etc. They cannot understand you and may not side with you at all. How could they, having never had an experience like yours? Remember, *they are analyzing your actions and decisions based on reason and logic.* On the street, events often transpire so rapidly that reason has no opportunity to assert itself. Most certainly you were not in that mode. Instinct took over, setting aside reason and logic in favor of survival.

Understand from the get-go that you are being judged by a different set of rules in a vastly different environment than the one the altercation occurred in. Is it fair? No, it is not. Deal with it. This is one of the best reasons to avoid these situations. It's easy to sit back in your comfortable chair, scratch your head and thoughtfully choose between options 1, 2, 3, and 4. This is precisely what the jury may be instructed to do and they will want to know why you didn't do the same. I bring this up, because it is impossible to judge this type of attack accurately and compassionately, unless you have a personal acquaintance with victimization. And this is utterly, completely, and undeniably, *a judgment call.* Ergo, it is difficult to predict the outcome. This is another excellent reason to have the best attorney you can afford.

Category Three: Consistent Defense Mode

5. *Did the actions by the intended victim escalate the conflict?*

This is where the posturing response to threat can get you into trouble. The words you choose to direct at an aggressor, your body language, gestures, objects you may brandish to ward off an attack can actually escalate the conflict and whether this happens or not, posturing can still be viewed as behavior that contributed to more aggressive action on the part of the attacker and lessen the sympathy a judge or jury may feel for you.

Just what is meant by the term "escalation" in a legal setting? Escalation is a step–by–step process, leading to increased levels of aggression alternating between antagonists. It reminds me of a tennis match, where each shot is delivered more rapidly and with greater force until one of the players misses the ball. For example, Joe looks down the bar and makes direct and prolonged eye contact with Ed. Ed asks Joe what the hell he's looking at. Joe says, "Looks like there's a chicken-shit sitting in my bar." Ed fires back, "Why don't you come over here and say that!" Joe promptly gets up (this is actually what he's been waiting for), walks over and pushes Ed off the barstool. Ed picks himself up and charges into Joe, striking him in the face. Joe yells, "I'll kill you, mother****!" and dives at Ed, who steps sideways, draws a knife and plunges it into Joe's liver, mortally wounding him. Wouldn't it have been easier for Ed to have left the premises the moment it became obvious a fight was brewing?

If we are aware of our surroundings, if we are attuned to the people around us, it is possible to interrupt the process of escalation and even reverse it. If such an opportunity arises and you fail to take advantage of it, rest assured that failed opportunity will re-visit you in the courtroom. If you purposely escalate a situation and if this can be proved in court, you will lose the advantage of claiming self–defense. In fact, you may even hand it over to the assailant. This is a common occurrence in court.

6. *Did the intended victim use more force than was necessary to stop the attack?*

One of the most important aspects of the self–defense argument is that it has a non-negotiable upper limit. **The purpose of self–defense is always and only to stop the attack.** It is not retribution, punishment or even justice. Those are issues for the court to decide. Stopping the attack and getting to a safe place is your only concern legally—and if you go just one step beyond it, you can, and probably will, be held accountable.

Because the claim of self-defense is the most common excuse to justify an altercation, the law defines it narrowly. If your use of physical force in a defensive situation does not *clearly* conform to these six tests, you may expect a difficult time in front of a judge or jury. It is an unfortunate fact that in our legal system, the truth itself may not be enough to grant you justice. Very often, what determines the outcome is how the truth is portrayed, how it is recorded and how it is presented.

Let's spend a moment looking at the information trail that leads from the aftermath of an altercation to the point in the process where a suspect is formally charged with a crime:

The Aftermath of an Altercation

1. Officers question participants and any eye-witnesses or persons with corroborative evidence.

2. Officers collect evidence; take written statements and record verbal testimony.

3. A decision is made by the officers whether or not to take one or more participants into custody.

4. Officers file an incident report and decide who will be informally charged, listing as many charges as they can reasonably apply. (This gives the district attorney plenty of options to pursue, as the case is developed over time.)

5. The District Attorney reviews the incident report and decides if and how the suspect will be formally charged.

Hopefully, you can see how crucial the impressions of the on-scene officers are and how important the incident report actually is. This third arena is of special interest to me because the self-defense courses that are taught around the country involving full-spectrum survival response tactics desensitize the students to the dysfunctional aftereffects of adrenaline. This could increase the complexity of navigating the legal highway, especially when it comes to how an officer perceives the intended victim's level of genuine fear. I do not believe individuals should be penalized for learning to protect themselves just because they do not exhibit the effects of fear in quite the same way others do.

Take the case of my good friend Pete Norton. Pete is a gentle, socially conscious man who once chided a friend for having a bumper sticker on his vehicle that read, "Gun control means using BOTH HANDS." He is an artist and a poet, a tremendously compassionate human being. He is certainly not prone to violence; rather, he abhors it. One afternoon, I received a phone call from him and after exchanging pleasantries, he related to me that he had been involved in a verbal altercation with a much larger neighbor, who threatened him with physical harm. This experience left him feeling disempowered, guilty, in doubt of his manhood and angry. Pete enrolled in my Survival Response program, to deal with how he felt—mostly about himself—and because now he saw the clear need to have the ability to physically defend himself, should it become necessary to do so.

During the program, Pete proved very capable of protecting his body and adept at verbal self–defense. By the end of the class, he understood the subject we are discussing here. (I cover self–defense law thoroughly in every course I teach and I would be remiss not to. Every self-defense instructor should be well–acquainted with the basic principles and legal issues associated with the subject, especially in the local area, because as you will see, the law varies from one locality to another.)

Several months after graduating the Survival Response class, Pete was visiting some friends in upstate New York. He, a second man, and three female friends were walking down a small town street, when a group of younger people on the opposite side challenged them over a wine bottle Pete happened to be carrying. One of the women in Pete's group responded by yelling back, "This is America and you can't tell us what to do!" At this point, a woman from the group across the street ran over, jumped into the air and kicked her to the sidewalk. Pete immediately jumped between the two and pushed the attacker away, resulting in her losing her balance and falling to the sidewalk. One of the men (presumably a friend of the attacker) approached Pete in a threatening manner and Pete, raising his left hand, told him repeatedly that he didn't want any trouble. The man then rushed Pete and struck him with a closed fist. Pete, still holding the wine bottle, struck the man with it, knocking him to the ground, at which point the female attacker, having regained her feet, sprayed Pete with mace.

Shortly thereafter, the police arrived. Pete was arrested and spent five days in jail. He was never given the opportunity to consult an attorney, even though he asked for one repeatedly. After he had agreed to pay the hospital expenses for the man who attacked him, assault charges were dropped. Sound ridiculous? It is! But for our purposes this is an excellent example of why we need to be careful in the third arena.

The key to all this is understanding that your perspective as a defendant in a case involving self defense is different from the perspective of the officers who arrive at the scene, or even the jury who will decide the verdict. Prior knowledge of these mindsets is invaluable, both in determining your actions on the street and later, in the courtroom.

Let's begin by looking at the scene of a hypothetical altercation from the officers' perspective. The officers respond to a call from dispatch reporting an assault. As they arrive at the scene, they see two people: one lying in a pool of blood and another sitting on the curb with head in hands. Question number one: *Who Committed the Crime?* Both will tell different stories and eyewitnesses may not agree with either of them. Someone is going to lie to them. It happens every day. This process understandably causes law enforcement officers to be highly suspicious, and doubtful of the statements and stories they hear. Expect them to doubt you. In court, you are innocent until proven guilty; on the street you are guilty until proven innocent. Consider that police officers routinely deal with the worst 10 percent of the population 90 percent of the time and this alters their perception.

Accept that your mindset is different from theirs. You are relieved to have them arrive because for a law-abiding citizen like you, they represent safety and security, *but it is a mistake to assume they are your friends.* To them, you are a suspect until there is sufficient evidence to prove otherwise. Their job is to secure the area, question the participants and any possible witnesses, make a preliminary decision as to who appears to be culpable, take that person into custody, and file the incident report.

The officers' assessment of the scene, your statement and the incident report all have profound and lasting significance for you. Officers are trained to spot inconsistencies in the behavior, demeanor, body language and verbal testimony of those they question. They know full well that an innocent victim of a physical assault is likely to be experiencing psychological trauma in its immediate aftermath and they take this into account. For them, its absence is significant.

Just how much information should you volunteer to the officers at the scene in the aftermath of a violent confrontation? Some experts will tell you to say nothing without an attorney present. Silence may seem prudent and safe, yet there are two concerns I have with this approach. First, while it is a mistake to assume that the officers will take your side, it is vital that you gain their respect, and this will not happen if you display combative, adversarial behavior. *It is crucial to gain their sympathy.* Second, there are several advantages that you will lose by default if you do not act to preserve them.

This was illustrated quite clearly to me by an assault I witnessed some years ago. I was in the parking lot of a health club I frequented when an argument broke out between a man who was leaving the premises and another who, it turned out, had been waiting for him at the entrance. As the first man attempted to disengage from the argument, the second man threatened him with death, drew a knife and tried to stab him. The intended victim turned out to be a Special Forces retiree who disarmed the attacker—breaking his arm and knocking him unconscious in the process.

Immediately after subduing his assailant, he called 911 on his cell phone. When the police arrived, he identified himself and said, "I'm the one who called." Pointing to the assailant, he said, "He attacked me, and I want to press charges. There is the knife he tried to stab me with, and those three people over there, and that man over there (me) saw what happened." At this point the officers began to ask him for details, but he told them that he was too upset to talk any more about it. Then he promised them he would fully cooperate within 24 hours after speaking with his attorney. The witnesses confirmed his account and the officers allowed him to leave.

I got to know this man in the aftermath of the event, and I asked him how he managed to communicate under pressure as clearly and succinctly as he did with the police officers. He told me that although he was a combat vet he had learned about deadly force encounters and the law during a course he had taken from Massad Ayoob, one of the world's leading experts on the legalities of lethal force self defense scenarios. I later confirmed that Ayoob does recommend the actions that this man took, because they represent the best balance between cooperating with the police and exposing yourself to needless vulnerabilities. Let's break down just what these steps are:

Anchoring Your Advantage at the Scene

1. **Call first:** Whoever makes the call is assumed to be the victim, until the facts prove otherwise.

2. **Identify the attacker:** Identifying the perpetrator from the start establishes clarity for the officers by defining the roles of the participants.

3. **Indicate your desire to press charges:** As with the initial call, the first person to tell the police they wish to press charges gains a powerful advantage. The strength of their argument is subtly enhanced in the minds of the officers: a type of "first impression."

4. **Point out any witnesses:** Waiting for witnesses to volunteer a statement is a mistake, because with every passing second, the desire to escape entanglement in a situation that the witness did not anticipate grows. Pointing them out to the officers right away puts the initiative to secure the witnesses in the hands of the police. It makes their job easier and they will appreciate it.

5. **Call attention to physical evidence:** Physical evidence can degrade, be misplaced and even disappear. Evidence that may clear you is of such importance that you must ensure its prompt collection. Calling their attention to it makes the officers' job easier and cements the credibility of your story.

6. **Agree to full cooperation within 24 hours:** You may experience some pressure from the officer/s to give a statement at the scene. No one likes delays, and officers are no different. It is inconvenient for them to have to come back to get a statement. Take a moment to weigh their inconvenience against your freedom and it will all come into balance. Remember, they see these things regularly and your worst nightmare—that you are reliving at this very moment—is familiar and normal to them. I invite you to consider: Is this the best time to give your version of the event, when your testimony has the potential to be used against you in court? The law itself recognizes this vulnerability and in most states you are not required to give a statement for a full twenty-four to forty-eight hours afterward. Make sure you use it. In fact, besides giving your name and securing the six recommended advantages listed above, the only thing that should come out of your mouth besides your breath are the words, "I thought he was going to kill me!"— Eight words that will save your life in court.

The reason for this is simple. In defining a self-defense scenario, one of the most important factors is the level of fear the intended victim feels. If you are truly in fear for your life, shock and adrenaline reduce the capacity to think rationally. You are sitting on the curb, gasping for air, and your mind is still in "Oh my God, Oh my God, Oh my God" mode. If you are able to calmly, rationally answer mundane questions, your level of primal fear becomes suspect. It is natural for you to exhibit confusion, anxiety and short attention span. The presence of these emotional behaviors validates the authenticity of your experience.

It is very common *not* to remember details and even if your memory is clear, the tunnel vision and auditory exclusion that are trademarks of the adrenal dump may greatly reduce your perception of what really occurred. A really sharp police officer may ask you specific, detailed questions precisely to test you. You have the right to remain silent. After a cooling-down period, after consulting with an attorney, give a written statement with some thought to the six legal tests mentioned earlier.

Another pitfall to avoid is making the assumption that police officers conduct investigations uniformly. I believe that the overwhelming majority of officers are honest, smart, dedicated, courageous public servants. Sometimes I wonder if people see uniforms or human beings. The point is, these officers are individuals and subject to the same passions and weaknesses as the rest of humanity. Some are idealistic; most are realists. Some are kind; a few are cruel. Many are faithful and principled; a handful are corrupt. Some simply care less than others.

Unless you live in a very small town, you have no idea who will show up at the scene. Most likely it will be a dedicated, compassionate public servant, but perhaps not. Since it is possible, in theory, that the officer on the scene may be less than sympathetic, is it not in your best interest to accept that possibility and prepare for it?

Know this: If you are the graduate of a survival response conditioning program, your behavior in the wake of an attack and the way you unconsciously portray yourself in its aftermath may not be in line with what the investigating officers' view as normal or common. Given their pre-disposition to suspicion, (often justified) it doesn't take a lot of gray matter to see the importance of minimizing these differences. I am not suggesting dishonesty. I am strongly urging caution. It is none of their business that you have training; that is personal, private information and the emotional turbulence following a violent attack on your person, or one of your loved ones is not an appropriate setting to reveal information that may complicate an already complex situation.

In addition to all this uncertainty, predators or those who exhibit predatory behavior can be exceptionally slippery at the scene. In all probability, they have been there before and know by instinct and experience just how to represent themselves most favorably. They are adept manipulators and very smooth liars. If you combine this with the occasional occurrence of poor police work, the result can be at best, a very ugly reminder of how vulnerable the average citizen is, and absolutely horrifying at worst.

Consider a story related to me by Rebecca, an acquaintance of mine for many years. One afternoon, as her ex-husband was picking up their three-year-old child for his weekly visitation, her boyfriend showed up unexpectedly and initiated a verbal conflict with the ex-husband. Words were exchanged, and the boyfriend charged her ex, who was holding his son in his arms. Attempting to protect the child, he endured a savage beating while pinned in the car door, unable to mount a defense. He later stated that if an off-duty police officer who happened to be a neighbor had not arrived when he did, he was sure he would have been beaten to death.

The boyfriend, aware of the approach of the officer, instantly became tractable and apologetic—in great contrast to the outraged ex, who gave full, aggressive vent to the emotional overload he was experiencing. The disparity in their behaviors was so pronounced that it confused the officer regarding who the real aggressor was. The boyfriend, in spite of Rebecca's statement to the officer, managed to be convincing enough that he was not charged with a crime, even though two eye-witnesses fingered him for aggravated assault and battery, and extreme, reckless endangerment to a child.

This same attacker had previously killed a man in another state and was still wanted for questioning in that case. He had beaten and abused his son from a previous marriage and nearly strangled the boy's mother to death with a coat hanger. He is a psychopath, capable of unleashing volcanic rage one moment and mild personable demeanor the next. This chameleon-like flexibility, combined with sub-standard police work, is the reason he is not in prison right now for these crimes. Had the officers done just a little digging, they would have quickly discovered that his story needed a much more thorough investigation. Remember the story of "The Edge" from the beginning of this book. The most adept predators are often not caught.

Let's pause for a quick review:

1. A strong grasp of the six tests for the self-defense argument is essential.

2. Being familiar with the laws that pertain to this subject in your locality is not only strongly advised, it is your civic duty.

3. No matter how friendly officers on the scene are, if you are a participant, you are a suspect until the other party has been formally charged or the charges are dropped.

4. Do not give a statement at the scene. Use all the time legally available to you.

5. Eight words will save your life in court: "I thought he was going to kill me!" Except for contact information and securing the advantages discussed above, do not utter a single syllable more at the scene.

6. Unfocused, distracted, distraught behavior is normal in the aftermath of a violent altercation. Calm, rational responses are the exception, and officers look for behavior that does not match the existing conditions. Beware.

I strongly advise the readers to avail themselves of some good legal counsel regarding self-defense law as soon as possible. Any police officer will tell you that ignorance of the law is not an excuse for breaking it. As a citizen of this wonderful country, it is your duty and responsibility to be familiar with its laws but sadly, the average citizen is not. Failure to be informed could lead to great expense, loss of time, loss of freedom and possibly even the loss of your own life. I cannot count the number of times I've heard someone say, "If only I had known, I would have done things differently!" Well, they could have known, and they should have known, and now, they do know. It is a "pay me now or pay me later" environment, and later is *always* more expensive.

All of this really points to one conclusion: unless you or your loved ones are in extreme danger, avoid at all other cost physical altercation because you do not know what it will escalate into. Negotiate, negotiate, negotiate and when that fails, walk away! If escape is impossible and you must use physical force to defend yourself, then strike suddenly and with complete commitment. If you must risk error, then err on the side of your own safety with a clear awareness of the precarious position this can put you in. When all is said and done, it is still better to be judged by twelve than carried by six.

*   *   *

Up to this point the focus has been on you, the adult parent. The subject of institutionalized victim mindset, its causes and the relevant effects, have been explored in depth and a solution offered that is effective and readily available. I have underscored that your personal experience is *everything* to your child's safety, and urged you to go and get this experience for yourself. You can do it in one day.

STOP PROCRASTINATING AND GET THE TRAINING NOW!
www.safetyfirstpps.org

Your perspective as a fully aware, experienced, resourceful counterpredator is the *essential* ingredient for success as you engage in choosing and executing the best working plan for your children's safety. Without it, you cannot be as effective in protecting your children as you could be. You may not think you need this for yourself, and you may be right. However, your children deserve your absolute, best effort. Do it for them.

A word of caution:

There are hundreds, perhaps thousands of commercial martial arts schools across the country whose sole purpose is to make as much money as possible. To that end, these businesses commonly provide "tack–on" programs to gain short–term customers who would not be attracted to their regular, long–term curriculum. Sadly, in recent months the term "adrenal self–defense" has begun to crop up in their advertising. What they offer to an unwitting general public bears absolutely no resemblance to what I have introduced in this book, other than the gear used by the armored attacker. Therefore, unless Survival Response Conditioning is the primary focus of the business providing the training, I would not trust its quality and neither should you. If you have questions regarding a specific program and are experiencing difficulty getting satisfactory answers, you may contact me through the website at www.counterpredators.com. I may be able to recommend a program in your local area.

We are located in Tacoma, Washington and you can sign up for our program at www.safetyfirstpps.org. I would be thrilled to work with you personally but recognize that it may be impractical for you to travel across the country to do so.

I'll see you on the other side.

Part III Endnotes

Chapter 9

[1] Aleksandr Solzhenitsyn, *The Gulag Archipelago*. (New York, Harper & Row 1973) 14

Chapter 10

[2] Laurence Gonzales, *Deep Survival: Who Lives, Who Dies and Why*. (New York: Norton, 2003) 92

[3] Gonzales, *Deep Survival*, 133

[4] Bruce Siddle, *Sharpening the Warrior's Edge: the Psychology & Science of Training*. (Belleville, IL: PPCT Research Publications, 1995) 27

[5] Gonzales, *Deep Survival*, 127, 169

[6] Norman Doidge, *The Brain that Changes Itself: Stories of Personal Triumph from the Frontiers of Brain Science*. (London: Penguin Group, 2007) 42

[7] Michelle Kodis, *Love Scents: How your Natural Pheromones Influence Your Relationships, Your Moods and Who You Love*. (New York: Dutton, 1998)

Chapter 11

[8] John Leach, "Why People 'freeze' in an Emergency: Temporal and Cognitive Constraints on Survival Responses," Aviation, Space, and Environmental Medicine Vol. 75, No. 6, June 2004, Page 539-542

[9] Forrest Church, Sermon, *"The Law of Unintended Consequences"* public address Feb. 9, 2003 New York, NY

Chapter 13

[10] While statistics may be manipulated to reflect any viewpoint, the overwhelming preponderance of evidence points to women

being the victims rather than the perpetrators of violence historically, socially and in every culture. I found the following article particularly enlightening: MALE VIOLENCE IS FUNDAMENTALLY DIFFERENT FROM FEMALE VIOLENCE

In domestic law on November 29, 2010 You can find it on line using this link http://angelzfury.wordpress.com/2010/11/29/male-violence-is-fundamentally-different-from-female-violence/

[11] Gavin DeBecker, *The Gift of Fear: Survival Signals that Protect Us from Violence.* (Boston: Little, Brown, 1997) 70

[12] Gavin DeBecker, *The Gift of Fear,* 6

[13] Rudyard Kipling, *Three and an –Extra* (Plain tales From the Hills, 1888)

[14] Gavin DeBecker, *The Gift of Fear.* 26

[15] Gonzales, *Deep Survival,* 119

IV

The Wolverine Club

Chapter 16

Basic Instincts

"Wolverines are small, highly intelligent animals that adapt to new environments quickly. They are known to regularly thwart the traps set for them. Wolverines are fearless, daring, curious and tough. While fiercely independent, they also have a playful side—but once engaged their savagery is legend—they will confront and defeat predators many times their weight and size..."

–Active Safety for Kids training manual

The primal power of knowing you have successfully defended yourself produces intense pride. This is completely natural. There is a reason that from time immemorial, celebration follows victory on any and every field of battle. Surviving deadly threat is proof of the right to live at its most basic and instinctive level. The focus here is not the moral right to live, because, in that arena, all creatures in nature are equal. I am speaking of the law of nature, independent of and separate from any human effort to define it. Nature bequeaths the right to live only as long as its inhabitants adequately protect themselves. The strong, the quick and the intelligent earn the right to live *solely by their performance.* They celebrate each victory in the moment, because their future holds no guarantee.

This war dance is a potent swirl of emotion combining the passionate exultation of the survivor with the quiet joy of gratitude *for the gift of life itself.* At core, it is the ultimate validation of our identity and existence. I am reminded of the sentiments expressed by John Dunbar, the character portrayed by Kevin Costner in "Dances with Wolves," in the immediate aftermath of the battle with the Pawnee when they attacked his village.

A professional soldier, no stranger to war, he describes a battle *unlike anything he has experienced before.* While the physical components of combat were familiar to him, the difference in motivation could not be more striking. In prior engagements, Dunbar had felt a strong belief in a set of principles, had a passionate sense of mission and a commitment to fulfill his professional obligations. In contrast, this had been far more intimate and personal: a mortal struggle to protect the lives and futures of loved ones in his immediate presence. It was a transformational event for him, and he eloquently speaks of the pride he feels when he is acknowledged by his Sioux name. It is *then* that John Dunbar begins to embrace a new and powerful understanding of who he really is.

A robust sense of identity is at the root of all human empowerment. Without it, we are sick, weak and unfit for the rigors of surviving a predatory environment. If you acted on my advice at the end of Part III and took the training that is the subject of this book, then you have had a powerful experience which has allowed you to re-shape your identity. You have been re-connected to your truest self, welded to nature through 10,000 years of trial by fire. This experience is now a part of who you are, and it cannot be taken from you, ever. It is a beautiful, powerful gift and only those who possess it can see and *feel* the true importance of finding a way to pass the benefit of the adrenal advantage on to their children. You will not be detoured by a weak and faulty ideology, regardless of how popular it is. You are able to see right through it. Now that your eyes have been opened, it is easy to understand how you have been sold a bill of goods regarding your children's true abilities. This awareness can and will enable you to enter into a whole new understanding of what true protection—the kind that actually prepares them to survive, actually is.

It is important to define just what is meant when speaking of preparation in this context. What I am suggesting, is a training format that produces an experience that is hard-wired into a child's neural network, so that when he or she is confronted by a threatening set of circumstances, the right choice is instantly and instinctively made. It is similar to the adult program we discussed in the first half of this book; a conditioning process that for reasons we will delve into later, is actually easier for a child to acquire than an adult.

The difference between our children and young in the wild is that, in the wild—the natural environment—instinct and parenting combine to *prepare* the young to survive. From day one, the learning process is dangerous, harsh and difficult. Human children are kept *as far from risk as possible* and enjoy all the advantages society can provide for them. Every effort is made to make the learning process as easy as possible. As a result, the moment they find themselves outside the protective shroud we have provided for them, they present easy, vulnerable targets to anyone who might wish them harm.

The objective of the rest of this book is twofold. The first objective: correctly and accurately portraying children's true potential when properly conditioned in an adrenal format. The second objective is to help you gain a working knowledge of the training methods and programs that will give your children the skill and experience to fight for their life and succeed, just as you did.

Before we get into the meat of this discussion, I want to clarify a very important point. Conventional wisdom tells us that it is impossible for most children to physically resist an adult and it is rare for them to be able to out-smart one. As adults, we receive daily reminders of the unforgiving nature of "adult on child" crime. We clearly see that most children are vulnerable and naive. The outcome of these situations appears to be a foregone conclusion. But does it have to be that way?

As things presently stand in our society, there is some truth to the belief that the average child is helpless and vulnerable to a predator. Why wouldn't they be? Children who have been sheltered, shielded and protected all their lives, with little or no exposure to the real world will always find themselves an easy mark. They are easy to spot, easy to manipulate and easy to subdue. They are either terrified, intimidated, confused or blissfully unaware of the danger. Our children seem defenseless.

Parents and children—all of us in fact—have been conditioned to accept this "truth." As long as this remains our default understanding, it will continue to be a self-fulfilling prophesy. Remember entrenched assumptions? What we believe has the powerful effect of establishing itself as a fact. In this artificial environment, the examples of children who act decisively and powerfully to save their lives are presented as the exception rather than the rule. This is why they are given hero status. They are viewed as *doing something out of the ordinary*, even though their behavior is in concert with their natural instincts. I share with you the wonder and admiration I have for these little warriors who, in spite of society's pampering, succeed against the odds, yet I am deeply offended at the notion that the resources they tapped into are only available to an elite few. This is not just a lie; it is a damned lie that is responsible for the victimization and death of thousands upon thousands of our children.

In truth, the assets of nature are available to every child; they are born with them and they have the right and the duty to use them. It is our responsibility as parents to introduce our children to their own primal skill set and provide them with the permission, access and training that wholeheartedly endorse their acquisition of the adrenal advantage.

The rest of this chapter will be devoted to revealing what children are truly capable of, when in harmony with the full array of their natural assets. The terms "Animal Mind," "Wild Brain" and "Cornered Animal Nature" all refer to specific aspects of the same phenomenon: a switch from conscious brain processing to the default condition of the subconscious mind when confronted by life–threatening circumstances.

* * *

On the Fourth of July 2007, not far from my own home in Tacoma, Washington, a terrible tragedy took place. Zina Linnik, a slight, blonde twelve year old was returning from a fireworks display in her neighborhood. It was just after dusk, but there was still enough light to walk by. Zina had gone to the display a short time earlier, accompanied by five of her eight siblings, but had left early because the noise of the exploding fireworks unnerved her.

At 9:45 p.m., her father, Mikhail and Zina's older sister, Nina, heard a piercing scream coming from the back yard, which they recognized as Zina's. Mikhail Linnik sprinted toward the sound, and saw a gray van driven by an Asian male disappearing around the corner. Through the gathering gloom, he managed to get a partial license plate number. In the alley, lying on the ground was one of Zina's red flip-flops. Two days later, police arrested Terapon Adhahn, a legal immigrant who was a level one sex offender. Shortly thereafter, he led officers to Zina's body in a field near Silver Lake.

Two weeks later, I received a call from a friend who is one of the nation's leading defensive tactics instructors for the military. His grandchildren were very good friends with the Linnik family and Zina in particular. This tragedy continued to devastate them. The children were suffering from nightmares, and the parents were sick with fear for their children.

My friend asked me as a personal favor to put the whole family through the Adult Survival Response Program to help them come to terms with their fear. At first I was very reluctant to do this. The adult program is extremely intense and no place for these children, who ranged in age from nine to thirteen. Normally we never allow anyone under the age of sixteen to attend without informed parental consent which means the parent must be a course grad or willing to accompany the child through the program.

Because of the unusual circumstances, we decided to make an exception to our policy. This was not decided lightly—nor was it supported unanimously by our staff. We were taking a risk and we knew it. I will never forget that program. The youngest, Molly, was nine years old. She weighed about eighty pounds, and it was clear from the beginning that she had been severely traumatized by the abduction and death of her friend. Although enough time had gone by for the initial shock to wear off, the fact that she would never see Zina again was still present with her.

As the day progressed, I watched her continuously as she bravely endured one scenario after another. It was difficult to get her to fully engage. The size and power deficit between her and the Ghouls was so enormous; she seemed helpless against them. She cowered behind her mother whenever she had the opportunity. Her strikes and voice power were not equal to the task. I had felt misgivings about her participation from the first moment and all my reservations seemed justified. This was the risk that our staff had been so concerned about taking: that we would be responsible for re-traumatizing her, without any positive benefit in empowerment or acquired skill.

Toward the end of the program, we did a lowlight scenario in which two Ghouls attacked a student. This was the limit for Molly, and she refused to participate. We had her stand to the side as one by one her family members completed the exercise. Molly grew more and more agitated, and when her mother's turn came, she began to pace back and forth, more and more rapidly. In the dim, shadowy light, I could see that her face was wet with tears. With all my heart, I wanted to send Molly's family members to comfort her but something kept me from doing it.

What happened next will never be forgotten by anyone who witnessed it. Had I not seen this myself, I would have hardly believed it possible. As Molly's mother engaged the Ghouls, both of which towered over her, Molly suddenly launched herself at her mother's attackers. With piercing howls of fury, she drove into them like a small hurricane. You could clearly hear the impact of her blows landing with perfect accuracy. Had it not been for their protective armor, she would have hurt them badly. Her onslaught was so sudden and unexpected that it caught one of the Ghouls in mid-stride and knocked him to his knees. She instantly whirled around, planted herself between her mother and the second Ghoul and screamed that if he touched her, she would kill him *"Dead! Dead! Dead!"* Then Molly took her mother's hand and without taking her eyes off the Ghouls, backed out of the arena.

This was the most amazing and complete transformation I had ever witnessed. In retrospect, I believe two things made it happen. First, Molly reached her saturation point—that moment when fear-driven rage filled her so completely that it exploded into action. Second, she had the focal point of a loved one to defend. Combined, those two motives took her straight into what we call "Cornered Animal Nature." In this mental state, logic does not exist; odds do not count and fear is the fuel that morphs the intended victim into unstoppable counterpredator. Molly became an elemental force, for the love of her mother, for the memory of her friend Zina and for her own outraged emotional self. This is pure and undiluted empowerment, one of the lifesaving benefits of the adrenal advantage.

From that moment on, Molly became a different person. She had found her power. Once she regained her composure, she was tired but no longer timid and paralyzed by fear in that environment. She became a hero; an inspiration to her family and the rest of the class. You are reading about her now, because she made an indelible impression on every staff member who was there, myself included.

What is important here is that Molly's experience is not unique, either in this program or in life. We have found that extreme fear is often a tipping point, especially in the training of children who are by nature subject to easy imprinting. Time and again, children in the Active Safety for Kids program have broken through this same barrier—but under more gradual and age-appropriate conditions. Molly's experience proved to me that the same methodology is effective under even the most severe and stressful training scenarios.

It is important to note that reaction to extreme fear can go either way. Fear can become fuel, or it can become a roadblock. What produces a positive result is whether or not a child is *able to take action that has a positive reward* while in fear mode. This is what turns fear into power. Remove action and reward from the equation and a child will become a rabbit in the headlights.

Take Katie, Lisbeth and Pam. All of them went through the A.S.K. program with the same casual attitude that you might expect from girls in the nine to twelve age bracket. They acquired a skill set in all the modules that was barely above average—normal performance for that age group in an environment their parents were more excited about than they were. For all three of them, a complete change took place the first time we unleashed the Ghouls and allowed them to push the girls' fear buttons, once again in a low–light setting. By definition, this means there is barely enough light to see. Things are confusing, loud, jumbled and chaotic. These conditions trip the automatic triggers that release nor-adrenaline into the system, and galvanize the body into action.

When the girls believed that the attack was real—when they became emotionally engaged— it supercharged their performance. They were *better than they ever had been before*. This was a genuine reality check for them; it was obvious because they were all crying and shaken when it was over. They had also pounded the hell out of their attackers, and they knew it. That experience changed them: their outlook was different, their performance notably improved, and most of all, their attitude became serious and bold. Like Molly, they had found their power.

All this leads us to the conclusion that given the right perspective and environment, our children are capable of far more than our society gives them credit for. I will augment what I have presented here with several real stories of children who *without training* took action far beyond what we would expect of them.

Alana Miller

When the 911 call came in, Petty Officer William Cummings of Naval Air Station Whidbey Island, heard a small voice say, "Mommy ouch." Alana Miller, age two, had watched her mother collapse from what she thought was a severe migraine headache. Erika Miller, a volunteer for the Red Cross, had shown her daughter how to dial 911 but never dreamed Alana would be put to the test so soon. When Cummings arrived, he found Miller unconscious on the floor and Alana in another room getting a blanket for her mother. Paramedics arrived and transported Miller to the hospital, where she was released, later that day. "I was shocked to hear my two-year-old had the ability and knowledge to call 911," she said. "I'm so proud of her!"[1]

Daniel Rivas

It took three full weeks for wood-shop teacher Fred Sotcher to recover from the infection that almost killed him. The San Jose teacher owes his life to an eleven-year-old boy, who realized he was in trouble and persistently refused to ignore his intuition. Daniel Rivas noticed his teacher was shivering and pale. Even though Sotcher said he was okay, Daniel didn't believe him and called the front office. At first the nurse was skeptical but Daniel stubbornly refused to back down. When she did arrive, she wasted no time in calling an ambulance to John Montgomery Elementary. Fred Sotcher spent the next four days in intensive care. According to Sotcher, Daniel had the courage to challenge authority when he believed he was right. His combination of instinct, initiative and persistence in all likelihood saved his teacher's life.[2]

Keither Dodds

On August 2, 2003, Edie Dodds, returning home from a trip to the park with her two children, felt her shoulder self-dislocate. The Oakland mother was driving a minivan downhill and the sudden and excruciating pain caused her to lose control of the vehicle. The mini-van collided with a parked Volvo and flipped over. Dodds immobilized and in great pain, could hear her six year old daughter, Eden, crying. That's when Keither Dodds took charge. The nine year old fourth grader unbuckled their seatbelts and helped his sister out of the car. Then he returned to rescue his mother. He was in a hurry because he could smell gas and thought the car might catch on fire. Keither had her halfway out of the car, when several by-standers came to his aid, as his mother's weight was too much for him. Dodds remembers Keither telling her not to worry and that everything would be okay. He then borrowed a cell phone and called his dad, an Oakland policeman. Young Dodd's remarkable composure is not surprising to those who know him, or to Keither himself. At Joaquin Miller Elementary, he is a natural leader. "I solve problems as a conflict manager," Keither said. "I break up fights and help, like when my friend scraped his knee."[3]

Titus Adams

The truck that seven year old Titus and his sisters were passengers in veered off the road and flipped over five times before coming to a stop. It was Thanksgiving Day, 2002, just outside of Greeley, Colorado. Titus Adams' mother had lost control of the car rounding a curve on their way home from the holiday dinner. She had been thrown from the vehicle and lay crumpled and unconscious in the snow. All three children were miraculously uninjured but they wore only pajamas and Titus was barefoot. The two girls, Tiffany, four, and Tierra, one, were terribly upset but Titus comforted them and instructed Tiffany not to let Tierra cry. He told Tiffany that he was going to get help, and he promised her he'd be back. Then, he squeezed out the window and began to run. It was twenty-three degrees. He crossed an open field, wiggled under an electric fence and broke through the gate on a second fence. After more than half a mile, he encountered three dairy workers, who called the state patrol. Titus' mother, Tammy Hill, was rushed to the hospital with a broken neck, a broken back and ten crushed ribs. She survived because of the quick thinking and bravery of a seven year old boy who was determined to rescue his mother.[4]

Alexis Goggins

Life has never been easy for Alexis Goggins. She suffered a stroke before her first birthday and has a mild learning disability as well as epilepsy. On December 1, 2007, the heat went out in the Detroit apartment that Alexis, then seven, shared with her mother, Seliethia Parker. Just before midnight, Parker called a friend, Aisha Ford, who decided to bring the mother and daughter home to stay the night with her. As Parker and Alexis entered the vehicle, Parker's former boyfriend, Kelvin Tillie, who had been hiding in the dark next to the building, forced his way into the car at gunpoint.

Tillie, an ex-convict on parole, had been stalking and harassing Parker for weeks. The women were terrified but Ford kept her wits about her. Hoping to create an opportunity to get help, she told Tillie she was low on gas. Ford then turned into a gas station, where she knew she would have to go inside to pay the attendant. Tillie gave her $10 and told her not to spend more than $5. As she left the vehicle to pay, Aisha Ford called 911 on her cell. She used every excuse she could think of to stall for time.

Tillie, enraged at Ford's delay, pointed his pistol at Seliethia and shouting that he would kill her, squeezed off two shots. Alexis threw her tiny body over the seat, between Tillie and Parker, and screamed at Tillie, "Don't you hurt my mother!" Kelvin Tillie then shot Alexis six times, hitting her in the eye, chin, cheek, left temple, chest and right arm

Police arrived and arrested Tillie at the scene. Alexis and her mother were rushed to the hospital, where Alexis was listed in critical condition. Initially, she was not expected to live, but to everyone's amazement, Alexis got stronger. Even though the doctors told Parker her daughter would never walk or talk again, after two months in the hospital and six surgeries, she was doing both and doctors expect her to make a full recovery. Parker, shot in the head and right arm, was released a few hours after the incident.

Alexis does not think she is a hero. When asked how she felt about what happened to her, Alexis said she was not afraid. To her, it was simple: "I love my mother and I didn't want a bad thing to happen to her." Seliethia Parker said, "My baby is just an angel to her mother. I thought as the mother, I'd be saving my child. I never thought my daughter would be saving me."[5]

Chapter 17

The Bones of the Earth

"Children need models rather than critics"

–Joseph Joubert

Training children successfully using Survival Response methodology requires a unique combination of knowledge, sensitivity and flexibility. This is a subject in which it is more important to ask the right questions than to possess all the answers. If you are a Survival Response grad, you will have an intuitive grasp of what your child needs to know, as well as specific ideas about the way in which he or she should be trained. I have made it clear throughout this book that I consider the expertise of the parent regarding the predatory environment to be the primary hedge of protection for every child. Possessing this experiential knowledge will answer many of the commonly asked questions automatically. If you are not yet a grad, I hope that as we focus on children (and the crucial role nature intends parents to play), the remainder of this book will motivate you to become one.

Even if you have become your own expert, the task of preparing your children to navigate threat is so important that you need all the help you can get. Also, it is important to recognize that your experience as an adult will not directly transfer to your child. It is crucial to recognize and honor the differences between training children and training adults. When considering whom to partner with in educating your child to navigate a threatening environment or situation, begin by asking yourself the following:

Does this individual or organization know and understand the real world environment? What is their background? How did their program evolve? What are the underlying principles that support their methods? Are they teaching self-defense from a traditional martial arts perspective, or is their training streetwise and preventative in nature? How does mental and emotional conditioning play a role in the training process? Is the program designed to cover a broad range of situations? Will the lessons be permanently programmed into a child's consciousness or soon forgotten? What percentage of the training is devoted to physical combat? To establishing strong boundaries? To honoring intuition? How is a child's relationship with fear treated in this program?

Does this method allow for differences in the way children learn? Is the format modular, or is each lesson dependent on grasping the one that preceded it? Is all of the training integrated into one or two concepts? Do the trainers attempt to motivate me as much as my child? Do they believe that children are capable of more decided and successful resistance to a predatory environment than is commonly accepted? Will my level of knowledge and understanding of the subject be expanded and improved along with that of my children?

The reason these questions are so important is that there are many "child safety" programs available out there, and almost all of them have severe deficiencies. In my opinion, many of these programs are dangerous because they are incomplete. They are based on the wrong premise, and they promote false confidence. There are three categories of these inadequate programs. First we will explore their differences and then we will take a look at their similarities. I have listed them in order from the least effective to the most effective, based on intensity, realism and retention. It is also worthwhile to note who conducts these classes, and the instructor's background, experience and outlook.

Safety Education Programs

This term describes both private programs and those that are either mandated or available through the school system. Sometimes these programs are more accurately called "life skills" (L.S.) classes. Often they are conducted by teachers, counselors or businessmen, depending on whether the program is government-sponsored or comes from the private sector. (The private programs have products and services to sell, and are normally broad-based from a scenario standpoint.)

While the instructors may be trained in conflict–resolution skills and have some knowledge of the curriculum they are teaching, they generally have no experience in the necessary physical skill set and know little or next to nothing about the predatory environment. The major difference between this type of safety program and the programs based on martial arts (M.A.) and self-defense (S.D.) has to do with ideology. Both M.A. and S.D. programs teach children to fight off an attacker to protect themselves, while the L.S. programs emphasize negotiation, avoidance and a very passive approach.

It is actually quite rare for M.A. and S.D. programs to be taught within a school curriculum because of the prevalence of pro-passive bias on the part of the administrators. They seem to prefer the life skills approach because it is closely aligned with pro-passive ideology. Often, especially with school programs, children are indoctrinated that it is wrong to fight to defend themselves, especially against peers who bully them. A common trait of the life skills approach is that it is based on authority figures (parents, principals, etc.) providing protection to the children under their charge.

The net effect of this approach is disempowerment. To make value judgments against children, who defend themselves *as a last resort*, in an environment where they are a captive audience (the school system) and many times because the adults in charge dropped the ball, is a despicable betrayal of trust that violates decency and common sense. These methods roundly and soundly fail to prepare children to be self-sufficient in an unfriendly environment and form a major section of the assembly line in the victim factory.

Self-Defense Programs

Almost always, these programs are very short–term in nature, in the 8 to 12 hour range, and often taught over a weekend. Many times, they are taught by law enforcement or military personnel and focus on a limited number of physical techniques. Because of "zero tolerance" violence policies, they are rarely included in a school's curriculum, unless it is a private school. Comparatively little is taught with regard to de–escalation and preventative strategies. Due to their background and experience, the instructors are familiar with the adrenal environment but very often lack the conditioning methodology to transfer that benefit to the individual students. Since the course is of such short duration and is taught solely in a conscious–brain learning format, lack of retention is compounded by the instructor's attempts to crowd too much information into the time allotted. Students walk away from the experience with the impression that the instructor is skilled and gifted, but suffer "systems overload" and retain only a fraction of the experience.

Martial Arts Programs

This type of program is a conscious–brain learning format that emphasizes physical combat. Many of the techniques require fine and complex motor skills to execute and are too complicated to succeed under adrenal influences. To the best of my knowledge, there is no traditional martial arts program available today that adequately prepares the student for the emotional stresses generated by genuine confrontation. In addition, the emphasis placed on combatives often eclipses the much more important preventative strategies that in many cases would make the physical tactics unnecessary.

Many martial arts instructors have never been in a real fight for their life and have no personal acquaintance with how quickly things can go wrong in the real world. Or, they are very tough individuals who have a wealth of personal experience in the threat navigation milieu, but, because of the traditional learning format, have difficulty transferring their personal toughness to their students. Yet, they are viewed as experts on teaching self-defense by an equally ignorant general public. These gifted individuals are indeed experts, but they are experts on the mat, rather than the pavement. Children, who take these classes, often emerge with confidence in a skill set that is unequal to the environment they circulate in. When disaster strikes, not only are they at physical risk, but must also deal with a devastating hit on their self-worth because of perceived failure.

I am reminded of a young man who trained with me personally and was an important member of my staff. He had previously trained for several years in Tae Kwon Do and had earned a black belt in that discipline. One night in Seattle, he was jumped by a couple of young thugs and was unable to fend them off. Arriving home, he promptly went to the closet and threw his black belt into the garbage. The whole thing was a depressing memory for him until we became acquainted and he learned the truth: He was not incompetent—his training method was the problem.

Since there is so much focus on martial arts as a self–defense option, and because what I have stated above appears so critical, I want to explore this type of program in greater detail. Our modern era has been referred to as the information age, but in the field of personal protection, it would be more accurate to call it the disinformation age. Books, newspapers, television programs and films abound with images of men and women with martial arts training who appear to be invincible. With perfect timing and blinding speed, they execute flawless techniques and often defeat several opponents simultaneously. Martial arts schools have sprung up on every street corner, all claiming to teach discipline, respect, self-defense, physical conditioning, meditation and other worthwhile pursuits.

Before I continue, let me say that I have a profound respect for the martial arts community in general, the individual instructors and students in particular that I have had the privilege to know personally. They are some of the hardest working, honest and genuine people in the world. I believe the study and practice of the martial discipline is an honorable and wonderfully beneficial endeavor. It has molded me into the person I am today, and I would not trade that experience for any amount money. I am a life–long exponent of the martial arts. I want to state this as emphatically and as forcefully as I can, so that the critical view I express regarding certain aspects of training that have become popular will have some temper.

Most martial arts schools train their students for sport competition. There are several benefits to this kind of training, such as physical conditioning, confidence, sportsmanship and discipline. However, unless the instructor understands the difference between sport karate and the type of street self-defense that includes adrenal conditioning, and trains students in both arenas, these students will assume that their experience will translate into street-readiness. This is always a grave mistake and occasionally a deadly one. I would add that it is very difficult, if not impossible, to integrate full–force survival response conditioning with sport karate, as they are polar opposites.

Perhaps you are scratching your head and asking the puzzled question, "But isn't that what martial arts is all about?" The martial art milieu's genesis began with the effort to systematically train soldiers for battle. Yet, right here is one of its greatest weaknesses.

Combat by its very nature is a fluid and formless reaction to the "flight" or "fight" response to danger. Let's take a moment to look at the full evolutionary process one goes through to master a martial art. In the beginning, there is a state of "no knowledge." The student is a creature of instinct, knowing no rule but the street, no law but survival. Nothing distracts from this prime directive. The street fighter is an extremely dangerous animal because he reacts without thought to threats. There is no lag time in the reaction process. He doesn't worry about controlling punches and kicks; *landing them* is all he is concerned with. All his actions are governed by this purity of purpose. It is the secret of his power.

Now, deciding he wants to improve his skills, he enrolls in the karate school of his choice. Right away he is told that he must re-learn how to breathe, walk, move and think. He becomes a victim of "systems overload" because his instincts are in conflict with his training regimen. Two separate drives are competing for mastery, and it can take many months and even years before programmed response is welded to natural instinct. Unfortunately, it is at this stage that many students quit their study for a variety of reasons. They have good head-knowledge but it has not become instinctive. In other words, these students think they are prepared but their preparation is lacking a key ingredient. Bruce Lee used to say, "Half-way cultivation leads to ornamentation," and this is exactly what he was talking about.

If the student perseveres and continues his study, gradually the martial knowledge rewrites his physical instinct program. When the process is complete, he has regained his purity of instinct but now it is augmented by truly superior technique. In other words, the techniques become instinctive in *a training environment.* It would appear at this point that the process is complete, but this is another mistake. In order to come full circle, the student must now pare away the bad habits that his martial training produced, and become conditioned to the environment in which he may someday be forced to apply his skills. Here, I will part company with some of my associates.

> *It is a law of the mind that as we train, so we act.*

For example, in sport karate, students are taught to pull their punches and kicks as an exercise in control and also to avoid injuring their sparring partner. This practice becomes so ingrained that in a moment of sudden surprise, when adrenaline shuts down the brain and nothing is left but instinct, the body automatically does what it has done 10,000 times before. The result is that the strikes do not have the desired effect.

Lt. Col. Dave Grossman, who wrote "On Combat: The Psychology and Physiology of Deadly Conflict in War and Peace," relates a story told to him by an officer who had practiced gun disarms with anyone willing to accommodate him. After each repetition, he would hand the gun back to his partner so they could practice the maneuver again. One day, he responded to a distress call involving an aggressive man in a convenience store. As the officer stepped around the end of an aisle, a man holding a drawn gun confronted him. Instantly, habit took over, and the officer was able to wrest the gun away. Unfortunately, still on autopilot, he handed the gun back to the aggressor, *just as he had done hundreds of times in practice*. Luckily his partner was able to shoot the suspect, before the man was able to fire his weapon.[6]

This story is a great illustration of the power of a conditioned response and the serious consequences attached to poor methodology in training. Over confidence (or lack of real world experience) combined with sub-standard method is an obvious recipe for disaster. Thankfully, it is now standard practice at many police academies to refrain from handing the weapon directly back to "the aggressor" when practicing disarms.

Another problem with sport karate is that vital striking targets on the human body, essential for the purpose of self-defense, are not allowed. They are off limits. Of eight targets providing maximum damage with minimum effort, only one, the solar plexus, will score points in a match. Striking the other seven will either score no points or get you disqualified. Again, as we train, so we act. A third problem is that certain techniques that work well for the purpose of sport karate can get you killed on the street.

Then there is the grappling issue. Approximately 90 percent of all altercations end up on the ground. The vast majority of martial arts styles are strike-oriented, and dependent on the student's ability to keep on his feet. Even an experienced martial artist can be defeated if he can be maneuvered into unfamiliar territory. Deprive a bird of the ability to fly and it can easily be caught. Take a person with no ground fighting experience to the ground and there is a good chance that the traditional martial arts background he is familiar with will be ineffective.

There are some martial arts systems that are more well-rounded than others. By this, I mean that they teach ground fighting skills, striking skills, locks, holds and throws. Hapkido, Pentjak-Silat and Kempo are three examples. While these are excellent systems, the deficiencies that I referred to above apply to them as well and should not be ignored, especially if the objective is to prepare the student to survive on the street. Without survival response conditioning, they may not be equal to the task and could fail the student in a moment of need.

Simply put, the difference between a martial art and self-defense is that with a martial art you are expressing yourself through perfection of technique. You are developing mind, body and character, seeking wholeness through discipline, health through exercise, and peace through meditation. These are marvelous goals and worthy of our attention. Self-defense is much simpler—it concerns our survival. The subject of personal protection is the study of two types of individuals: those who use violence to accomplish their goals and those who must respond to violence to preserve their lives. One must prevail, for there is absolutely no common ground, and never will be. It is this understanding that defines the nature of street survival.

Let's review a list of the <u>martial myth busters</u> that we have discussed:

1. Sport karate does NOT double as self-defense.
2. In combat, conscious judgment rarely supersedes instinct.
3. In an emergency, the switch from no-contact to full-contact is unreliable.
4. Good martial artists seldom win fights defensively.
5. Even good martial artists need ground fighting ability.
6. Competitive targets in sport karate are NOT sufficient for self-defense.
7. It does NOT take long periods of training to become street-safe.
8. You do NOT need be physically fit to defend yourself.
9. Mental discipline alone CANNOT cancel out the effects of fear.
10. Reaction seldom beats action.

Just because you have a black belt in karate, doesn't mean you will win an altercation. We martial artists are often guilty of living in a cocoon, woven by our own training methods and philosophy, and it can be difficult to escape. To one degree or another, all three of these types of programs share the following common denominators:

1. **They are opportunistic.** To sell their products and services, they magnify and play on the fear of parents when, in fact, these solutions do little or nothing that is *preventative in nature*. Exploiting the subject of missing children and greatly exaggerating the number of stranger abductions are just two examples of these outrageous scams.

2. **Their focus is post event.** Most, if not all, of the "solutions" that are offered by these groups revolve around reacting to a tragedy. I.D. kits, dental records and reward insurance, are useful only after a child disappears. However, they sell extremely well.

3. **They lack depth and effectiveness.** The situations covered are not dealt with in a realistic manner, nor do the methods used to instill the lessons leave a lasting impression. The instructors teach rather than train and train, rather than condition. These safety courses are not comprehensive, i.e. they only deal with the most obvious and common situations. Often the solutions presented are unworkable in the real world. Predators are constantly evolving, and most safety programs are so far behind the curve that the instructors can't even see the same horizon.

4. **They are designed to facilitate the comfort envelope of parents and educators.** The one thing programs like this excel at is making parents and educators feel good. After all, they are doing something, which is more than the great majority—who are apathetic or indifferent because denial has blinded them to reality. However, doing something is worse than meaningless if that something is the wrong thing, or if it is ineffective, *because then we relax*. Once we decide to place trust in an instructor or a program, it is easy to allow our minds to file awareness and concern into a nice, compact little box

that doesn't take up too much of our attention. The truth is we all want peace of mind. Yet, I am compelled to ask if we have *earned the right to peace of mind* because we are actively engaged in training our children by the best methods available; methods that arm them with the awareness and skills needed to keep them safe?

I believe it is a moral imperative to rise above the sleazy commercialism, faulty ideology and shallowness of the modern child safety milieu. As parents and as human beings, I know you are with me in desiring the absolute best for our children. I urge you to turn your back on the apathetic mindset that makes excuses, passes the buck and languishes in comforting denial. Kick those thought patterns in the backside and *demand* something better! All of this starts with insisting on higher standards, and you cannot be successful in this endeavor unless you start with your own thinking processes. This little acrostic has been personally helpful to me, so I will leave it here with you:

Improvement

Constant
And
Never-ending

My research and experience has led me to conclude that a truly outstanding and effective child safety program must be based on five principles. When combined, they form a powerful and unique methodology that my organization has found to produce consistent, superior results. All of the lessons we teach are an outgrowth of this integrated foundation.

Safety Program Basics
1. Positive modeling
2. Structured emotional empowerment
3. Effective strategic planning
4. High–pressure interactive scenario-based exercise
5. Instinctive conditioned response

There are two basic methods of opening a child's mind to the predatory environment. The first approach is reactionary. It consists of graphically portraying numerous examples of predatory behavior in an effort to help a child avoid contact with a predator. I call this "finger wagging." Most of the safety advice that is given to children by well-meaning adults falls into this category. An extreme example of this methodology is the "scared straight" type of program where children are taken into the prison system and introduced to criminals, who tell them exactly what they would do to them if not for the bars between them. While this may achieve some success in motivating children not to enter the criminal world, in my opinion, it does little to help them avoid victimization by criminals themselves. More commonly though, the advice given to children by parents and other well–meaning adults is ineffective—it does not impact them in a way that leads them to change their perception of reality.

The reason so many resort to this method, is that it is easy to do, it requires no planning and allows parents and educators to respond to perceived threat *in the moment*. It makes *us* feel as if *we* are doing something positive about the problem right when we are affected by their vulnerability most acutely. However, there are a number of complications with this method. Many of these stories—and the warnings that result from them—originate from urban legends and are inaccurate and untrue. Children have an uncanny knack for exposing these untruths and the net effect is distrust of the *sound advice* you give them. Often the net result of finger wagging is fear and distrust of exactly the wrong people, and misplaced confidence in people they have been taught are "safe." Quoting facts and statistics to children with short attention spans and giving them advice that is meaningful and important *to us* does not mean that they view it the same way, or that they will retain it like we might.

The second approach is diametrically opposed to finger wagging. Instead of reactionary lecturing, "direct immersion" is a well–planned strategy that is focused on real world scenarios and children's emotional response to them. As you will see, this results in profoundly changed behavior, not because the parent desires it but because the child does.

When we consider the disparity between the sophistication of a predator's web of deceit and the innocence and naivety of most children, the task of preparing them to out-maneuver a predator's advances seems at first overwhelming. It would be impossible to cover every situation a child could face, for the simple reason that these criminals are evolving, adjusting and changing tactics like hunters that change camo patterns with the terrain. There is no strategy that can *guarantee* success. There is no way to make our children's armor completely seamless. There are simply too many variables. As soon as we accept that reality, the importance of making them *the hardest target possible* becomes apparent.

Positive Modeling

The good news is that there is a way to do this, and it is simpler and more effective than most would believe. I call it positive modeling. It is the same method that the Secret Service uses to train its agents to recognize counterfeit currency. Secret Service trainers do not focus on examples of counterfeiting. The method they use is to have trainees study genuine currency so carefully that when they come across a counterfeit bill, they recognize it as a fake immediately. They may not see at first what is wrong, but they instinctively sense that *something* is. Then they are able to zero in on that bill, until the discrepancy becomes apparent. It is a remarkably effective technique, and I am sure you are already making the connection.

It is not necessary to traumatize our children with all the bad and sneaky things that predators might say or do. That would give exactly the wrong message. Teaching children not to trust people is a terrible mistake that will adversely affect them all their lives; especially when the vast majority of people are well-intentioned or at least harmless. What we need to do is focus on, teach and demonstrate normal adult-child relationships. We need to train them to know the real thing, and know it well. *Once they are familiar with how a healthy, balanced adult-child relationship feels and what it looks like, any anomaly, no matter how subtle or slight, will generate an uneasy feeling.* It doesn't matter what the predator does, the moment there is a mismatch internal alarms will ring.

Structured Emotional Empowerment

The next step is to train our children to trust their feelings, and this requires both adults and children to view emotions in a different light than they may be accustomed to. Often we reject, deny or otherwise qualify our feelings before we accept and act on them. As human beings, we have a tendency to view ourselves through the filter of social approval, and if our peers consider an emotion to be negative, our automatic response when we experience that emotion is to deny and reject it. This trait is imprinted on our children from infancy. *Structured emotional empowerment is the strategy of training children to re-interpret the emotional signals their body produces under threatening or unusual circumstances in a way that aids them in making powerful choices.* When you combine positive modeling with structured emotional empowerment, you are helping a child become familiar with the radar system that nature instills in all of us from birth. First, we train them to know by experience what a normal, healthy adult-child relationship looks and feels like. Then, we condition them to recognize and act on the emotional triggers that signal departure from that norm.

Effective Strategic Planning

The third principle, effective strategic planning, *revolves around identifying the common denominators in the stratagems employed by those who would harm our children, and designing tactics to neutralize them.* To accomplish this with credibility requires great creativity and ruthless dedication to reality. We must continually question, testing the limits commonly accepted by society and experts in two general areas. First, what is a child capable of under extreme stress physically, emotionally and mentally? Second, how far are we willing to go to ensure their safety? To justify this approach, I would ask, "Are you satisfied with the job the experts have done so far and are you willing to allow the status quo to define your child's education with regard to safety issues?" No? I didn't think so!

Once effective tactics have been established and tested, we need to turn our attention to the question of how best to instill them in our children. We need a method that facilitates a high level of retention and produces instinctive action. What is the most effective learning format?

Common learning formats	Retention
Reading / hearing	5-15%
Sight	10-20%
Auditory /verbal	40-50%
Personal experience	90%

Give a child a list of facts and it will go into one ear and out the other. Give them an experience and they will remember it for a lifetime. Howard Hendricks, the longtime professor at Dallas Theological Seminary who wrote, "Teaching to Save Lives," believes *"maximum learning is directly linked to maximum involvement."*[7]

As you can see, personal experience is by far the most effective learning format but is 90 percent enough? What if the 10 percent they missed happened to be the exact information they need to maintain their safety? Based on our exploration of Survival Response Conditioning for adults, we know there is a way to supercharge an experience so that it is permanently imprinted in the memory, and then, responded to automatically and instinctively. Let's review it briefly:

High Pressure Scenario Based Exercise

The basic concept behind this technique is to re-create a situation in the real world that a student can be taken through under high stress. During the exercise, the student's actions and reactions can be altered and improved at a sub-conscious level, resulting in an instinctive response under similar circumstances in a real situation. The U.S. military uses this method to make its training the best in the world. Anyone interested in the scientific evidence backing these concepts should read "Sharpening the Warrior's Edge" by Bruce K. Siddle, which you will recall from our discussion in Chapter 6. For now, let me share a fascinating glimpse into the subject as Rush W. Dozier Jr., the author of "Fear Itself," sees it:

"Powerful emotions often create exceptionally clear memories. ...Think of your brain as a thick wax tablet and experience as a sharpened pencil. Experience creates memories by making marks in the wax.

But if the wax is cold, it is hard. The tip of the pencil can only make shallow scratches... that are easily rubbed off. But when we receive a severe shock ...the priming signal heats and softens the wax. Any immediate experience written into the wax ... will be deep, easily made, and once the wax cools will last as long as the tablet itself."[8]

This is the premise behind Survival Response Conditioning, considered to be the best way to improve an adult's self-defense skills for the past thirty years. Now, how can we adapt this methodology to benefit children?

Conditioned Instinctive Response

Survival Response Conditioning must be adjusted when working with children because predators do not usually approach children the way they approach adults. With children, persuasion rather than intimidation is the predator's preferred lever. Adults can be conditioned in an extremely short period of time, because their training involves fear immersion. Taking adults into the fear environment and training them to act decisively when under its influence is extremely effective. As we discovered in previous chapters, a well-run and effective program can produce permanent results in as little as a day for most adults. This is an intense and emotionally exhausting experience, unsuited to most children.

Conditioned instinctive response is a more gradual and repetitive approach, better suited to children because they are dealing in most cases with a friendly persuader. Conditioning them to fear by degrees is preferable because it mirrors the predator's tactics and protects them from unnecessary trauma during training. Make no mistake, the children who benefit from these classes are still having their fear buttons pushed, but not in the horrific way that adult Survival Response grads experience. Over a relatively short period of time, they will acquire the same basic physical skill set that an adult has, adapted to the methods predators use to ensnare them. Even so, it is astonishing how quickly children are able to acquire these skills.

To illustrate, allow me to make an analogy. Consider the difference between kiln-fired pottery and sun-dried adobe. As the clay is subjected to intense heat in the sealed environment of the kiln, it takes on permanent characteristics, becoming hard and impervious to moisture—so much so that it is able to contain and control that which previously weakened it. With proper glazing, the beauty of the clay is revealed for all to see. It is a rapid process, accomplished in a couple of hours.

In contrast, adobe dries slowly in the sun, and must be coated with stucco to protect it from adverse weather conditions. With proper structure and protection, adobe can be used to construct walls that will last for decades. If we compare the kiln-fired pottery to adult Survival Response Conditioning, then the process of creating adobe becomes an apt metaphor when describing conditioned instinctive response for children. It is a gentler, less intense approach.

Both methods refer to subconscious, instinctive processes that produce permanent results, rather than the familiar, conscious–brain learning format with its retention issues. Because of this, it is easy to make incorrect assumptions about the effectiveness and practicality of these methods. The speed with which a good skill-set can be acquired is out of all proportion to the time and effort invested. We are used to the slow, plodding progress of the conscious brain. The subconscious is lightning fast and, as we learned earlier, children are much more receptive to its signals. This is the *primary* method by which young children acquire knowledge.

In the natural world, it is the primal, instinctive, sub–conscious mind that often makes the difference between those who survive and those who do not. Nature gives this advantage to the young precisely because they are most vulnerable. Ironically, it is the adult world that teaches children to rely on slow, logical processes and to regard them as superior.

The depth and effectiveness of any program based on the above five principles is clear. In light of this, what specific lessons should we focus on, as we use this strategy to prepare our children for partnership with risk?

Chapter 18

What Powerful Children Know

"Absolute safety has its consequences. It's like practicing being dead."

−Forrest Church

Helping children to intuitively sense threat and define it so the proper action can be taken is the focus of the first half of the A.S.K. (Active Safety for Kids) program. This course is designed for children aged seven to twelve and taught in ten modules that repeat over a twelve week period. Like all Safety First Personal Protection Strategies programs, A.S.K. was created by staff, based on empirical evidence and years of hands-on experience.

Note: If these exercises are treated as information and taught solely in a conscious–brain learning format, they will have limited effectiveness! It is not only the information—*but the method by which information is imparted that counts in life–or–death situations.* Lessons acquired in adrenal format are the only ones that imprint deeply enough to be truly effective for a child in the moment of primal necessity.

Lesson One: Normal Relationships

Street smart, empowered children with strong self-images are not likely to be selected by predators. Accordingly, the first and most important, positive relationship for children to have is with themselves. By highlighting and under scoring children's uniqueness and special talents, by helping them to feel loved and appreciated, we draw closer to the goal of having children *like* themselves. Therefore, we seek to make children in this program feel important and valued. The issue of self-image is one of the major pivot points that determine whether a child is targeted or ignored by a victimizer. A child who is emotionally healthy is hard work for opportunistic predators. Because of this, our program is designed to foster positive, proactive behavior in their relationships with themselves, peers and adults.

The desire to be liked and accepted by their peers is another vulnerability that children experience. However, we never use the term "peer pressure" in their hearing. To most children, those words are a trigger signaling the approach of a lecture and their receptiveness instantly diminishes when they hear them. Instead, we speak of leadership and *we train them to lead*. This is something most children find desirable. As soon as they believe it is achievable, motivating them in the pursuit of excellence becomes much easier. Children who have a mentor relationship with their parents or other strong adult role models, who have a healthy self–image and who demonstrate positive leadership aptitude within their peer group, are statistically unlikely to become victims.

To transition children from easy victims to hard targets, it is imperative to train them to have an instinctive knowledge of what a healthy adult-child relationship is. *Normal adult-child relationships are low-key, casual and non-exclusive.* Most importantly, they trip no internal alarms. Many children raised in a healthy, balanced family environment never really think about these things at all. They rightly assume that this is just the natural order of things. When a child begins to wonder and question these matters, it is usually because there is a legitimate concern. As parents, are we paying attention?

Lesson Two: Emotional Alarms

When I speak of emotions in the context of personal safety, I am narrowing the focus to intense, powerful emotions felt in the body, like joy, ecstasy, fear, outrage, guilt, apprehension and anger. When an emotion is powerful enough to be felt in the body, it is because our subconscious mind is red-flagging us and it is *always* important. As I facilitate safety programs and interview individuals, I am repeatedly confronted with a curious block when I ask them how they felt about emotionally charged situations they have experienced. Almost without exception, they tell me what they thought instead of what they felt. Often I am forced to repeat the question by telling them pointedly that I am not concerned with their thoughts at this juncture, rather, I want them to recognize how their body physically felt in the heat of the moment. This illustrates clearly how addicted we are to re-interpreting, analyzing and judging what the subconscious mind—through the body—is trying to tell us. Long ago Marcus Aurelius directed us to seek original sources:

> *"...What is it in itself, in its own constitution? What is its substance and material? What is its causal nature?"*[9]

Instead of making a judgment call when we experience a strong emotion, instead of responding with denial, we should ask ourselves why we feel this way. We should trust our splendidly complex, accurate radar and carefully examine what it is telling us. Clarity leads to power. Stop for a moment and say to yourself, "I love my child and my body is giving me signals that something is wrong here!" Instead of treating your feelings like some cheap street vendor trying to sell you something you don't want, honor those feelings *and teach your children to do the same,* because it will greatly strengthen their emotional health. Someday, honoring their feelings may even save their life.

In my mind, there are no negative emotions. All of our emotions serve a particular purpose, especially with regard to safety. The emotion itself is neither positive nor negative, but action based on that emotion can have positive or negative results. What we need to do is re-write our own emotional programming and give our children definitions for these so-called "negative emotions" that will prepare them to make sound decisions under pressure; decisions that result in their doing, as Laurence Gonzales says, *"the next right thing."*[10]

Let's take an emotion that is universally vilified: *fear.* Webster's Encyclopedic Unabridged Dictionary of the English Language 1996 version defines fear in this way:

> *" A distressing emotion aroused by impending danger, evil, pain etcetera, whether the threat is real or imagined; the feeling or condition of being afraid."*

I must admit that a more negative description could hardly be imagined, and I would like to thank the publishers for making my point. This is exactly the way fear is commonly viewed by the public at large, and I would be willing to bet that you do, too.

In contrast, I would like you to consider an alternative interpretation: a definition that is positive, powerful, accurate in nature, and most importantly, it is the one that best serves your child's safety. I was first introduced to this definition by Dr. Jeff Alexander, the founder and C.E.O. of Warrior Spirit, a Washington State based nonprofit dedicated to empowering children and adults. During a children's safety program, he asked a group of youngsters aged six through ten to tell him what they thought fear was. A seven year old boy said it like this:

> *"Fear is a feeling in my body that tells me about my environment so I can make the right choice."*

These are his exact words, unaided and unprompted by an adult. Sometimes children see these things more clearly than we do. If someone could manufacture a pill that could achieve this, he or she would make millions and be a publicly acclaimed hero, but because fear is uncomfortable, we tend to associate it with what it points to and reject them both. We imprison the messenger because we don't like the message.

When children have been trained to think of fear with this new, more accurate definition, it acts as an insulator against a number of disempowering self-worth issues by giving them subtle yet powerful affirmations. Here are some examples:

1. I am smart. (Cowards are ruled by fear. Intelligent people use their warning system to avoid danger.)

2. I am valuable. (We feel threat only because of the possible loss of what is important to us.)

3. I am worthy of being loved. (We fear because we love. If we love, we can be loved.)

4. I am unique. (What is rare is precious; what is unique is priceless.)

5. Other people love me. (I am valuable to them.)

Seen this way, fear becomes an asset because it does exactly what nature intends it to do. It is the opposite of what society proclaims it to be—an agent of empowerment rather than paralysis. As a bonus, children who have this understanding, this relationship with fear, are more likely to become leaders within their peer group, which prepares them for leadership in life.

While we are addressing this subject, I would like to examine two other emotions that often get bad public press: *guilt* and *anger*. Again we'll go to Webster's (the same version quoted earlier):

"Guilt: a feeling of responsibility or remorse for some offense, crime, wrong, etcetera, whether real or imagined."

In our society, guilt has an even more tarnished, ugly and negative reputation than fear. I have personally heard counselors, psychiatrists and mental health workers label guilt as a worthless, wasteful negative emotion, which no healthy person should waste their time with. The consensus seems to be that since guilt is about the past and we are in the present looking toward the future; there isn't much we can do with it. However, there are two distinctly useful things we can do when we experience the emotion of guilt: We can learn from it and we can use it to fuel action to make a course correction. So the thing that guilt does for us, the thing nature intended it to do, is to act as a moral compass, guiding us in maintaining emotional health and balance. Seen in this light, can you really imagine what a world without guilt would be like? Wait, we already have that picture: prisons overflowing with sociopaths!

Now we can create a new, accurate and much more constructive definition:

> *"Guilt: a feeling in my body about a choice I've made, that arouses my conscience!"*

For the purpose of this book, I'm not concerned with whether or not psychiatrists and counselors agree with me, because I'm not coming from their perspective. I am concerned with doing what works best with regard to a child's safety, mainly from human threat. Guilt is a tool that predators use with great skill and effect and they imprison their young victims with it emotionally. It is their objective to make victims feel dirty, worthless and helpless; to strip them of both the energy and desire to ask for help. We know that this is a potent strategy because child predators often succeed in victimizing many, many children before they are caught. Interviews guaranteeing complete confidentiality and immunity from prosecution, conducted by Emory University psychiatrist Dr. Gene Abel[11], uncovered that:

- Male offenders who abused girls had an average of 52 victims each.

- Men who molested boys had an astonishing average of 150 victims each.

- Only 3% of these crimes had ever been detected.

Next to love, anger is the most commonly expressed emotion between parents and their children, especially as they enter puberty and beyond. In the arena of safety, anger, rightly understood, is important and useful, because *it is almost always about the perception of being wronged*. Children come into this world equipped to trust adults and expecting to trust them. When a predator (or anyone else for that matter) breaches that trust, the fear and guilt that result often turn to anger when the child realizes he, or she has been wronged. Deep seated, smoldering anger in a child is very often an indicator of perceived betrayal, and as such, parents should be on the lookout for it.

Once again, let's compare Webster's definition with a more outcome-oriented understanding:

"Anger: a strong feeling of displeasure and belligerence aroused by a wrong; wrath; ire."

Anger seems to be a more comfortable emotion; meaning that we are more used to engaging it and its lesser minions, frustration, irritation and vexation, on a day–to–day basis. Because we are a bit more familiar with it, I think you will see a correspondingly closer connection between the two definitions:

> *"Anger: a feeling of energy in my body about something wrong that I can use to create change."*

It is a mistake to tell our children not to feel or express an emotion they are experiencing. By doing this, we are actually training them to deny a part of who they are. It is like an electrician with hands shaking from the effects of hypothermia inserting his screwdriver into a live circuit box. We are ignorantly tinkering with a failsafe that nature has implanted within our children for their protection. The consequences of not allowing them to be authentic are predictable and unpleasant, as Alice Miller and Mary Pipher discovered. Instead, meet your children where they are. Accept at face value that, right or wrong, *this is what they are feeling in the moment* and ask them what they are going to do with these feelings. Listen, accept, suggest and guide.

By harnessing and channeling the energy produced by anger and directing it into achieving a solution, we are teaching our children about responsibility, honesty, fairness and justice. We are preparing them to adopt the empowered mind.

Nature has provided us with an array of highly sensitive and accurate mechanisms capable of detecting the most subtle abnormalities in the behavior patterns of those around us. Emotion serves as powerful warning beacon that is designed to alert us to threat. We possess this system. Our children have it too. It is hard-wired into the subconscious mind. Our duty as parents is to acquaint them with it and to train them to become an expert in its use—the same expertise that they demonstrate every day playing complex computer games.

Training our children to know by experience what healthy, stable adult-child friendships consist of, and putting them closely in touch with their feelings, makes it possible for them to execute an end run around a predator's game plan. It transforms them from easy victims into hard targets.

Lesson Three: Proper Boundaries

Under normal conditions, a child's radar array will detect an anomaly while it is still a little way off. Nature designed it to be so, to give a child some time to muster a defense at a specific point. We call these points' boundaries. In order to obtain a clearer, broader understanding of boundaries, I prefer to describe them as fences. A fence is not used to deny access, rather it is erected to limit invasive overtures and direct them to a checkpoint where access can be denied or granted. These "gates" are the control mechanism that all human beings, young and old, use to monitor intimacy in relationships.

In the real world, whenever somebody scales a fence instead of knocking at the gate, it can be safely and automatically assumed that their intentions are suspect. In that moment, no time need be wasted deliberating the circumstances, as you might do when deciding whether or not to open a gate. Someone is trying to breach your security. Period. The real value in a fence is that it justifies an *automatic* alarm and forces you to pay close attention to it. The issue here for all of us—and our children in particular—is speed of correct response under duress. We need to teach our children to watch for those who attempt to climb over their fences and to respond: "Hey! Stop that! Don't climb over my fence! Ask my permission at the gate or get out!"

All child predators have one thing in common: They are opportunistic. Their attraction to a child is in direct proportion to that child's vulnerability. Every predator has four objectives which must be met, before he reaches the goal of remaking a child into a victim. Usually these objectives come in the same order:

Predator Objectives

1. Information
2. Access
3. Interaction
4. Physical contact

A predator needs information to plan a successful approach. If he plays his cards right, this will give him repeated access, which he will need to develop rapport. This interaction is his basis for creating levels of trust that will make the child vulnerable to his excesses.

You might call this the predator's game plan. In studying these objectives, it becomes obvious why *ninety three percent* of the children who are molested, raped, abducted and killed know their abuser[12].

The first three objectives—information, access and interaction—are, to one extent or another, already achieved. It's just so much easier.

To make children safe or at least turn them into very difficult targets, each of the predator's objectives must be met with uncompromising rejection. This can be really difficult for children, especially when the predator is someone close to them. We need to give them tools that they can use to their advantage, and we must train them in such a way that they feel no guilt in erecting these boundaries around themselves. Remember that good fences make good neighbors.

The Privacy Fence

To counter the predator's need for information, our children should be taught to value and even love *privacy*. This is the first, and in many respects the most important of the four boundaries, because everything that follows is rooted in its rich soil. When someone asks a child for information that is personal, our children need to be able to tell that person very firmly, and without hesitation, "*That* is none of your business." This is one time that it is absolutely necessary for your child to not only verbally resist an adult, but to ju-jitsu him.

Having stated this, I would like to devote a little attention to a more obscure but no less important side to the "information" debate. The knee-jerk reaction that many adults display regarding children giving out personal information to strangers is understandable. It excites our darkest fears. Yet right here, the vast majority of us miss the boat. Our children will be giving information about themselves to those they don't know for the rest of their lives and very, very rarely is this hazardous to them. We treat this subject as if the information itself is the issue, when nearly always it is the *circumstances* under which information is asked for and given that determine whether or not there is cause for alarm.

In dealing with the privacy "fence," we need to go several layers deeper than just telling our children not to give out personal information to others. It is far more beneficial to train our children to ask themselves questions like, "Why does this person seem so persistent?" or "Why do I feel uneasy when I'm around him?" "Why does this grown-up seem more like one of my friends?" and especially, "What does this person want with me?" *The fact that he made an approach means that he wants something.* If this person's objective is not clearly and immediately spelled out, then it is likely that whoever is making the approach is up to no good.

Very often people with predatory intentions will reveal private things about themselves as a way to get a child to open up. Predators understand very well the age-old principle of "quid pro quo" and use it effectively to guilt their mark into quickly revealing things about themselves that under normal circumstances might *never* come to light.

> *It is a law of the mind that when a private matter is revealed, especially to a new acquaintance, it is a covert offer of intimacy, with an expected return on investment.*

The subtext here is: new adult acquaintance offering intimacy to a child. It may not be harmful, but it is certainly not normal and, therefore, deserves our undivided attention. Remember, predators want to get information that will give them an edge in grooming a child. It is their attempt to manipulate that gives them away. Teaching children to value and respect their own privacy, as well as the privacy of others, erects a roadblock across the predator's journey down the information highway.

The Proximity Fence

The second fence necessary to a child's security is *proximity*. How close should a child allow a stranger (or anyone for that matter) who provokes a feeling of uneasiness in him or her? In my mind, the issue of proximity has two facets—the obvious physical side and the obscure emotional side. Human beings in general and children in particular have a natural inclination to create distance between themselves and anything that produces a feeling of distrust. This human love affair with "personal space" is one of the best built-in safety mechanisms available to us, and yet parents unwittingly rob their children of its free exercise from infancy.

I remember an occasion from my not too distant past that illustrates this point clearly. My friend and radio broadcast co-host Mic Stump and I were conducting a live broadcast on child safety. As he was conversing with a caller, Mic made the comment that at gatherings of extended family and friends, he often hears parents telling their young children to "give your uncle a hug goodbye" and how it bothers him that they try to coerce their child into obeying them in this, *especially* when the child seems reluctant to do so. Mic went on to tell this gentleman that when he finds himself in this awkward position as the "uncle," he tells the parent that he does not want the child to express affection to him unless the child is freely willing to do so. Affection cannot be forced, and repeated attempts to do so, only dull nature's finely tuned machinery until it is rendered useless. A child's perceptions and feelings are the only internal alarms they possess, and as such should be respected. Never attempt to force children to express affection they do not genuinely feel, for two reasons: First, it teaches them that dishonesty is OK and second, it can leave them vulnerable to the advances of a predator.

On a physical level, the amount of distance between a child and a perceived threat is conditional to the severity of the threat. Children should be taught that the instant an internal alarm is triggered, they should move out of lunge range, normally about fifteen feet. This is a minimum. More is better, obviously. Of equal importance is maintaining that space, no matter what. For every step the threatening person advances, the child should retreat two, while verbally resisting the aggressor. Some might object by pointing out that verbally resisting the predator is interacting with him, which is his next objective anyway. However, this is not the kind of interaction he wants. Almost all child predators depend on *persuading a child to trust them.* A child who directly confronts him is a severe complication and highly unusual—it throws his agenda into chaos. Very often it is enough to cause him to desist and choose an easier mark.

The Language Fence

It is a profound and deadly mistake to believe that a child can verbally outmaneuver a seasoned and manipulative adult predator. This is why the possession of a strong *language* fence is *the crucial component* in a child's armament. It is the only defense they have at this point, and if it fails, that failure will lead to either physical combat or physical submission. Since children have neither the verbal skills nor the life experience to engage a predator on his level, they must resort to instinct and something I call panoramic perspective. Have you ever heard the expression, "He missed the forest for the trees?" Predators are adept at disguising what they are doing in plain sight by cloaking both their intentions and their actions with the "ordinary." They skillfully get us to believe what we want to see rather than what is actually happening. Panoramic perspective is the ability to see the big picture; the context—what is really happening as opposed to how we are normally diverted by the subtext. The good news here is that, surprisingly, it is easier for a child to grasp the "how" of this than it is for an adult.

In order to understand how the language fence functions, it is necessary to take a closer look at the predator's game plan. Child safety experts recognize that there are six stages to "grooming."

Six Stages of Grooming

1. Targeting the victim
2. Gaining the victim's trust
3. Filling a need
4. Isolating the child
5. Sexualizing the relationship
6. Maintaining control

Every one of these steps is interactive except the first one—targeting, which is conducted in secrecy. Therefore, specific language in the form of suggestions used by predators can be identified and revealed to children as "red flags" that should trigger awareness that all is not right. These suggestions can be classed into five basic categories corresponding to the interactive stages of grooming listed above.

1. **Division**—*gaining the victim's trust—(instead of, or in addition to, the parent who has earned it)* the process of bonding with the victim in a way that is calculated to supersede the parents' influence. Its operating mechanism is any suggestion or statement that leads a child to replace trust of parents, family or friends with confidence in a "special friend." Example: "I know your parents may not understand what you're going through, but I do and we can

talk about it anytime." These are dangerous suggestions and should be rejected immediately.

2. **Secrecy**—*filling a need*—Predators know that gifts, special attention and interest are all red flags for informed parents and extended family, so they persuade the victim to allow them to fly under the radar with these things, early on in the relationship. Any suggestion that a secret be kept from a child's loved ones should be treated with suspicion. Why would anyone who truly cares about a child want to disguise their feelings? This is what you drive home to your children—it is because they know that what they are doing is wrong, and you will not approve of their inappropriate attentions.

3. **Exclusivity**—*isolating the child*—in this context the only one who has the right to the suggestion "just me and you" is the parent. Any other adult who says this to a child, without the express knowledge and consent of the parent, is usurping his or her place, and that is a threat of supreme malevolence. Any language suggesting or promoting time spent alone together is abnormal and could be dangerous. The real questions here are, Why? What good can come from this?

4. **Challenge**—*sexualizing the relationship*—appealing to children's curiosity, willingness to take a dare, expanding their horizons or challenging their limits in ways that they suspect are wrong or that their parents would not support. This is *always* indicative of predatory intent. Of the children who are targeted, two personality types are especially vulnerable to these tactics:

    - A Type 1 victim is a "passive, apathetic introvert." Type 1 children have a poor self-image, are socially starved and are willing to break rules because they no longer care. These children are what predators consider MRE's: meals, ready to eat because they have so little prep work to do.

    - A Type 2 victim is what I class as a "curious rebel risk taker." Type 2 children are over-confident; they express denial masked as bravado and are willing to break rules on a dare.

Note that the common denominator between these two personality types is that they are willing to break the rules. Ergo, they are easier to persuade. In both cases, a predator who suggests to a child that even though his or her parents may not agree, *he* knows that they are much more mature than they are being given credit for; is going to be listened to. He is giving them something they are incredibly thirsty for—recognition as someone special. Unless these children are brought into a more healthy personality balance and trained to instinctively recognize these language fence breaches, they are likely to be an easy mark should the predator's cross-hairs find them.

5. **Threat**—*maintaining control*—the moment a child crosses the line and commits an act that he or she is ashamed of, a measure of control passes over to the predator. With each submission, the guilt and helplessness increases and along with it, the desire to escape the relationship. Predators are adept manipulators of the emotions, especially guilt and fear, and their language reveals this as the relationship changes between predator and prey. At this stage, children know full well that their special friend is in reality their worst enemy, but since he has convinced them that they are at least partially to blame, fear, shame and guilt paralyze them and it becomes exceedingly difficult to extricate themselves. What they need to recognize, is that the threats a predator makes are a window to his own fear and weakness. Parents and society will almost always side with a child victim: The predator knows this and his objective is to keep the child from revealing his secret. Ironically, it is when the predator is most vulnerable that the child feels the fullness of his power. Children need to know with unshakeable certainty that they will always have a parent's unconditional love, no matter what the predator has done and no matter what they have done. Like the prodigal son, they must realize that a loving parent's worst criticism is far better than the praise of a predator.

So, let's recap. The language fence is a powerful tool for children because it provides verbal triggers that allow them to see the larger picture (panoramic perspective) rapidly. These verbal triggers are divided into five categories: division, secrecy, exclusivity, challenge and threat. When welded to instinct, they produce an emotional response rather than a logical one. This is vital because, *especially in children, emotion controls behavior.* Many times I have had parents tell me that they fear for their child because he or she seems completely unafraid of strangers, even when warned about the dangers of being too friendly. Children as a matter of course equate feelings of fear with danger. In their eyes, if they feel no fear, there is no danger. The key to all this is instinctively acting upon the emotional perception of threat, resulting in their doing, saying or thinking *the next right thing* as dictated by the situation.

The Physical Touch Fence

Physical contact, the last and innermost fence, is the boundary least taught by parents. However, despite our reluctance to introduce this topic to children, it is the fence most easily erected by a child. Time and time again, as I have conducted training sessions for children, I have witnessed them automatically and instinctively lean away from someone who violated their personal space boundary, and this is at the beginning of the training session before anything has been taught. Children have an innate sense of right and wrong when it comes to space and touch limits. Never-the-less, it is important to cover this subject so that what their bodies tell them and what their conscious brain signals to them are in perfect accord.

What our children really need is confidence: boldness to use verbal skills to both articulate their feelings and to forcefully check anyone who violates their person. *They need to feel that they have permission to enforce these limits.* It is essential to role-play these situations under increasingly stressful conditions in order to imprint instinctive verbal and physical responses. When we teach these classes, we use a long-sleeved *empty* glove to simulate a human hand and arm. This helps the instructors realistically portray a predator without violating the child's touch boundaries themselves. It reinforces these sacrosanct body boundaries by saying, in effect, that *even in a training scenario* it is not permissible to touch another's private places.

When children are engaged by an individual with predatory intent we teach them a five step response. Imagine a child seated on a park bench waiting for a friend. A man approaches and instead of seating himself on the other end of the bench as a person normally would, he sits down right next to the child.

Step 1. The child scoots to the other side of the bench. Now the man slides over, reclaiming the space he usurped earlier, and places his hand on her knee while attempting to engage her in conversation.

Step 2. She tells him in a loud and strong voice that she does not want to be touched.

Step 3. She removes his hand from her knee.

Step 4. She immediately gets up and tells the first person she sees; turning and pointing him out, making sure he sees what she is doing.

Step 5. As soon as possible, she tells her mother.

The best preparation actively establishes the following boundaries:

- **Privacy**

"I will not give out personal information because it is none of your business."

- **Proximity**

"Respect my space—its mine, not yours, and I will protect it."

- **Language**

"If you're not comfortable saying it in front of my family, don't bother."

- **Touch**

"My body is off limits; this means you, no exceptions."

These boundaries are necessary to block the four-step approach of a child predator. First, they need information. Second, they will use that information to gain access. Third, they must begin successful interaction in order to have physical contact. This holds true whether they are active or passive predators.

NAVIGATING THE DANGER ZONE

Type 1 Child

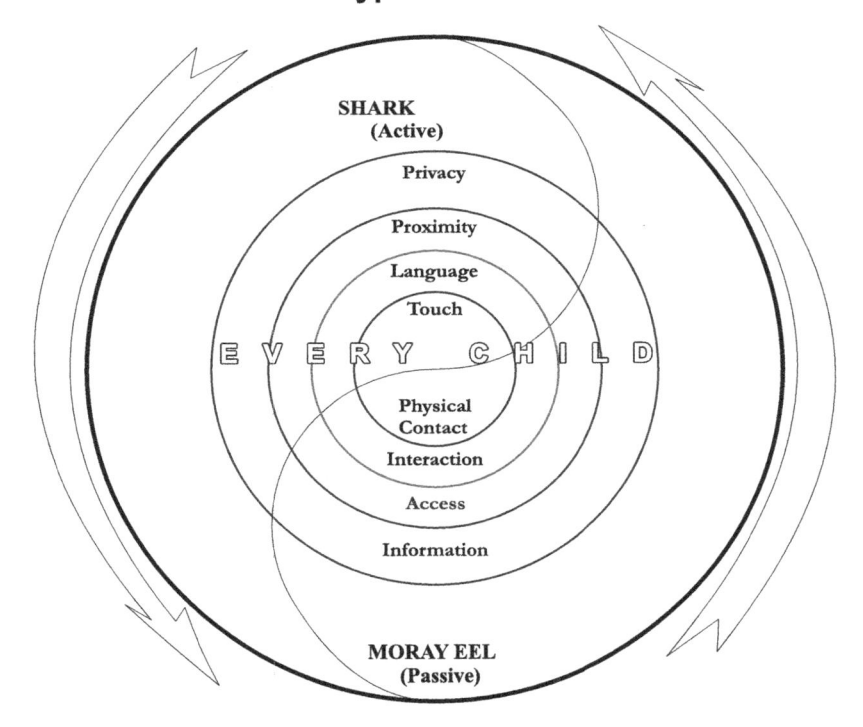

SHARK
(Active)

Privacy
Proximity
Language
Touch

E V E R Y   C H I L D

Physical Contact
Interaction
Access
Information

MORAY EEL
(Passive)

Type 2 Child

Fig. 6

CHILDREN AT RISK

TYPE 1
<u>Passive / Apathetic / Introvert</u>
Have poor self image, are socially starved,
willing to break rules because they no longer care.

TYPE 2
<u>Curious / Rebel / Risk Taker</u>
Over-confident, denial masked as bravado,
willing to break rules on a dare.

Both types can be permanent traits or temporary phases.

CHILDREN AT RISK

NAIVE unaware of the environment, overly confident or overly trusting, overly curious, life experience insufficient to accurately access threat

CARELESS driven by apathy or rebellion, will yield to pressure for information, willing to break rules to be accepted

DISCOURAGED shy, fearful, friendless, alone, introverted, sad, passive, poor self-image

SKEWED physical appearance panders to attention getting, poor posture, lack of concern regarding personal hygiene, grooming etc., physically passive

SAFE CHILDREN

AWARE of danger, alert and intelligent, make good choices

GUARDED in their manner, socially inter-active, have numerous healthy friendships

POSITIVE & confident, balanced and strong self-image, able to verbally resist an adult

BALANCED with good posture and hygiene, physically active, have will to retaliate physically based on self-worth

Lesson Four: Identifying Predators

This can be a difficult lesson to instill because predators are identified by their behavior, which they hide until it is advantageous for them to reveal it. By then it is usually too late: They have already succeeded in turning their mark into their victim. However, they have certain characteristics and behavioral patterns, which can be spotted, if a child knows two things: How normal adults (and people in general) treat children and how accurate their own internal radar is.

It is equally important for them to see a clear difference between healthy adult-child relationships and the type of relationships children have with each other. Often predators attempt to conceal the relationship they are trying to have with a child by giving them the same kind of attention that their friends do. This makes them seem "cool" because they appear to be able to relate to the child in a different, more appealing way than most adults do. But viewed in its proper context, this attempt to cross the age barrier is a warning. It is not normal and a well-trained child's feelings will alert him or her to this. An adult who wants to have a "kid" relationship with a child, who is willing to alter his normal behavior to do so *and* who also wants to have alone time with the child could easily be a predator.

* * *

What follows is a simplified and condensed version of what we teach our young students in the Active Safety for Kids program regarding predators:

Active Safety for Kids High Points

Sometimes predators are strangers who try to persuade you quickly, but *usually* they are nice people whom you know.

Question: How do you tell a predator from a normal person?
Answer: You can't tell by what they look like. You can't tell by whether or not you know them.

It is what people *say* and *do* that tells us what kind of person they are.

Predators are very good at:
- Being your best friend
- Being kind
- Being understanding
- Being "cool"

Here is how you tell:

1) They try to persuade you (win you over; get you to change your mind, opinion, habit, etc.).
2) They get you to keep secrets from your family and friends.
3) They try to separate you from your family and friends.
4) They try to spend time alone with you.
5) They lead you to do something questionable (not sure whether it is right or wrong).

This might not happen all at once. They may take a long time to do their thing. Watch them. It's OK to resist an adult who you think is doing something wrong.

Good news:

You will get warnings!
The feelings in your body will help you sense the presence of danger.

Question: What feelings are we talking about?
Answer: Here are some of them:

- Uneasiness
- Weirdness
- Something is not quite right
- My stomach feels funny
- I'm afraid
- He's so nice, but for some reason, I feel strange

Predators count on your not recognizing these warnings, or ignoring them when you do have them.

This is very important!

Predators will try to confuse the friendship they are attempting to have with you by giving you the same kind of attention that your friends do. This makes them seem "cool" because they pay more attention to you than most adults, including your parents. But this is *really a warning.* It is not normal, and your feelings will tell you so. An adult that wants to have a kid friendship with a kid *and* wants alone time with the kid — "just the two of us"— could very easily be a predator.

KID FRIENDSHIP WITH ADULT

+

LOTS OF ALONE TIME

=

UNHEALTHY IMBALANCE

It doesn't always happen this way, but whenever it does, it happens *right here*. Normal, safe adults want you to play with other kids.

Chapter 19

What Powerful Children Do

"The energy which makes a child hard to manage is the energy which afterward makes him a manager in life."

–Henry Ward Beecher

The focus of the second half of the A.S.K. program is conditioning children to initiate powerful, correct and timely action after having acknowledged internal warnings of danger. Lessons five through eight provide children with behavioral templates that will help them to: Take an active part in their own rescue if they become lost, succeed in verbal self defense, thwart an auto-abduction and go to another's aid when aid is needed.

Lesson Five: The Lost Child

In the human arena, threats to our children come from five general sources:

Five Sources of Threat

1. Familiars
2. Strangers
3. Situations
4. Peers
5. Themselves

Up to this point our focus has been on children's interaction with strangers and familiars. In subsequent chapters, we will address their relationship with peers and themselves. This lesson is designed to help children become more self-reliant when they find themselves in the frightening situation of being alone and vulnerable. We will use two scenarios as examples: first, a child lost in a busy city (what we could call "separation serious") and second, a child lost in a wilderness area (a.k.a. "separation acute").

Six year old Bobby Thompson is with his parents and older brother on a family outing in Pike Place Market, Seattle, Washington. It is Saturday, just before the noon hour, and the market is packed. The family decides to have lunch in a small bistro and is soon seated at a table. As they are perusing the menu, Bobby's brother Mike, who is twelve, tells his parents that he has to go to the bathroom. The nearest available public restroom is around the corner and down a ramp, one level below the bistro. Mr. Thompson tells Mike to take Bobby with him because Bobby is making tell-tale squirming motions in his seat. Bobby is not to leave Mike's side.

When they arrive at the restroom, the boys find it so crowded that there is a line extending into the aisle. To make matters worse, Bobby suddenly says he doesn't have to go and besides, the place stinks. It looks slimy. No way is he going in there! Mike, who does have to go—badly—tells him not to be a moron and to stop wasting time being a crybaby, but Bobby puts up such a fuss that Mike, embarrassed, relents and tells his brother to wait for him on a bench just across the aisle. Bobby, seething with resentment at being bossed around by Mike, decides to show his brother that he *won't* be ordered around. He looks around for something interesting to do—and before he realizes what has happened, he is at least two levels lower and has made a number of confusing turns. Everything looks strange. Bobby has never been to Pike Place Market before. He does not know that some parts of this market are several levels deep. He is hopelessly lost, in an underground maze, crowded with strangers he has been told never to talk to.

As Bobby's level of fear and desperation increase, so does his vulnerability. Before he realizes he is lost—while busy exploring—the energy signature he puts out is normal and does not attract undue attention. From the standpoint of a predator, Mom or Dad could be right around the corner and probably within earshot of a shout.

However, the moment his fear becomes tangible, he becomes a much more attractive target. Here's why:

First, the fact that he is exhibiting fear tells a predator that Bobby believes his parents are nowhere around. Second, he is hesitating to ask for help because he is afraid to. Bobby has been told all his life that he should never talk to strangers and in his mind strangers are BAD, SCARY PEOPLE who want to hurt him. All that is necessary for a predator's success here is to be friendly. A friend is exactly what Bobby would most like to have right now, and it is easy to persuade him *because he wants to be persuaded.* This nice man is going to take him to a policeman and soon he'll be safe with Mom and Dad. Bobby dries his eyes and takes the hand of his new friend as they step around the corner. Bobby's family never sees him again.

Nikki Bolton and Jordan Sear planned the camping trip for weeks. Best friends since kindergarten, they are both sixteen and eager to exercise their freedom muscles. Both Nikki's parents and Jordan's mom are unaware of the trip the girls are taking; had they known, they would have forbidden it. Jordan's mom thinks she is spending the weekend with Nikki and her family. Nikki's parents believe she is spending time with Jordan and her mother. The girls are sure the ruse will succeed because Nikki's parents will be away for the weekend celebrating their 20th wedding anniversary.

Of the two, Nikki is the outdoors person and the trip was her idea. Jordan is involved only because Nikki is her friend, and she is mildly curious about "roughing it." Now they are having a serious disagreement. At the last moment, Jordan is backing out of the trip. She has blabbed to her boyfriend, and he has pressured her not to go so that he can spend an uninterrupted weekend alone with her. Nikki is sick with disappointment and not just a little angry. Her stubborn streak becomes fully engaged, and she decides to go by herself. The hell with selfish Jordan!

Now, a day into the trip, Nikki is in trouble. The girl's chosen campsite was closed when Nikki arrived and she was forced to drive farther north. Several valleys and many miles of mountainous terrain now separate her from where Jordan and her boyfriend, the only ones in the world who know about this trip, believe she is. Without realizing it, Nikki has taken a wrong turn on an already unfamiliar trail. She can't find the campsite she was heading for on her map. Worse, *nothing* on the map bears any resemblance to her surroundings. She has left the trail because it is getting dark and she is desperate to find a place suitable for the night, before she is overtaken by darkness. Now she has no idea where the trail is, and she does not know how to find her way back. She has enough food to last for two more days, three if she stretches it. She has moderately warm clothes; she can make a fire, and she has a tent. However, the weather has changed; she is cold and beginning to feel the edge of panic. She knows she is in serious trouble, and she does not know what to do about it.

Although these situations appear entirely different, they share three common denominators relative to a child's safety:

Children Break Rules

They ignore instructions, and they have a burning, unquenchable desire to expand their comfort zone at the expense of their parents. It is called growing. We know this. We know that our children will break our rules, yet how many parents take the additional and necessary steps to prepare their children for difficulty, for the consequences of their own actions? In this situation, most, if not all parents, play the odds with their children's safety, betting that they will be obedient, praying that nothing major will happen when their instructions are ignored. We combine denial and hope into a potent cocktail, sip it steadily and are snockered. When reality asserts itself, when tragedy strikes, we are as unprepared for it as our lack of follow-through has left our children.

In both of these scenarios, the parents' protection failed their children because it was incomplete. Their understanding of the situation and its relevant hazards did not translate into action that would adequately prepare these children for the consequences of breaking the rules. Here is the reality check: We are completely responsible as parents because *we know they will break the rules.*

Ignorance of Environment

Not knowing what to do when things go wrong, when there is a crisis or emergency, leads to hesitation, confusion, denial of reality, indecision and finally, panic. The definition of panic is fear out of control. Panic robs human beings young and old of the exercise of good judgment—exactly the ingredient that is needed to survive. Without good judgment, no one can make wise choices. It is crucial that children have a game plan in these situations, precisely because it eliminates or greatly reduces the downward spiral into panic.

It is important that we as parents understand that *the situation is not the enemy.* Almost every child at some point or another is going to experience being lost. It is a natural component of growing up. In reality, this situation is a proving ground that tells us whether, first, our training plan for our children is effective and second, how well they have absorbed the preparation process. The real enemies here are hesitation, confusion, indecision, denial and panic.

Dependence on rescue

Because children often lack specific knowledge of the hazardous environments they occasionally find themselves in and have no game plan for dealing with the inherent dangers, they are left with *no other option* but rescue. Waiting for help that either does not come or comes too late is, in my mind, one of the most disempowering and deadly traps children can fall into. It forces them by default into a mindset that is the exact opposite of self-reliance. If panic can be replaced with confidence, the greatest hazard in these situations is greatly reduced. I simply cannot say this plainly enough: *Confidence comes from knowledge of a skill-set learned by experience.* It is important that children feel they can choose between the options of waiting to be rescued or taking initiative themselves. It would be extremely foolish to consider that one option is in general more viable than the other. Circumstances alter cases. The situation itself always provides the context for that choice.

We have looked at the three common denominators in our lost child scenarios. Now, let's explore the specific things we should be training our children to do, should they ever find themselves in like circumstances.

Lost in the city

Had Bobby been properly trained, it is very likely the story would have ended differently. The moment he realizes he is lost and needs help, Bobby would remember his game plan and put it into action. He would begin a specific search for someone to help him. He would understand that the vast majority of people have good intentions or at least are harmless. Bobby would know that his best choice would be a woman with children. Statistically, she would be the least likely to be someone with predatory tendencies. Also, because he is the one doing the choosing, he further tips the odds in his favor. If a strange adult approaches a child under these conditions, there is a fair chance that the person has unsavory intentions. However, if Bobby chooses with training and intent, the chance that he chooses the one person who might mean him harm, out of hundreds or thousands of decent people, is infinitesimally small. Bobby has been taught to be a chooser, not a loser.

Let's look at the remaining choices on Bobby's list from a statistical perspective. The second choice would be a woman alone. Third would be an elderly couple together. Number four would be a man and a woman together, hopefully with children. If none of these choices is available, he should look for a man walking in the opposite direction, who is busy doing something else, like talking on a cell phone. Bobby should walk right up to him and interrupt his conversation with a request for help. If he is grouchy and abrupt, he is more likely to be a good choice. I'm sure you can see why. Bobby could also enter any store or business and ask the manager to call 911.

I have heard many parents tell their children that if they are lost, to go find a policeman. This is impractical. Additionally, it is easy for a child to mistake a security guard for a policeman, and that would not be a wise choice. Many individuals with predatory intentions seek employment in that field, because it is easy to get into and gives them a level of public trust and authority that could be misinterpreted by a child. This is a good example of how poor advice combined with a child's lack of confidence can result in a tragic outcome—which in many cases is entirely preventable.

Children have been taught the dangerous and misleading half truth, "Never talk to strangers," instead of the rule that is truly helpful: *"Never talk to a strange person who tries to talk to you first."* Teaching children to take action based on trustworthy information is the game plan that best serves their safety.

Lost in the Wilderness

Nikki's plight is much more complex than Bobby's, even without the complication of a human predator. As a result, her game plan needs to be a little more involved. This is a subject that could be a book all by itself. My purpose here is to open a window for you to look through; one that will give you some idea of what constitutes a basic game plan for a child in this situation. Let's dispense with blame and recriminations for Nikki's venturing out without notice or permission. Remember, we have accepted that our children are occasionally going to break our rules. We will assume that Nikki has been thoroughly and properly trained for this hazard, but has had an initial lapse in judgment. Where does she go from here?

Like Bobby, Nikki's immediate and deadly enemy is panic. She knows this and so her first action is to sit down right where she is and accept the fact that she is lost, and that this is OK. This is her way of giving herself permission to think, calmly and carefully, about her game plan. When she has control of her emotional body, she must ask herself THE QUESTION that all Safety First students are taught to ask themselves in this situation: *"Does someone know where I am going and when I expect to return?"* Everything that follows depends on the answer. If it is "Yes," then Nikki's best choice is to focus on keeping warm and dry. Once this is accomplished, she should stay right there and wait until help arrives. She should only move about when necessary, to conserve her energy. This is crucial, because her ability to reproduce energy is directly linked to her food supply, which in this case is limited. This is an excellent game plan and is the right choice in approximately ninety percent of these lost–child scenarios.

Unfortunately, Nikki's answer to THE QUESTION is "No." It will be at least two days before anyone realizes that Nikki may be missing. Since Nikki's parents will be gone for another four days, and Jordan knows Nikki is angry with her, it is quite possible that nearly a week could go by before all the players put their pieces together and realize that Nikki is missing. Even then, they will start looking in the wrong place and they will be miles off in their search. By this time, Nikki's food will be long gone. Given these facts, it is clear that she must play a part in her own rescue.

Nikki knows the rule of 3's: *You can die of exposure in three hours, thirst in three days and hunger in three weeks.* Nikki is lucky because she has portable shelter and some warm clothing. Unless there is an ice storm, exposure is not an immediate threat. Therefore, the search for water will define her game plan. Nikki is also fortunate in that she has a map. Even though she cannot use it to define her immediate position, she knows from studying it that all of the rivers and streams in this part of the mountains flow east and eventually lead to the highway she drove on to arrive at the trail head. Between the highway and her position, wherever that is, are dozens of gravel logging roads.

Nikki starts a fire and makes herself a cup of soup. While the water is heating, she quickly sets up her tent. The best she can do right now is to rest up and not worry: a good night's sleep is necessary for what she has decided to do. She feels better after having made a decision. She hopes it's the right one…

The morning dawns, and the weather is crisp and clear. Nikki stirs the embers of the fire she carefully banked the night before and prepares a quick breakfast. She decides to leave everything she can spare, to reduce weight in her pack and also to mark her camp. She tears a page from her journal and writes a brief note explaining her situation and what she intends to do about it. If searchers find her camp, they will have a better idea of how to search effectively for her if they know what her objectives are. She reads it carefully one more time, especially the step–by–step game plan:

1. Walk down-hill to find water.
2. Walk down-stream until I find a bridge, a road or a trail.
3. Walk down-hill on the road or trail until I come to a "Y."
4. Check the "Y" to differentiate between the "branches" and the "trunk."
5. Walk down the "trunk" and away from the "branches."
6. Eventually I will hit the highway.
7. As soon as I flag down a car, I will ask the occupants to call 911.
8. I will wait there until the authorities pick me up.

Satisfied, Nikki puts the note inside a used sandwich bag and wedges it into the bark of a fir tree, at eye level. She hopes whoever finds it will know what she means by "trunk" and "branches." She remembers how cool she thought it was when her instructor told her class that trails, roads and rivers in the mountains have one thing in common: They fork or "Y" out as they go deeper into the mountains, which means you can tell which direction to take.

Without a trail to follow for the first part, it takes Nikki two days to make it to the highway. She is dirty, tired and hungry, but uninjured and in good health. Search and Rescue is just beginning to look for her. By taking the initiative, by acting on good information and believing in herself and by using fear as fuel instead of allowing it to paralyze her, Nikki has not only saved herself, she has minimized the potential risk to her rescuers.

Lesson Six: Voice Power

A pioneering study at UCLA indicated that up to ninety-three percent of communication effectiveness is determined by non-verbal cues (Mehrabian, 1971). Another study determined that non-verbal messages are seen as more reliable than verbal messages (Zuckerman, DePaulo, and Rosenthal, 1981).

If the ninety-three percent figure is accurate, then the seven percent that *is* verbal assumes importance out of all proportion to its numerical value in the threat environment. In my opinion—after a lifetime of study and thirteen years of direct empirical research—a child's ability to find his or her voice is so important that it is second only to intuition. This is because bold, passionate verbal expression is welded to robust self-concept in all healthy, confident and assertive children.

Voice power deals with what you say, how you say it, when you say it and why you say it. These parameters apply whether you are a child or an adult, but they are much more critical for children because of their vulnerability. Adults have had a long period of time to know themselves and the world they inhabit, and to establish their personal identity. Children have a knowledge deficit, lack understanding and experience and, therefore, have lower levels of true confidence. What they lack in all these areas must be made up for in their ability to project passion or spirit. The more unmanageable a child seems, the more difficult a target he or she will be for a predator. Let's face it, without the conditioning that is the subject of this book, most children don't have the physical size, depth of knowledge or real experiences to match an adult predator, but they can be loud, unruly and most of all—unpredictable. Timid, passive children are an easy mark. Aside from body language, the ability to project this "too much trouble" factor is the exclusive territory of the voice. The good news is that it can be both easy and fun to help children find their true voice. Let's briefly examine the four basic components of voice power:

Voice Power Components

1. Content (What You Say)

Remember that predators operate differently when the intended victim is a child rather than an adult. In these scenarios, successful persuasion is the predator's objective. Understanding this is the key to teaching a child effective, verbal resistance. He or she must become difficult to persuade. The instant children detect an attempt to persuade that makes them feel uncomfortable; they must deny the suggestion completely and *specifically*. For example:

>**Predator:** "Hey Kid! I have free video games to give away. C'mon over here and have a look!"
>
>**Child:** "No! I don't want *your* video games!"
>
>**Predator:** "Why, what's the problem?"
>
>**Child:** "It doesn't matter! Go away and leave me alone!"

Notice that the child denied this suggestion specifically and personally. Here's the breakdown: "No" is the general denial. "I don't want video games" is the specific denial and "I don't want *your* video games" is the personal denial. The predator then makes a second attempt, this time to negotiate the denial. Once again the child denies him utterly by refusing to give an explanation, and this refusal is not because she is intimidated, but because she is direct and street–wise. Clarity leads to power: *"Go away and leave me alone!"* This response is so pointed it leaves no room for negotiation. This child has cut the predator's verbal legs off at the knees. Right away he sees that she is extremely resistant to his advances—he's been ju-jitsued, and he knows it. Clear, precise words underscore awareness, determination, intelligence and the refusal to be manipulated or dominated. They spell disaster for the predator's game plan. The more pointed the response, the more powerful the child.

2. Mechanics (How You Say It)

Even when a child uses the right words and is very specific, the delivery of the message must not be mishandled, or it will be his or her undoing. Predators are always measuring responses to see if they are genuine or if the intended victim is "fronting." To remove all doubt and deliver a clear, convincing message, body language must be in sync with verbiage. We must teach our children to have integrity in this and every other context, *to mean what they say*. The earmarks of a forceful message in this context are eye contact and voice volume. The power of a statement is multiplied many times over when the person making it is looking you right in the eye. Kids who communicate with lowered voices and hanging heads are sending a message, but it is not the one that enhances their safety.

Voice volume should be taught in three stages as dictated by the escalation of the situation: at first, **firm** and if that does not cause the persuader to cease and desist, then, as Gavin DeBecker says, "skip several levels of politeness"[13] and be **rude**. Finally, and as a last verbal resort, go **ballistic**. Our children have been taught all their lives that politeness is the desired behavior in nearly every situation, but *it is the deadly enemy of their survival in these scenarios*. Children need to know that their fear, anger and even rage are justified and perfectly natural in this arena. It's not wrong, and they are not going to get into trouble—they are already *in* trouble, and *this* is the way out of it.

When the stakes are high, specific language, eye contact and intensity (volume) must be like the three amigos: always together. When teaching this concept to children, the focus should always be on being honest. This is necessary because, *in the moment of peril*, thinking about the right things to do in order of priority takes too much time and is distracting. Their responses need to be natural for two reasons. First, the predator will have no choice except to interpret the message they are sending as authentic. Second, to be honest is to accept the reality of the situation, and to respond *emotionally* to it. If they do this, the right message will automatically be sent, *if it has been trained in an adrenal format*. This eliminates unnecessary confusion and the resulting hesitation, which the predator will interpret as vulnerability or weakness if he detects it. So far, the winning formula is:

SPECIFIC LANGUAGE

+

EYE CONTACT

+

VOICE VOLUME

=

VOICE POWER

3. Timing (When You Say It)

The third component of voice power, timing, is probably the most crucial and difficult concept to grasp and to apply under pressure, particularly for a child. Yet, this is only true if we are considering traditional training methods, which rely on a conscious–brain learning format. Using Survival Response Conditioning methodology, what is normally a dangerous deal-breaker *is easy because it is automatic!* When training children to use voice power, it is not necessary to try to outmaneuver a predator over the timing issue—as long as adrenal format is the training method. The emotional triggers that signal danger and threat are designed to prompt action instinctively, and only our denial and self–image issues prevent us from engaging in an *immediate response*. Remove these barriers and the timing issue goes away. We—and our children—will say what we need to say, in the way we need to say it, at the very moment it is most needed.

The good news here is that children grasp this quicker and with far less resistance than adults do because our inhibitions have had more time to strengthen their hold over us. Children have a fresh, clean slate and are much more easily conditioned by a competent trainer. As parents, we are prone to adopting the mistaken belief that, because a thing is difficult for us, it is nearly impossible for our children. In fact, the exact reverse is true. Children learn and adapt with incredible speed. We have forgotten what that is like because we have lived in our own adult world for so long.

4. Rationale (Why You Say It)

The primary reason for engaging voice power is to put an aggressor in verbal check. Additionally, voice power is a time–tested method of super charging your entire defensive array, allowing you to explode with both physical and emotional energy. There is a reason why athletes grunt, yell and shout. The voice becomes the focal point not only for releasing explosive and uncontrolled bursts of energy, but for controlled bursts, as well.

When I and my staff are running programs, we have been able to demonstrate that physical energy output is directly proportional to voice volume. That may not be so surprising to a thinking person, but what is remarkable is that this is *not* voluntary: the louder the shout, the greater the power of the blow. In other words, it is not possible to strike with all your power when you are yelling at less than full volume. The voice becomes like a volume control dial on a radio. This is especially valuable to a child, because of its simplicity. To train them to strike with *all* their power, teach them to yell their lungs out. Kids love to make noise, it is *natural* to them. When true fear (as opposed to anxiety) is the motivating force driving voice power, the results can be the same as what happens when, under adrenal forces, a human being performs a superhuman act, such as lifting a car off a loved one.

The bottom line is: *voice power is real.* Children are capable of releasing devastating blows, just like adults, provided they are emotionally motivated and know how to channel voice power. Giving children access to voice power is easy. It helps them to be balanced and emotionally healthy, it improves their self-image and gives them a profound edge in a predatory environment.

Lesson Seven: Automobiles and Amber Alerts

Nowhere is the practice of preparation more neglected and yet more needed than in this scenario. In late 1993, the Criminal Division of the Washington State Attorney General's Office undertook a 3-1/2 year research project, partially funded by the U.S. Department of Justice, Office of Juvenile Justice and Delinquency Prevention, to study the investigation of child abduction murder cases. The research was published in 1977 and in 2006 the Attorney General's

Office released a follow-up study[14], including 175 additional solved cases. The additional cases generally reflect and support the findings in the original report, including the following key findings:

- In 74 percent of the missing children homicide cases studied, the child murder victim was female and the average age was 11 years old.

- In 76 percent of the missing children homicide cases studied, the child was dead within three hours of the abduction—and in 88.5 percent of the cases the child was dead within 24 hours.

Society teaches us that our children are helpless against an adult predator. Very few children escape once an abductor gets them into a car. Taken as a whole, this information has led us to the entrenched assumption that survival for a child in this situation is virtually hopeless. We don't tell our children this, but deep down inside, we believe it. When we hear of an Amber Alert, we get a sick feeling, not just because of the abduction but because of how the story so often ends.

As a result of our *acceptance of hopelessness*, we limit children's exposure to this aspect of the predatory environment by simply telling them never to get into a car with someone without our knowledge and consent. Children are not shown how to prevent an abductor from physically forcing them into a car or what to do afterward if their effort to resist fails. The silence of the child-safety and self-defense world on this subject is deafening, given the attention that the media and parents place on child auto-abductions. This is a crystal–clear example of the powerful, negative effect of entrenched assumptions that we explored together in the beginning of this book.

In spite of the media's hyperbole, auto-abduction is statistically rare. However, we are dealing with our children's perceptions and to instill confidence in them, we need to give them a working game plan, just like we did with the lost–child scenarios. If our children's anxiousness were the only reason for dealing with this issue, it would be enough. And to be truthful, what do statistics matter if it happens to *your* child?

If you took my advice and graduated from a Survival Response Conditioning program, you know how limited your thinking was regarding your true abilities prior to the training—and you discovered within yourself an unlimited reservoir of courage and determination to survive. The Survival Response instructors and staff did not provide you with it. All they did was facilitate your passage through an experience that revealed what was there all along. Where did this latent power come from? Did you gain it at some point in your life as an adult? No, you were born with it, you had it as a child, *and so do your children.*

In presenting this lesson, I will not attempt to go into minute details; an over-view is enough at this point. This is one situation where the parent truly needs the services of a real expert whose specialty is this scenario. In addition, the solutions to these life-threatening situations are violent, graphic and require parents to carefully consider that they are training their child to engage another human being in a life—or—death struggle in extremely close quarters.

If that happens, there will be trauma. In the real world, your child will not emerge unscathed, either physically or emotionally, and will most likely require a long healing period. This is a crossroad. Your commitment to your child's present and future safety will be severely tested by the methodology used to secure it. Here is where it is easy to buy into the denial of reality, and hope that your child will beat the odds. Yet I am compelled to ask, "How does this serve both your family's safety and your own peace of mind?" Would you rather spend time helping them heal, or visit them one last time in the morgue? Personally, I am convinced that the reward is worth the risk. I put my own daughter through an adult program when she was twelve years old, and it was one of the best things we have ever done together—we both benefited from it. I want my children to *live*, as free from fear as awareness of their environment will allow, and if the price of survival is some scar tissue, I will be there to help them heal. Together we can face anything.

Okay, I have given you the warning—now let's talk benefits. While learning this lesson is tough, you and your child will have a new, better perspective on safety. You will have more peace of mind, and so will your child if you both know that he or she has a game plan that has a reasonable chance of success in a scenario that is often deadly. Your child will possess confidence based on experience, the same winning combination you experienced as a Survival Response grad. It is the greatest gift; a legacy of courage handed down from parent to child for a thousand generations—before we lost our way and allowed our culture to strip us of our birthright. You will have ensured that they never, ever give up and passively accept becoming a victim. You will have a shared experience that unites you in a way that others may not understand but that you both will come to love.

Now for my final observation: The motivation for having your child learn this lesson using these methods cannot be fear. Only the deep commitment that comes from self-sacrificing love qualifies as a genuine and effective motivator.

*   *   *

Not long ago, I was driving home from some evening classes when I noticed a middle aged man drawing abreast of me in his vehicle. It was a warm, sunny evening and both of us had the windows down. As I watched, his left hand drifted idly to the back of his head. It was a slow and relaxed motion which, on contact, became a sudden, violent slapping and flailing with both hands. I was forced to brake rapidly to avoid his vehicle, which was swerving all over the road. He managed to regain control of the car, pulled over and instantly jumped out, still slapping and yelling in a panic. As I pulled away, I could still see him in the rear-view mirror, bent over and apparently searching for something in his vehicle.

Can you guess what happened? I can. The same thing had happened to me just a few days before with similar results. Encouraged by the warm weather, a large wasp had made its way from where it had been hibernating and crawled into my hair, where my subconscious mind triggered an internal alarm that something unusual was afoot. Unaware of the source of the irritation, I reached back to scratch the tickle and my hand came in contact with a small, vibrating shape which my very conscious and fearful mind identified as a threat, capable of producing a painful sting.

I suddenly found myself trapped in a steel cage, traveling at forty miles per hour, which I nearly lost control of and couldn't possibly exit from quickly enough. After managing to stop and conducting a harried search, I discovered to my dismay that I couldn't find the dratted thing. Embarrassed *and still fearful*, I was forced to re–enter the vehicle, wondering if the wasp was buzzing angrily somewhere under the seat, thirsting for revenge. Luckily for me, there were no police officers along my route home because it was a very rapid commute from that moment on, let me tell you. I never saw the wasp again.

This tiny insect, which didn't have the ability to do more than sting me and which I outweighed hundreds of times over, was able to change the situation completely and it wasn't even trying to attack me. What if it had been a small dog that had somehow been driven by fear to attack? What if it had been a child?

Let's revisit the auto–abduction scenario and examine it anew, from the standpoint that a seven or eight year old child has more intelligence, better tools and a far more comprehensive understanding of the human dynamic than a wasp or a small dog is capable of. My first observation: The predator is likely to have the same concept of helpless children as the rest of us do. He is used to being in control and would never question his own ability to enforce his will on a child. Like most of humanity, the predator defines his reality by his previous successes, and this makes him more vulnerable than it might, at first, appear. He doesn't expect to be surprised—a sudden and determined attempt to disable him and bring his vehicle to a stop, is the last thing on his mind after his initial success—and he will be unprepared to deal with it when it occurs.

Secondly, I invite you to consider that a moving vehicle is actually a restrictive cage that will only allow the driver to defend himself with his right arm, while he must maintain control of the vehicle in a manner that does not draw attention to the situation. This is one of the few places where an unrestrained child has a physical advantage over an adult. If a child is trained to engage him when he is most vulnerable—while executing a left–hand turn, the odds are very much against the driver. Any parent who has ever driven a car while two children are engaged in a severe cat-fight knows just how dangerous and distracting it can be—and their bad behavior is directed at each other, rather than mom or dad. It is almost always necessary to pull the car to the side of the road to regain control of the situation. If that happens, the primary objective of the child's attack, stopping the car, has been achieved.

For those concerned with the risk of an automobile accident resulting from the use of such tactics, I would say, "I share your concern." We all have to make choices pertaining to the amount of risk our personal comfort zone will allow. I have concluded—and there are many, many parents who would side with me—that in this awful situation I would want my child to fight back. It would be better for her to take a risk, without a certain outcome, where there is a fair chance of survival, than allow the driver to reach his destination, where her fate is virtually sealed. When it comes to child auto-abductions, we need to address four physical challenges:

Auto Abduction Scenarios

First: Training children to prevent an abductor from getting them into a car

Second: What to do if the predator gets them into the back seat

Third: A game plan for the front seat

Fourth: The game plan for the trunk

First Challenge: Do Not Enter!

If a child verbally resists a predator who is trying to persuade him or her to get into a car, the predator is left with a choice. He must either give up and move on to a more passive victim or escalate the situation by attempting to force the child into his vehicle. A child who is grabbed by an adult needs an edge to counter the adult's superior strength and speed. In this scenario, the only physical common denominator is the presence of a vehicle. As the struggle against containment by the predator ensues, a well-trained child can use the vehicle itself to escape the predator. For example:

Kristen has been grabbed from behind and taken off her feet. The predator begins running with her toward his car. The driver's side rear door has been left open by the predator in anticipation of a quick getaway. As Kristen comes within range of the car, she suddenly kicks out against the door frame with all her might. The predator, already overbalanced by supporting her weight, and unprepared for an abrupt reversal in direction, loses his balance and is thrown violently backward. Kristen reverse-head butts him in the face, bicycle-kicks him in the groin and rolls to her feet. She is out of his view in five seconds.

Another possibility is that she is able to kick the door closed, making it necessary for the predator to shift her weight to his dominant arm in order to re-open the door. He is now vulnerable to the Survival Response tactics Kristen learned in the back fight scenario. All this resistance is interrupting and interfering with the smooth execution of his plan. The problem for the predator here is, in order to execute a successful abduction, he must cram his victim through a relatively small hole, while she is fighting him tooth and nail. Even if he manages to get her inside, he must then turn his back on her and climb into the driver's seat. This limits his ability to protect himself from an enraged and desperate adversary who has been trained under very high levels of stress for this very situation. This is a radically different picture from what a parent might imagine when he or she thinks of abduction and I guarantee the predator is unprepared for it as well. His tactics are designed around the idea that his victim will capitulate out of fear, shock and intimidation.

Second Challenge: Containment in the Back Seat

Whenever a predator uses force to get a child into a car, speed and convenience make the driver's side rear seat his first choice. All he has to do is pause briefly while he tosses his victim into the back and then hops into the front. This way he can be driving off in less than five seconds. His only objective at this point is to get his victim contained and get moving. We must assume that he has succeeded in doing this before and anticipates no real problems after this goal is accomplished. He has her. He has won.

Let's go back to Kristen. We will assume that in spite of her fierce fight, he has succeeded in locking her in the back seat. The instant the door closes she should scoot to the other side and try to get out. She may succeed if he has neglected to remove the handles or if the car does not have child-proof locks controlled from the front seat. She will be able to get there first because he will have to run all the way around the car to block her escape. For the sake of argument, we will assume that she is trapped. Now she must appear docile, and he will expect that because it is the natural or default position of those who realize they are trapped.

Kristen is well-trained and has a game plan. She is terribly afraid, but because of her training, she has been emotionally conditioned for this situation and fear is now her fuel. She is enraged that this man is going to keep her from getting home to her family. She is wearing a strong belt, as she has been taught. Moving directly behind him so that he cannot watch her all the time, she carefully removes it and passes the end through the metal buckle. She now has a noose. He is trying to talk to her; to calm her, and she answers him in subdued monotones—waiting for the moment to strike. She thinks of all the times she practiced this and how, when she passed all the tests, she was given a special tee-shirt with a wolverine on it. She knows she must become a wolverine now.

He arrives at a busy intersection and moves into the left-hand turn lane. He is watching her through the rear view mirror when the light changes. He looks left—then right—then left again and begins to turn... NOW! Kristen lunges forward and loops the belt over his head and around his neck: It settles over the head rest, and she pulls and pulls and pulls. Voice power makes her unstoppable. Her feet are braced against his seat back. He is struggling, making gurgling noises and bucking up and down and then there is a tremendous crash. Things have stopped moving, and it is silent, except for a hissing sound, and a funny, croaking noise—and the smell of gasoline. There are people all around... Her hands are bleeding but she can't seem to let go of the belt, and then other hands, kind hands are reaching through the broken glass— someone has her and it is not HIM and she is safe...

Even though this is a brutal and graphic depiction, I would rather have this ending than a policeman's knock on the door and a trip to the morgue—wouldn't you?

For those of you who still doubt that it is possible for a child to engage and thwart an adult during an auto-abduction, I include the following true story about a five-year-old boy who pulled it off with no training at all.

Sacramento Car Thief Gets More Than He Bargained For

Randy Barnes, 24, thought he could make a quick score when he saw Mimi Alexander leave her car running in front of the donut shop. Jumping into the driver's seat, he took off down Del Paso Boulevard, taking Mimi's five year old son and 6 month old infant with him. The boy lost no time in attacking the strange man, punching and choking him with such ferocity that the man was unable to steer the car.

According to Sgt. Daniel Hahn of the Sacramento Police Department, Barnes "...ran into a parked car then took off again, drove recklessly and even jumped out of the car while it was still moving... The car eventually came to a stop running into a telephone pole." Barnes was charged with kidnapping, auto theft and parole violation. The children were unharmed.[15]

Third Challenge: Containment in the Front Seat

When an abductor puts a child into the front seat, it is usually because he or she has not put up much of a struggle or the abductor has completely subdued his target en route to the vehicle. Either way, the abductor has *enough confidence* to take time to walk around the front or back of the vehicle in order to access the driver's seat. This is significant, because his success or failure is measured in seconds. Therefore, it is reasonable to assume that he is not expecting determined resistance. If, under some pretext, the victim has been fooled into entering a vehicle, perhaps lured by a family friend, a moment will come when she feels that things are going terribly wrong. Under these circumstances, a child who has been well trained will not allow the abductor to know she suspects. Instead she will covertly adjust her position by curling up into a ball with her feet up on the seat, as far away from him as she can get.

Right here we need to focus on what the real situation is rather than what we have been conditioned to believe by society. The minute he climbs into the car and drives off, his physical advantage over her lessens considerably. His attention is partially diverted. At least one arm is engaged in the task of steering. His feet and legs cannot be used to provide the full body leverage he is used to enjoying when struggling with a victim. He must be careful in his conduct so that other drivers do not pay him or his vehicle undue attention. This is particularly important if he knows an Amber Alert has been broadcast. *His only assets are the threat of violence and his right arm.*

The child he has abducted has the full array of her defensive armament available to her. She has superior motivation. She possesses the element of surprise, and she does not have to worry about attracting attention in this setting, indeed, it is one of her primary objectives. There is only one thing she must do: unleash a focused, ruthless attack with all her power, the moment he is least prepared to deal with it. Like in the previous scenario, he is most vulnerable when executing a left-hand turn, preferably at a busy intersection.

She has curled herself into a fetal position, with her legs drawn up, her back against the passenger door and facing his profile. As he looks left—away from her—following the direction of his turn, she will lash out with her feet and legs, augmented by full voice power in ballistic mode. Her primary targets are his right elbow, right hand on the steering wheel and the gear-shift lever. If he is holding the wheel with his right hand, a strike to the elbow will cause the steering wheel to rotate right. This will have immediate, devastating consequences in the middle of a left-hand turn. Smashing his hand between her foot and the wheel has nearly the same effect and targeting the gearshift lever is self-explanatory. Also, the effect of these strikes will cause him to turn and lean toward her, bringing the right side of his face and neck into the range of her powerful kicks. Her intention should be to hurt him as badly as she possibly can. If it is possible (and we have found in full force re-enactments that it usually is), she should then launch herself at his face and eyes, using her fingernails and teeth to rip him apart. Remember the wasp and the little dog. It is her life or his.

We train our students to consider themselves dead already in this situation, that they have absolutely nothing to lose, except the chance to make the predator pay. The combination of anger at a lost life; the injustice of never seeing their family again, and *revenge for the pain their death will inflict on loved ones,* is just the fuel children need to help direct a superhuman effort against a physically superior foe. Under these horrific conditions, rage is more useful than despair. The goal in this scenario is to secure the same ending as the previous one.

Fourth Challenge: Containment in the Trunk

This is the most difficult situation from the standpoint of the primary objective of the other challenges: stopping the car. The victim has no physical access to the abductor and must rely on either breaking out of a locked prison or on other people noticing that something is wrong. In addition, fear of the dark and the loss of the ability to see, compound the situation exponentially. If the predator has managed to get the child into restraints, it becomes terribly difficult.

Worse, the predator is not the only enemy here. Some trunks are virtually airtight, and the child can die from asphyxiation, even if the abductor intends no initial harm. Another lethal hazard is heat and humidity. If the weather is hot, the temperature inside a closed trunk can reach 175 degrees within a half hour, and the victim can literally be baked alive. Twenty to twenty-five percent of trunk entrapments end up being fatal to the victim, whether they are accidental or intentional.

For all these reasons, *anyone*—children especially—should fight to the death rather than be stuffed into a trunk. If that happens, *there is no waiting for rescue*; they must act immediately to extricate themselves. Parents should make sure their children have *experience* in executing the following game plan:

Trunk Escape Game Plan

1. Stay calm, breathe slowly and don't hyperventilate.

2. Feel for a trunk release button or lever.

3. If there is no release mechanism, look for the trunk release cable, usually under the carpet on the driver's side of the car.

4. Pull out all the wires that you can reach and try touching the bare ends together to short out anything you can. If the tail lights are out, the driver may be pulled over by the police and then it is time to use voice power.

5. Look for anything that can be used as a tool to punch out the tail lights. If nothing is available, use your hands and feet even if you get injured doing it. Stick your arm out of the hole and wave it around to attract attention.

6. If you have succeeded in opening the trunk, time your escape. If possible, wait until the car has slowed down enough that you can jump out without too much injury. Don't jump at freeway speeds or if you are on a bridge or viaduct. If the car is stopped, wait until you think you can get away without getting re-captured.

The following story is a factual account of two children who succeeded in escaping the circumstances we have just described:

8 Year Old Girl Foils Kidnappers, Saves Brother

During a home-invasion robbery, three men stuffed Diamond Nguyen, eight, and her brother Jack, six, into the trunk of the family's Lincoln Town Car. The men had knocked on the door of Dong Nguyen's Burnaby, B.C. home, and forced their way inside when Mrs. Nguyen answered the doorbell. Mr. Nguyen was not home. After ransacking the house in search of cash and not finding any, they became enraged and drove away with the children trapped in the trunk. At some point during the ninety-minute ordeal, the driver stopped and forced Diamond to call her mother on a cell phone and warn her that they would be hurt if she called the police.

When the men arrived at their destination, they entered an apartment, leaving Diamond and Jack locked in the trunk. All late model Ford vehicles have an illuminated trunk release, and Diamond knew how to use it, but she bided her time thinking, "I have to wait until I know they are gone." After a few minutes of quiet, she released the trunk. As she was helping her brother out, a passing couple stopped, curious as to what they had been doing in the trunk. Diamond quickly outlined the situation and the couple, Sherrold and Marina Haddad, escorted them to a safe location and called 911.

Mrs. Nguyen, traumatized after Diamond's call, had obeyed her daughter's warning and not called the police; but neighbors, hearing the shouting and sounds of violence coming from the Nguyen residence, had done it for her. Burnaby police, receiving both the neighbor's and the Haddad's calls, converged on the Lincoln Town Car and arrested one of the men as he returned. The other two men escaped.

Diamond and Jack did everything right. First, *Diamond's parents had taught her how to escape that particular trunk compartment.* Second, she did not panic. Third, she chose the right moment to act, and last, she was able to explain the danger quickly and succinctly to the Haddads. But for her bravery and resourcefulness, this story could have had a very different ending. Police believe the perpetrators specifically targeted the Nguyen family. This was a violent home invasion combined with a daylight abduction; desperate acts executed by angry, frustrated criminals. Yet, these three adults were out-maneuvered by a brave, smart little girl who refused to lose her cool.[16]

In concluding this lesson, I recommend the following items that children should keep on their person, or at least close to them (in a school back pack for instance), at all times. Although some of these items are everyday objects of little intrinsic value, whenever possible they should be expensive, beautiful gifts from parents or loved ones; gifts that your child has great sentimental connection to and does not want to lose. Here is the list with a brief explanation of the object's use:

Abduction Survival Gear

- A 550 para-cord braided friendship bracelet, with a tiny, bright utility light attached. The bracelet could be rapidly and unobtrusively unraveled to use in place of the belt in the back seat scenario. (Shoelaces—if they are strong enough—could work as well, but have the disadvantage of making running away more difficult.) The light could make the difference between life and death in the trunk scenario.

- A cell phone with the latest GPS options. Ideally, the GPS function would be in constant activation mode whether the phone was on or off.

- A small multi-tool with pliers, screwdrivers, small knife, saw and scissors. The benefits are endless and obvious. Smaller is better (key chain size) —convenience is king if its purpose is every-day carry.

- A Marks-A-Lot indelible felt tip marker, 6-inch size. This is an invaluable resource: it can be used as a devastating close quarter striking weapon, as well as giving a child the ability to write messages that cannot be easily erased on virtually any surface. In the A.S.K. program we train kids to be able to write "HELP CALL 911," backwards while they are blind folded so that the message, when written on a car window, can be easily read by a passing motorist.

- A golf ball or pet rock and a pair of <u>strong</u> knee-high socks. These items should be kept in a back-pack permanently: a pet rock or golf ball slipped into a sock and swung with power can smash out car windows (or anything else for that matter), yet when separated, would never be viewed as a weapon.

Lesson Eight: Human Connection and Survivor Mindset

When we review Columbine, Virginia Tech and similar tragedies, the intended targets can be divided into two groups: those who waited for rescue, and those who acted to preserve their own lives and the lives of others. Unfortunately, those who choose to act under extreme pressure are always in the minority. As parents, we all want our children to be in this elite group, to have what I call "survivor mindset." The Survival Response Conditioning that has been the focus of the preceding pages will certainly help them make the right choices and execute the right actions, but it is clear that *the way survivors think is fundamentally different from the way victims think.* Their actions prove this conclusively. The real question is: do we want to raise children who give aid, or children who need aid? A proactive, powerful mind has a default position when confronted by a shocking threat—it is set to act, instinctively and decisively. Knowing what to do and having the confidence to do it are essential to survival, but it is the *character* that provides the true launching pad for all this.

In order to help our children possess these assets, we need to define just what "survivor mindset" and "victim mindset" means and explore their differences. Survivors have an empowered mind as their primary asset. This means they have formed the habit of having a "can do/will do" attitude. For them, danger, hardship and extremely difficult circumstances are challenges to be met. Victims feel disempowered. Hesitation and confusion take up valuable time in the decision–making process, producing responses that are too slow and ineffective. For them, fear is a roadblock that they often can't get around. When confronted by the unthinkable, both mindsets start at the same place: surprise and shock.

Disempowered minds respond to shock with denial, which leads the victim straight into apathy, and while they are waiting for somebody to do something, *it is happening to them.* Notice how vague and nonspecific the terms, "somebody" and "something" are. There is no plan, only helplessness and hesitation.

Contrast this with the path taken by empowered minds. They immediately recognize and accept the reality of the situation. It is very specific— "Look what's happening!"—Which leads them straight into decisive action, "I'm doing THIS, now!"

That is often what makes the difference in whether they survive the ordeal (take action) or become victims (inaction).

DIS-EMPOWERED MIND	EMPOWERED MIND
Shock: "Oh my God!"	**Shock**: "Oh my God!"
Denial: "This isn't happening!"	**Acceptance:** "Look what's happening!"
Apathy: "Why doesn't somebody do something?"	**Action:** "I'm doing this now!"

Fig. 7

The objective here is for your child to have survivor mindset. This comes from two sources: specific scenario–based training in an adrenal format, which results in their having a working game plan and general principles of living, which happen every day, day in and day out. These principles are both the support structure and the emotional fuel for taking the right action in spite of great danger and overwhelming odds. We have covered the first source in the previous seven lessons, and now we will turn our attention to the support structure because it is almost entirely the purview of the parent.

RESPONDING TO CRISIS

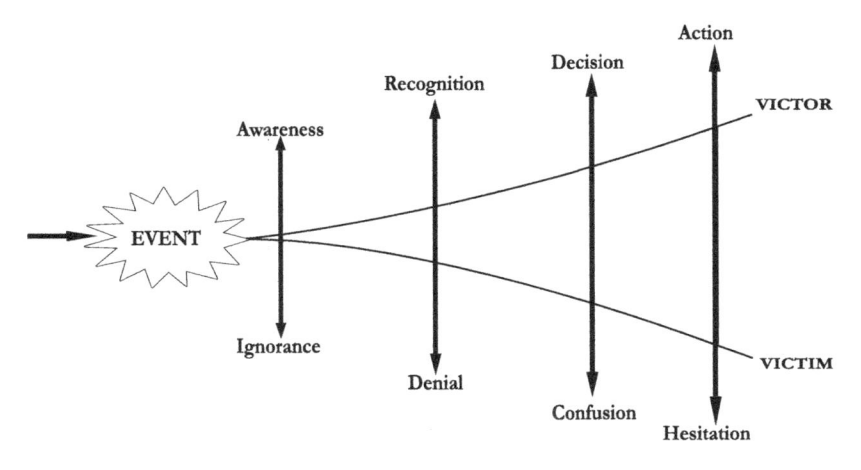

Fig. 8

The purpose of this support structure is to develop a powerful self-concept within your children. Their identity is established primarily by their relationship to loved ones. Survival experts have known for decades that survival is far more dependent on motivation than on knowledge. It is love for family, and desire to be reunited with them that turns a victim into a survivor. Stated simply, it is easier for children to defend someone other than themselves. Therefore, it is incumbent on us to teach our children to be *brave helpers*. If this is their default position, they will transition from shock to action in a twinkling because the urge to help is ingrained in them. These children will instinctively know what the right thing to do is, because they have been practicing it daily. It is *natural* to them. Love for others and the desire to help them will eclipse hesitation, confusion and fear. This is the perfect definition of a hero.

Another facet in a child's self-concept that is often neglected and desperately needed is *identity as a problem solver*. It is OK and even beneficial to set children up for failure occasionally so that you can teach them to view these things as "learning experiences." The idea is to help them to learn to love the challenge of solving a difficult problem. This will teach them to not be intimidated by failure. The resulting "can do" attitude is one of the cornerstones of survival, because it promotes a positive mental attitude that will benefit them for the rest of their life.

If you combine the image of a brave and friendly helper with the image of a problem solver, it leads to a third and vital identity: *a friend finder*. Children who are friend finders save lives, and the life that they save by default may be their own. Teach them to look for and befriend other children who are outcasts and misfits. The value of this habit cannot be overstated. **First**, it teaches them to be compassionate and merciful. **Second**, it gives them an opportunity to teach other children what they know. This will fortify the lessons you have taught them. It is an old principle that *you do not know something well until you teach it to someone yourself.* When your children help others by telling them how to be safe, you will know that they have internalized that lesson. **Third**, when your children reach out to other less fortunate children, they may be saving lives. These outcast children are the primary targets of most predators and your child's offer of friendship, freely given, could be the life-saving link that removes them from a predator's crosshairs. **Fourth**, nothing builds character like standing up for someone who is unpopular. When children are willing to do this, it is a sign that they are capable of withstanding peer pressure in other areas. Every one of these practices strengthens a child's self-concept, and together they form the planks in the support structure needed for survivor mindset.

There are literally hundreds of ways to introduce these concepts to your children and then re-enforce them over time. Use your creativity and knowledge of their personality to customize your approach. Here are three examples that you can begin with today:

1. Reward your children every time you witness them sharing what they know, especially if it has to do with their safety. Encourage them to tell you about instances that occurred out of your sight, so that you can reward them for those, as well.

2. Teach them to *expect* problems as an everyday occurrence in their lives and coach them in self-solving. This will encourage confidence, independence and self-reliance.

3. When you leave your children in the care of a "trusted other," make it a habit to endorse their character by telling this person that your children can help them if something goes wrong. Make sure your children hear you do it, because it will bolster their self confidence. Knowing that you trust them and think highly of their abilities, will cause children to want to please you, by making the right decisions or taking the correct actions, whether things go wrong or not.

I conclude this lesson with the following true story.

Bullets on His Birthday:

Wounded Teenager Overpowers Gunman

Just before classes began on Thursday morning, Jacob Ryker was seated in the school cafeteria with his girlfriend, Jennifer Alldredge, and several friends. It was his seventeenth birthday, and the Thurston High School junior thought a prank was being played when he heard what many described that day as firecrackers going off. It was school Election Day, and there were between 300 and 400 students present in the cafeteria. Jacob looked toward the sound and saw a fellow student, Kip Kinkel, dressed in a trench coat pointing a rifle. Then Jennifer took a bullet to the upper body. Jacob jumped up, shouting "Gun!" and was knocked over, shot in the lung.

Kip fired more than fifty rounds into the packed cafeteria, killing two students and wounding twenty-two others. From his position on the ground, Jacob saw Kip approach, stand over another wounded student and put the barrel to her head. Kip squeezed the trigger. Instead of a gunshot, there was an audible click, followed by two more as Kip repeatedly tried to fire the weapon. Jacob, familiar with weapons from hunting with his father and uncle, as well as N.R.A. gun safety courses he had taken, recognized that Kip would have to reload and seized the opportunity. Kip was only fifteen feet away when Jacob, with a bullet in his lung, charged and took Kip to the ground. In the ensuing struggle, Kip drew a nine-millimeter pistol and fired at Jacob's head, striking him in the hand as he grabbed the gun. At this point, several other male students including Jacob's younger brother Joshua pounced on Kip and subdued him.

Jacob Ryker and Jennifer Alldredge survived, but Ben Walker and Mikael Nicholauson were killed as were Bill and Faith Kinkel, Kip's parents. He had murdered them the day before. Kip was tried and sentenced to 111 years without possibility of parole. Even though Jacob does not consider himself a hero, his actions that day were heroic and "in character," according to Gary Bowden, his wrestling coach. While other students were diving for cover, Jacob Russell Ryker, weaponless and wounded, engaged a heavily armed gunman and saved the lives of many potential victims. On December 20, 1999, he was awarded the Carnegie Hero Medal.[17]

Chapter 20

When Bullies Meet Hard Targets

"In a time of universal deceit, telling the truth is a revolutionary act."

—George Orwell

The icy ball of fear rolled into my stomach every afternoon and coincided roughly with the ringing of the bell ending the school day. I could usually divert my mind with school work or a good book, but inevitably the ticking clock during fourth period study hall would remind me that I was on a collision course with another beating. It was April 11, 1974, a beautiful spring day. I should have been just another happy-go-lucky eighth-grader. I will never forget the events that transpired that day on the bus, for they made a lasting impression and proved to be a turning point in my life.

Their names were Richard Franks and Alan Grundle, and they were the reason I dreaded riding the bus home each day. Franks was big for his age; almost six feet tall and heavy set, with sullen, dark eyes. He was a hater, and his cruelty was legend in our school. When you saw Franks coming, you moved out of the way. Grundle was smaller and meaner than Franks. He reminded me of a cobra I once saw at the Woodland Park Zoo in Seattle. Unlike the other reptiles that remained still, staring through the glass windows with dead eyes, the cobra was in constant motion, ceaselessly weaving back and forth. I felt it was looking right into me, thinking of its next meal.

For reasons I could not understand at the time, these two had taken a serious dislike to me and would wait for me to take my seat on the bus with obvious relish. No matter where I sat, they would come swaggering down the aisle and bully the students sitting to my right and left until they gave up their seats. Franks and Grundle never said much. They let their fists and elbows thump out a "We hate you! We hate you! We hate you!" cadence, always striking above the hairline or below the collar so no bruises showed. One would watch the bus driver while the other performed the beatings, so they never got caught, and the other students were either too scared or indifferent to the plight of the skinny little geek with the John Lennon glasses. At any rate, nobody said a word to the bus driver.

As for me, it had never entered my mind to fight back. I was absolutely certain I stood no chance at all against either one, much less both of them at once. They knew that I knew this, and were supremely confident. They depended on my fear to make me their victim. I know now that my fear was the main event and the beatings were merely preliminary entertainment. The effects this systematic persecution had on me were profound. I withdrew inside myself and assumed a siege mentality. I would not meet the eyes of those around me. I became fearful, not just on the bus, but all the time. Loud noises made me jump, and once the others discovered how easily I was startled, I was fair game. They called me "Eek the Freak" and the few friends I had were afraid to socialize with me in public.

As I approached the bus that afternoon, fear enveloped me like a rising tide. I felt as if rivulets of the icy stuff were running down my body and collecting in my fingertips and toes. I could barely breathe, and it grew progressively worse as I trudged up the steps and looked down the aisle. Sitting there about two-thirds of the way back, on my left, was my younger sister, Heidi. It was the first time she had ridden that bus because she normally stayed for choir practice after school. I found out later that her practice had been cancelled and she had missed a ride with a friend's mom. She knew nothing about what had been happening, for I had told no one. I was ashamed. Now here she was, about to see me get flattened.

The second surprise of the afternoon came right on the heels of the first. Grundle boarded, but Franks was not with him. I had chosen a seat opposite Heidi and one seat ahead; Grundle flopped into the seat directly across from me, which put my sister right behind him. He had no idea who she was; she was beneath his notice. As a child, my sister was very petite. Even now, she has the tiniest hands and feet I have ever seen on an adult. At the time, she was less than five feet tall and weighed around ninety pounds.

As the bus lurched into motion, Grundle jammed his fist into the side of my head, snapping it back, and I went numb. I kept thinking, "Soon this bus ride will be over, soon it will be over and I'll

279

be OK, I'll be OK, I'll be OK"... And he kept hitting me and hitting me... In telling this afterward, my sister said, "I kept waiting for my brother to hit back, but after a while, I was pretty sure he wasn't going to, and I started to get mad. I thought, "If that boy hits my brother one more time, I'm gonna knock his head off!"

In my peripheral vision, I saw my sister put her books down on the seat next to her, stand up and tap Grundle on the left shoulder. He turned in surprise, right into Heidi's fist. She may have been tiny, but every ounce of her ninety pounds was behind it, and she unleashed a furious barrage of punches, smacking him every place she could reach until he went down. His glasses flew off, and he couldn't see well without them, so while he felt around to find them, she gave him two or three kicks in the ribs and face. It was a savage beating. When she was done, she calmly sat down, picked up her book and began reading again.

At the back of the bus, was a young girl named Briana Fuller. She was one of those loud, boisterous girls, irrepressible, full of life and motion. I had secretly named her "The Magpie" because no one could shut her up, ever. In the middle of all this, while I'm sitting there with my mouth open in shock, she began jumping up and down on the seat, screeching "Bus driver! Bus driver! There's a fight! There's a fight!" The bus driver looked back, saw my sister whipping the stuffing out of the worst trouble maker on the bus and he just yelled, "Aw, let 'em fight," and kept right on driving.

Grundle picked himself up and sat back in his seat. He didn't say a word, but Briana did. As Grundle sat dazed and crimson with embarrassment, she began to yell out, over and over, *"Alan Grundle got beat by a seventh grade girl!"*

Grundle never spoke to me again. Come to think of it, I don't remember ever seeing him on that bus again. Franks disassociated himself with Grundle and ignored me from that moment on, too embarrassed by Grundle's failure to want any connection with him. As for me, I was amazed at my sister's action and self-possession. She seemed fearless. I was older, heavier and stronger, yet I had been paralyzed with fear. I had done nothing—and she had acted. Why?

The answer is that the arena in which we find ourselves is not physical; it never has been and never will be. I "knew" they could beat me. They knew they could beat me, too and knowledge is power. The difference between my sister and I in this situation was simple. She believed—I did not. It was entirely in the mind. If we believe passionately that something is possible, then it is. The reverse is also true. This is an unbreakable law of the mind.

The truth is that if we want to succeed, we must risk failure: And more to the point, we must disregard failure completely. I'm sure my younger sister didn't think it through like this, but none-the-less she was galvanized into action because she had reached what I call the saturation point. It is the moment that fear is eclipsed by rage—and rage disregards consequences. In that instant, she *committed herself to a seemingly foolish course of action and caution became her enemy.* In the arena of the mind, she was ten feet tall. This incident is a perfect example of the outworking of an equation long known to martial artists and profession soldiers:

Ferocity combined with surprise and speed cancels out size and strength.

Under these circumstances, Grundle didn't stand a chance against my ninety pound sister. In that moment, she was transformed from a petite, seventh grade girl, into an elemental force of nature.

*   *   *

Given my childhood experience as a victim and the life I have lived since then, I am sure you can see why the subject of this chapter is of special concern to me. The phenomenon of bullying is nearly universal. At some point or another, all human beings have either witnessed it, been subjected to it or have been a bully themselves. There is no culture or period of history that is free from the pervasive influence of the bully. Because of this, I believe it is safe to assume that bullying is a part of the human experience in the same way that pain, suffering and adversity are.

When we think of bullying, the first mental images that come to the majority of us have to do with the childhood bully. We tend to view the subject through that filter, even though bullying often becomes a character trait that is taken into adulthood. Forward-thinking mental health experts recognize the importance of attempting to correct this behavioral aberration early and they have played an important role in directing the public's attention toward the goal of reforming childhood bullies. In spite of all the press, these efforts meet with limited success when they succeed at all.

In "The Sociopath Next Door"[18] Martha Stout, Ph. D., posits that 1 in 25 Americans are sociopaths, capable of doing anything at all without feeling guilty. Whether these individuals are born without a conscience or lose it due to environmental influences continues to spark heated debate, but whatever the source, it happens early. An estimated 2–5 percent of school–age children engage in what could be described as chronic bullying behavior. By superimposing the first set of statistics over the second, it is possible to conclude that a significant number of these bullies are, in reality, young sociopaths learning to flex their aggression muscles. This is a frightening thought because the vast majority of experts agree that it is nearly impossible to rehabilitate a sociopath. It would also explain why the numerous and varied approaches to solving the bullying epidemic have so little stopping power. It is like trying to convince a tiger that he's actually a zebra because they both have stripes.

Bullying is, first and foremost, a crime of power. At worst, it is an aggressive attempt of one will to conquer another, subdue it and keep it enslaved. At best, it is a misuse and perversion of the assertiveness that is necessary to succeed in any endeavor. Every bully has three audiences he or she desires to influence: first, themselves because it pleases them to feel powerful, which feeds their self–image; second, the victim—who must be brought to acknowledge the bully's superiority; and third, the bystanders, who will communicate what they witness to others and establish the bully's reputation.

In the beginning of this book, we explored the power of entrenched assumptions and we briefly covered what I call "pro-passive bias," which is the slant toward *passive response to aggression* that the media, government and academia attempt to present to the public as the "moral and legal high ground." I utterly reject this premise. It is the deadly enemy of the individual right to personal safety. If you don't clearly remember the concepts we discussed in that section, it would be helpful to return to Pro-Passive Bias in Chapter 3 and review them now.

We desperately need clarity here. Once again, let us begin with acceptance of reality. It is not possible to eradicate bullying, anymore than it is possible to stop people from cheating, stealing or entering a life of crime. In every social setting, human beings engage in power plays. There will always be someone who resorts to bullying tactics in the struggle for dominance. This is a fact of life. How we choose to manage conflict defines us as individual human beings, and it defines our culture. Decent, law-abiding citizens in every society oppose the use of violence to resolve differences among themselves. In every context except self-defense, violence is unacceptable, illegal and immoral. Yet, that exception is of profound importance, and when it is needed, *it trumps every other consideration*. The crux of the conflict over dealing with bullies is the failure of the ideologues to recognize and validate this point.

In an attempt to teach our children the value of peaceful conflict resolution, we have minimized the more important duty to assertively defend their personal liberty. This imbalance leads to fatal character flaws in our youth, many of whom will inherit the responsibilities of leadership in tomorrow's world. Where will we be without leaders who have the intestinal fortitude to stand up to those who would attempt to exercise despotic power over the vulnerable? What will we do when the average citizen is unacquainted with courage? A society that will not defend freedom does not deserve freedom and is doomed to rot from within. I am reminded of the words of Pat Condell, British political commentator and comedian in defense of freedom:

> "*...If we cannot bring ourselves to say what's in our hearts when it truly matters, then we've already given up our freedom and with it the freedom of future generations, which is something that we've got no right to do. We didn't earn this freedom; it was handed to us on a plate by people who did earn it with their lives. We don't own it; we're custodians of it: it's not ours to give away...*"[19]

Anyone who is being bullied is in danger of losing their freedom. Their self-concept is under attack—the life they want to lead and should be able to lead is being denied them in the most humiliating way imaginable. This is especially true in the case of children, because their self-concept is still under construction; it is a work in progress and should it be damaged during that vulnerable period of time; they may never fully recover. Over the past decade, the number of child suicides caused by bullying has increased so dramatically that authorities have actually coined a new word to describe the phenomena: bullicide. These poor victims actually lost their lives long before they took that final step *and because of it*. Suicide was merely the period in the sentence that ended their life.

From the time of our earliest origins, there has only *ever* been one way to consistently make bullies desist from their predatory and abusive behavior: fighting back. As long as human nature remains the same, this will continue to be true. Once again, the social engineers among us have mislabeled the problem. Fighting is not wrong—unprovoked, naked aggression is. There are times when it is morally wrong *not* to fight and there are things absolutely worth fighting for. Love and freedom are two of them. You cannot legislate the problem of bullying away, anymore than you can make effective laws against suffering, pain and adversity. These are problems that define the human experience and they must be *contended with and overcome*.

When victims engage oppressors, they are *always* fighting for their life, whether it is internal (self-concept) or whether the conflict is physical. This is pure self-defense and whether you are an adult or a child, you have a right to every form of self-care available to you. Anyone who attempts to interfere with this right is on the side of the aggressor and automatically forfeits any claim to commanding the "high moral ground." I recognize that there will be many who do not see it in this light. As a former victim, I would like to challenge those who subscribe to this thinking: put your own child in the place of the child whose life is made a living hell by their ideology and see how fast that child turns on you for your betrayal, for that is what it is. Or, walk in the shoes of adults who have been victimized by this ugly sickness. They are trying to regain their life from the person who is attempting to steal it from them. This is fundamentally an issue of having the right priorities, and sometimes it's easy to get confused by all the psycho-babble we are inundated with. For clarity's sake, I'll say it like this: if our principles put the needs and rights of the aggressor above the needs and rights of the victim, than either our principles are in error or we are aggressors ourselves. We need to think this through carefully and ask ourselves if our ideology has eclipsed our humanity.

I am writing this to you right now because a little girl had the guts to stand up to and beat down a bully three times her size. Witnessing that awesome and desperate display of love-driven courage changed my life and continues to motivate me to influence the lives of countless others. You are reading this book because of her. If she had been "politically correct" and followed "the rules," none of these positive benefits would have been realized.

I wish to state clearly and unapologetically: I am on the side of the victim. We can talk all day long about the societal causes of bullying and cry our eyes out for the "poor bully" we think is a victim too, but these arguments crumble in light of one simple fact: For every bully who *chooses* to continue the cycle of victimization, there are hundreds of other children who have suffered like *or worse* circumstances and have made the right choices *in spite of them*. For the sake of these little heroes and for the innocent victims of heartless bullies, **let's stop making excuses for predators in training.** They are committing a crime, and the ideology of pro-passive bias is enabling them.

Allow me to tell you a story that clearly illustrates the points I have made above. This is a recent, true story, and only the names of the participants and the location have been changed for privacy's sake.

JB'S Story

When I first met JB, he was a small eight year old boy, with flaming red hair and energy to burn. His parents enrolled him in my class when I was the head instructor at a karate school near Tacoma, Washington. JB trained with me fairly regularly over the next eight years. At the time this story took place, he was a brown belt in Isshin-ryu Karate, was five feet seven inches tall and weighed about 135 pounds. In addition to his traditional martial arts training, he had graduated from the age–appropriate Survival Response Conditioning program that I and my staff developed. JB was a sophomore at one of the roughest and largest high schools in Washington State. He had wisely refrained from telling anyone he had experience in a martial arts. He was an excellent student both physically and academically; he was respectful, dependable and conscientious.

During his sophomore year, Annie, a girl he had dated previously, began dating another student. This individual, Aldon, had been in and out of trouble with the law, was a year older and outweighed JB by fifty pounds. Apparently JB's ex-girlfriend was still upset over their break-up. She felt she had been wronged somehow and that JB should be punished. Aldon had a cousin who attended the same high school. Lewis had an extensive criminal record, including robberies, assaults and weapons charges.

Two weeks prior to the incident, Annie, Lewis, Aldon, and another male friend of Annie's, were at her house hanging out. Annie, still burning with resentment over her break-up with JB, instigated the others to teach JB a lesson.

They called JB's home and JB's younger sister answered. When the first and primary caller, Lewis, found out whom he was talking to, he called her unspeakable names and said they were going to rape her anally and then kill her. He said they would do the same to JB's mother. JB, who was listening on another line, told his sister to hang up and then he disconnected, as well. Lewis immediately called back and threatened to hunt JB down and beat him up at school.

The next day at school Lewis and Aldon confronted JB in the hall and to his face threatened to kill him, but JB was able to verbally de-escalate the confrontation. He reported the incident to his parents and to school officials. JB's parents were concerned. They knew these boys were thugs with a history of violence but the school authorities were unresponsive.

Tuesday and Wednesday were uneventful, except for hints through the grapevine of Aldon and Lewis's bad intentions toward JB. For whatever reason, JB didn't see either one of them, and that was just fine with him. The point here is that JB was not pursuing conflict with these individuals; rather he was trying to avoid it. In light of subsequent events, it is important not to lose sight of this fact.

On Thursday morning, between first and second period, Aldon again confronted JB in the hall. JB told Aldon he would not fight, and Aldon responded by saying he had no choice; Whether he fought back or not, JB would get his "ass kicked." JB remembers Aldon growing angry and shouting, "You better hope to God you have friends because you're gonna need them!" This confrontation took place adjacent to the janitor's supply room. On hearing the shouting, the janitor, who had been busy taking inventory, stepped outside and inserted himself between the boys. When he asked them what was going on, Aldon cursed and threatened him, but then retreated. The rest of the day was uneventful. On returning home, JB once again told his parents exactly what had happened.

The next day, Friday, JB's father visited the school and had a talk with one of the school counselors. He explained what had been taking place, and asked the school to do something about it. The counselor told him that since nothing physical had occurred, their hands were tied. Mr. B responded that a crime had already been committed against his son—more than once—and while they might take that lightly, he did not. Mr. B explained to the counselor that JB would not pursue conflict, but if Aldon or Lewis put their hands on him, he would defend himself. He said: "I will not allow my son to *accept* a beating by thugs in an environment where he has every right to feel protected. If you will not defend him, he must protect himself. This is your environment and you are responsible for controlling it. Do your job. Don't force my son to do it for you."

The weekend went by uneventfully, but JB and his parents were worried. Mr. B felt his meeting with the counselor had not gone well. He had no confidence that his concerns were being taken seriously. JB knew his parents were on his side; that they would back him up if he was forced to defend himself. In this, he was lucky. Many children in like circumstances are taught that fighting is wrong; that they are not to "reward violence with violence" and consequently they feel they have to choose between disappointing their parents and taking a beating. Although JB was spared this anxiety, he had the normal dread of conflict that all children do when faced with hoodlums like Aldon and Lewis.

When JB arrived at school Monday morning, Lewis and Aldon were waiting. They were hiding around a corner that they knew JB would have to pass by on his way to first period. As soon as they saw him, they jumped from their hiding place and blocked JB's way. Lewis was in the lead. Cursing loudly, he threw his backpack on the floor and began to crowd JB, repeating the threats he and Aldon had made the day before. Aldon was beside Lewis, and it was obvious to JB they both intended to engage him. Lewis was known to carry a blade, and in a rage, he screamed that he would cut JB's #%**! throat.

At that moment, a school security guard appeared from behind JB and seized Lewis. The guard immediately silenced Aldon and commanded JB to accompany him as he escorted Lewis to the principal's office. Along the way, Lewis subjected the security guard to a continuous stream of verbal invective. When they arrived at the office, Lewis and JB were separated. The guard took JB aside and told him that Lewis had both verbally and physically assaulted him. At that moment, the counselor invited JB into the principal's office and closed the door. Besides JB and Lewis, the principal, the counselor and the security guard were all present. During this meeting, the entire situation was discussed at length, with Lewis continuing his aggressive posturing and JB repeatedly stating he did not want any trouble. Right before the principal concluded the discussion, he asked both boys if they could put aside their differences. JB replied that he had never had anything personal against either Lewis or Aldon. Lewis said, "Well, we'll see about that." The content of the meeting, as well as its end, should have made it clear who was pursuing conflict.

Right after the meeting, Mrs. B received a call on her cell phone. The counselor informed her of what had happened and what her view of the situation was. The counselor said she was worried and that JB should be watchful and aware. "This is not over," the counselor told her, "I could see in their eyes that there was bad blood between them."

Mrs. B responded directly: "You are making this sound like JB and Lewis have a mutual, personal problem. Nothing could be further from the truth. My son just wants to be left alone. Lewis and Aldon have targeted him. He wants nothing to do with either of them. Under the circumstances, how dare you place them on an equal footing? One is breaking the law, and the other is innocent. Why are you people are looking the other way?"

That same day, in the lunch room, Lewis approached JB, called him a coward and a faggot and threatened him with death in front of a large number of students. This was reported to the front office, but again, nothing was done. In talking with JB after the incident, he related to me that as all this was going on, he was becoming more and more aware that a physical confrontation was inevitable. "These guys didn't care about the consequences. The school authorities could not make them stop. Even if they had been kicked out of school, they would have still come after me. At least at school I would not be alone with them—other students and teachers would be nearby, and could help me if I got hurt."

The next day, Tuesday, several students warned JB that Aldon and Lewis intended to attack him the next day with weapons. Lewis was absent from school because of court appointments on unrelated charges. JB informed both school officials and later his parents, who told him that perhaps he should skip classes the following day. By this time, however, JB was tired of all the turmoil and did not want to miss school. He decided to go anyway.

Wednesday morning, when JB arrived on the school campus, his friend Chris told him that Aldon and Lewis were waiting for him.

Because of the layout of the school, JB could not get to the office before passing the point where his antagonists lay in wait. Sure enough, as JB approached, they both attempted to block his way, but JB managed to shoulder his way past them. A long hallway lay between JB and the relative safety of the office, which was beyond a jog and around a corner, out of sight and hearing from his present location. JB didn't think he would make it. Both culprits were right behind him crowding and shoving, attempting repeatedly to get around him and once more cut off his escape. To JB's right was a stairwell leading up to the second story and a hall with his locker. Right over it was a security camera. JB took a sudden turn and raced up the stairs. Other students, sensing what was about to happen, converged on the stairwell and followed on the heels of his pursuers.

JB turned to face his tormentors. He was now directly under and in line with the security camera. As he backed toward the wall, JB was holding his cell phone in his left hand, which he passed to Chris. JB told the pair once again that he didn't want any trouble. In response, Lewis threw down his back–pack and cap and rushed JB, cursing. He threw two punches. JB ducked the first one and slipped the second. JB then fired back, striking Lewis in the face twice. As Lewis lunged toward him the second time, JB closed with him and threw him over his hip to the floor. Fearing his attacker would get up and re–engage, JB pounced on him and rained down several punches until Lewis cried out for him to stop. JB immediately let him go and gained his feet, intending to get away. At this point Aldon, who had been hanging back, charged JB from behind. Hearing Chris yell, JB spun around and intercepted Aldon's first punch, steered him into the lockers and struck him once in the left temple. This rendered Aldon incapable of further aggression. Bystander's helped him keep his feet, without which he would not have been able to stand. Let me remind you that both of these attackers were taller than JB, and had forty to fifty pounds on him.

JB dazed and in shock, intended to go straight to the office, but instead found himself heading toward his class. On the way, he was accosted by a female security guard, who asked him to accompany her to the office. JB complied willingly. When they arrived, the security guard asked JB to wait in an empty room in the office complex and locked the door behind her. Although JB had blood on his clothes and face, no one asked him if he was hurt, what had happened or what his side of the story was, and no one visited or checked on him for nearly two and one half hours.

The assault on JB took place at 7:10 a.m. and was over within a few seconds. It is safe to assume that by 7:15 he was cooling his heels in the office. The police did not receive a call from the school until 9:30 a.m., and didn't arrive on the scene until 10:45. Mrs. B was not contacted until almost 1 p.m. and was not allowed to speak to her son. Why the delay?

Because of the influence of "zero" tolerance violence policies, school administrators often make little or no attempt to differentiate between the aggressors and the victims in these cases. They are not concerned with guilt or innocence. Their primary concern is liability, and they immediately go into damage control mode. Who is injured? Can we treat them in-house? Might their parents sue? What happens if the incident goes public? Can the charge of negligence be attached to us in any way? Do we notify the police? If so, at what point? What evidence should we review before making a decision as to how we will present this?

Nearly every school district in America either has attorneys on retainer or has easy access to them. The sole purpose of these legal specialists is to defend the district, administrators, school board and the legal entity of the school itself against lawsuits. One of the first things that the administrators do in situations like this is to bring legal advice to bear on behalf of the school immediately. The attorneys are briefed and shown any relevant evidence, especially video footage and documentation of systematic student–to–student harassment that could be construed to indicate negligence on the part of the administrators. Both existed in this case.

The important question to ask here is, "From the school attorney's perspective, which parties represent the greatest legal threat?" We can immediately strike Aldon, Lewis and their parents off the list. Their claims are cancelled out by their criminal conduct both before and during the incident. They are vulnerable, and they know it. With their records, the last thing they would want is legal scrutiny, so any attempt to pursue legal action against the school on their part would be half-hearted at best. On the other hand, JB and his parents had a case, and evidence existed to prove it. Therefore, *they* were the threat.

If we take right and wrong out of the picture and focus solely on the tactical issues, as attorney's do, it is easy to achieve clarity. JB and his parents must be brought to decide not to sue. The strategy of choice in cases like this is to attack immediately, to catch the opponent off guard and to put him on the defensive. The idea is to make your opponent feel he has so much to lose he will spend all his time and money defending himself, rather than pursuing your client. This is very effective methodology and frequently produces a positive result for schools that use it.

In addition to this disgusting mess, these administrators are just as prone to making snap judgments based on subconscious programming as the rest of humanity. For example, whenever there is an altercation, people who did not see the events as they unfolded will typically and automatically reserve compassion for those with the most severe injuries. They see a person bleeding, and their mental programming says, "Somebody *did* this to them!" Instantly that individual is transformed into the victim. So in effect, a judgment is made but it is made without investigation and without regard to the involvement of the participants.

This is what was going on while JB languished away in solitary confinement. Lewis had a deep gash over his left eye, which the school nurse determined needed stitches. Aldon had a severe concussion. The principal, the counselor and the security guard were comparing notes, reviewing the video footage and interviewing the witnesses and participants. They were talking to their attorneys. It is significant that the school authorities questioned Lewis, Aldon and others at length but had no contact with JB prior to the arrival of the police. Both the principal and the counselor were well aware of the history of events leading up to the attack on JB. They knew that Aldon and Lewis were actively pursuing conflict with JB. Yet, all of this was swept under the rug because had it come to light, the administrator's negligence would have been exposed to public view. It was easier to discreetly sit on that information and let Aldon and Lewis's injuries define the assignment of guilt. The decision to use JB as the scapegoat was a natural and automatic response for administrators who believe that *a fight begins when the victim hits back*. JB was guilty until proven innocent.

At 9:45a.m. the counselor unlocked the door and presented JB with a blank incident report form she wanted him to fill out. He complied and asked her if he could telephone his mother. Her response was, "Not at this time." The counselor departed abruptly and JB was left alone again, this time for an hour and a half. Meanwhile, the police interviewed Lewis, Aldon and Chris at length. In situations where multiple witnesses and participants are involved, it is common for police officers to question last the individual they believe is culpable. This allows them to manipulate the interrogation with the intent of bringing great pressure to bear on the suspect and provide multiple opportunities to catch him or her in an untruth.

Finally, at 11:15 the police were ready to interview JB. He was escorted to another room by one of the officers; the door was locked behind them, and JB was read his rights. The officer then told him the room was sound-proof, that he had done something very wrong and that he was in serious trouble. As an afterthought, he remarked that JB would probably receive a felony conviction. This officer's questioning of JB was extremely brief and very general in nature. JB was given almost no chance to tell his story. Within five minutes of the police officer's entrance, JB was handcuffed and led to the squad car.

Let's focus for a moment on what was done to JB by this officer. Bear in mind that this was a 16-year-old boy who had never been in trouble with the law before, who for at least two weeks had been in fear of great bodily harm, and who had good reason to believe he was about to be stabbed, perhaps to death. He had gone to the authorities in good faith at least four times, and yet the situation continued to escalate. He told these hoodlums repeatedly that he wanted no trouble with them. When the altercation finally began, he did not strike first; rather, he avoided two wild punches before responding and then his only motivation was to stop the attack. He wisely and purposefully positioned himself beneath a video camera, so that an exact record of the event would be available to the authorities.

I am compelled to ask you, are these actions born of a guilty conscience? What more could have been asked of this young man? What would you have done? I asked JB what scared him most, the altercation—or the prospect of his life being tarnished with a felony conviction? He told me there was no comparison between the two. He was so relieved to have *survived the attack* that everything else seemed trivial. It was one of the reasons he was so calm and patient even after waiting several hours alone with no information about what might happen to him. He was experiencing great relief because he was safe.

When the officer entered the detention room, he had a plan. The objective was the psychological disempowerment of a minor who he had determined was guilty. Step one was to let him wait, alone with no information, to allow anxiety to build. Step two was to shock JB by reading him his rights with no preamble or explanation. Step three was to underscore his vulnerability by telling him that no one could hear him and that he could not get away; this officer had complete control over him and his situation. Step four was to pass judgment on his actions and step five was to pass sentence on him without allowing any defense of himself. All this was done without any legal representation for JB, which should have been obtained for him as soon as he was read his rights. As a parent, would you be comfortable with this if it had happened to your child? What if it happened to you?

If the officer expected these tactics to meet with success, he was disappointed. JB was made of sterner stuff. When he could see that JB was not going to have a meltdown and confess, he wasted no more time questioning him. The officer had another surprise in store. Snapping on the cuffs, he led JB to the squad car and put him in the back seat. Then he put one of JB's attackers, Aldon, in the back with him. There was no divider between the two. Unfortunately for the officer, this tactic was a miserable failure as well, for Aldon soon broke down, blubbering and crying to JB to forgive him. JB stonily told Aldon he could go to hell—he should have thought about all this before he and his buddy attacked him. The officer, listening, became enraged at *Aldon* and shouted for him to "Shut the f--- up!"

JB spent the night in jail—with the general population—in spite of the assurances the police gave to Mrs. B that he would be isolated from the other inmates because of his age. Mrs. B had been frantic upon hearing that her son had been arrested and was being detained in jail. After hours of waiting, she was only allowed to have a two-minute phone conversation with her son. He assured her he was OK, uninjured and in good spirits. He told her not to worry, but worry she did. The police officer she talked to told her that JB was to be charged with second degree assault and that it would be $25,000 to bail him out. Personally, I don't see how he could have come to that conclusion, since JB had not yet darkened the door of a judge's chamber.

The next morning, JB met with a female court-appointed attorney, who upon finding out what had really happened, raised such a ruckus that JB was released within the hour. All charges against him were dropped. The authorities had dropped the charges against Aldon and Lewis as well, *stating that the altercation was mutual* and, therefore, unlikely to produce a conviction. In this they were echoing the school system's policy of meting out equal treatment to predator and victim alike—an absolute and unmitigated failure of justice. Eventually, both Lewis and Aldon were permanently expelled from that high school, which was a small comfort to JB. Annie, the instigator of the entire sorry affair, assumed a very low profile as soon as the possibility of consequences became evident and she never interacted with JB again.

The end-cap to this story took place a month later, when the B. family received court documents telling them the case against JB had been re-opened. The authorities presented JB with a choice: go to trial, or accept binding arbitration involving JB being on two years' probation, and paying restitution to his attackers for their medical bills. This outraged them and they called to consult with me about this turn of events. I immediately connected them to an attorney who specializes in cases like theirs. Based on his advice, they were able to ward off this brazen attempt to re-victimize JB.

*   *   *

This nightmarish incident showcases just how far the authorities will go to protect themselves without regard to the collateral damage it causes. Why did this happen to JB and why does it continue to happen to countless others every day in a country that promises "justice for all"?

Zero Tolerance Violence Policies

There is a large volume of easily available information regarding this subject online, as well as an excellent book by Brian Schoonover, Ph. D., titled "Zero Tolerance Discipline Policies," available through www.iuniverse.com. Because of this I will only briefly touch the highlights here. Your first-hand local research is essential, due to the fact that these policies lack uniformity and vary significantly from district to district. A basic definition of a zero tolerance policy (Z.T.P.) might read, *"The policy of addressing undesirable behavior with an automatic, non-negotiable application of aggressive punishment for first and subsequent offenses without regard to the attendant circumstances."*[20]

Z.T.P.s first appeared in the early1980's and originated in the U.S. Navy as a disciplinary strategy to combat drug use among sailors. The initial success of these programs led politicians and educators to begin their adoption within the school system a decade later for the express purpose of halting the incidence of students bringing guns to school. Subsequently, educators greatly expanded the list of offenses punishable by Z.T.P.s and purposefully made the descriptive language as broad as possible. This allowed administrators to apply them as they saw fit and to use them in ways never intended originally. This led to a number of high-profile cases in which school boards and districts were sued for a long list of abuses, caused by the lack of justice in the application of Z.T.P.s. Early in 2001, the American Bar Association began uniformly opposing Z.T.P.s because of their basic unfairness and disregard of the individual circumstances of each case.

My research has led me to the following conclusions:

1. There is an almost complete lack of supporting research regarding the effectiveness of these policies. In many districts, violent crime continues to climb regardless of the Z.T.P.s in place.

2. At the same time that many of these policies were implemented, funding for them was cut, so they have never been administered with the necessary attention and focus due to the students governed by them.

3. Implementation of Z.T.P.s is required in order for school districts to receive federal funding, but there is no federal oversight, resulting in a complete lack of uniformity in the application of these policies.

4. Since evidence that Z.T.P.s are ineffective is growing, the reason for their continued existence seems to be political rather than educational. Statistically, students who have disciplinary issues tend to be poorer students. Quite possibly school administrators find value in Z.T.P.s because these policies give them a pretext to get rid of poor stu-

dents and thus raise the school's efficiency ratings. Either way, politicians and professional administrators love to bang the zero tolerance drum, because it makes them seem tough on crime while they actually relax their efforts to combat it.

5. Our children are being given an object lesson that *convenience trumps justice* by the very people who are entrusted with their education, demonstrated every day by educators who punish perpetrators and victims in equal measure without the application of fairness or even common sense.

Children who assertively embrace self-care (defend themselves) are bucking a deeply entrenched system and its supporting ideology—a system designed to reduce the administrator's work and to insulate them from personal responsibility and liability. This is a real threat to these educators, and they respond with the same vigor that law enforcement uses to go after those accused of vigilantism—and for the same reason. Taking the law into your own hands is equated with reckless disregard for the law itself. However, this whole construct collapses with a resounding crash when we take into account the inevitable result of the authorities' failure to protect those whom they are legally responsible for (*in loco parentis*) and who depend on their care. A victim's right to self-care trumps any policy, any system and any ideology—in fact it trumps the law itself. It is the supreme and prime directive of the human race.

What lessons can we learn from this story and others like it?

JB emerged from his ordeal with more confidence and less fear. His naturally sunny disposition was unaffected; if anything, he became more positively engaged with his peers. His fellow students who witnessed the incident talked about it and distributed the videos of the altercation they had taken with their cell phones to many others. The result of all this was that JB was given the "don't mess with him" respect that is so valued at his age. He now feels it is his responsibility as a former victim and a good citizen to step in and help others who are suffering as he did.

In the school social pecking order, JB became a hero and his tormentors became zeros. This is true education. We must learn the lessons that life itself teaches, and one of the most important is *always stand up to a bully*. At present, our society focuses on the down-side of fighting back and ignores its upside. We are going down a wrong path. JB's story is proof of this point. Individual and collective willingness to stand up to a bully is what causes a healthy, compassionate society to become a safe environment. It is what has made this nation one of the world's great leaders.

Children who fall into the behavioral template of passively submitting to a bully's torment become weak, disempowered adults who never achieve their full potential. As I mentioned earlier, some never make it that far because the process kills them off. The contrast between children who forcibly resist a bully—in spite of the consequences—and those who yield to a bully, because they fear the consequences could not be more pronounced. If you keep your focus on this profound and remarkable shift, you will not be misled by well-meaning, but ignorant individuals, regardless of their credentials.

Teaching your child to resist a bully, with physical force if necessary, will have some consequences that are negative, but the positive benefits so outweigh them, you can consider it an excellent trade. So what if they miss a little school! That is a small price to pay for acquiring a life-lesson that will help to mold them into powerful, successful adults. *Life lessons always trump academics!* How is it possible that we have lost sight of this benchmark principle?

Why Children Should Fight Back Against a Bully

1. To secure self-protection.
2. To bolster self-esteem.
3. Teaches a bully a valuable lesson he or she can only learn in this way.
4. Teaches bystanders a lesson.
5. Saves the bully's future victims.
6. Insulates them from the effects of victim mind-set.
7. Gives them an object lesson in courage.
8. Teaches them that action in the face of fear is almost always better than hesitation.

Negative Effects of Children Submitting to Bullies

1. Puts them squarely and surely in victim mind-set.
2. Teaches them to rely on others rather than taking responsibility for themselves.
3. Encourages and rewards the bully.
4. Encourages denial rather than acceptance of reality.
5. Puts them in physical danger both in the present and future.
6. Teaches bystanders all of the above.
7. Misses an opportunity to learn about courage by experience.
8. Teaches them to yield to fear out of balance reflexively, instead of responding to a real warning by doing the next right thing.

It is a mistake to assume that your child will tell you that he or she is being bullied. When it happened to me, I purposefully disguised the fact because I was ashamed. Take note of your children's behavioral patterns and moods, especially concerning school. Bullying does not always occur there, but since this is the place where they have the most contact with their peers, this is where it is most likely to happen. Any change in their normal behavior is significant; your job is to be sensitive to those changes and to discover the reason for them. Here are some of the warning signs:

- A sudden aversion to going to school
- A depressed attitude
- A lackluster report card
- More accident prone
- Chronically too sick to go to school
- An increase in the amount of money they need for school
- The occurrence of scuffles your child says he or she didn't start

If any two or more of these patterns become apparent *at the same time*, it is time to begin a thorough investigation. Do not stop until you are completely satisfied that you know the truth and that you are applying an effective solution. Remember, only very rarely does a child reach adulthood without enduring the abuse of a bully at one point or another. If you are prepared to defend your child effectively in the moment of real need, this experience can have the unexpected and pleasant side–effect of immeasurably strengthening the bond between you and your child. Listed below are some proactive things you can do to prepare yourself and your child to turn this challenge into a powerful life lesson that may ultimately be a defining experience in his or her life. Mine was—and you are reading this now because of it.

In these cases, school administrators respect and respond to three things: assertive, well-informed parents, legal action and bad press. I offer the following seven suggestions, which if acted upon, should aid you in mounting a successful campaign in your child's defense:

Seven Tips on Fighting for Your Child

1. Using the methodology described earlier in this book, teach your children that it is normal and right for them to fight back when targeted by a bully. They should know that when it happens, you are on their side and have their back—you can be depended on to be their best friend and ally. They do not need to worry that they will receive punishment or anger from you because they may miss school, or are expelled. Explain that the school system has a different values system than you do, that your family values are more important, and they come first.

2. Get a written copy of the zero tolerance policy at your school and read it carefully. This may be surprisingly difficult to obtain, but stubbornly persist in your efforts until you have it in your possession. Knowledge of its contents will eliminate confusion and will force administrators to treat you with respect as an informed parent.

3. Find an attorney who is a specialist in these matters and have his business card in your purse or wallet. It should only take a few moments of research and a short drive, but then it is done and you will have access to legal advice immediately, which is always a plus in an emergency.

4. Make contact with and get the business card of the human interest editor at your local newspaper. Keep that card in your purse or wallet, as well. Quick access to the contact information these business cards contain allows you to bring tremendous pressure to bear in the interest of your child right when it is needed. It is one thing to threaten legal action. It is quite another to put a face, a name and contact information into the mix. Brandishing that card will put real teeth into your words because someone who has taken the time to prepare is always a formidable opponent.

5. Write a certified letter with a return receipt to the principal of your child's school demanding to be instantly notified if your child is involved in a bullying or fighting incident. Include a photocopy of your attorney's business card in this letter. Then, the administrator will not be likely to exclude you from involvement (as was done to JB's mother).

6. Form a group of like-minded parents within your PTA. Share this book with them, and agree to support each other if your child or theirs gets targeted by a bully. This forces the authorities to take you and the incident much more seriously. They will not be able to discount you as a "problem parent" because they will be dealing with a group.

7. If you must confront school officials, be calm and direct. Tell them that you are counting on working with them to resolve the situation and if that does not produce immediate and desirable results, they will be speaking with your attorney. Tell them that they will be speaking with reporters, as well. Show them the business cards. This approach will be much more effective than screaming threats, because it goes right for their fear jugular. They will know you are in deadly earnest and the fact that you are calm will make your approach even more formidable.

With your help and support, a bullying incident—despite being painful and traumatic—may become the catalyst for powerful, positive character change in the child you so love.

Chapter 21

Mouse Jockeys: A Fresh Perspective

"Where questioning is rewarded, virtues are promoted, respect is demanded and love is central."

–*L'abri*

One of the most powerful examples of the flawed hypothesis of protection eclipsing preparation is the subject of internet safety and children. Press coverage inundates us with examples of crimes against young people committed by online predators. It is the fastest-growing venue for child victimization and the trend continues to expand exponentially. Obviously, what we are doing presently is not only ineffective; it is a profoundly dismal failure.

Over the last twenty years, computer technology has exploded with such rapidity that those of us who did not experience it during our formative years cannot keep up, unless it is our dedicated field of study. Conversely, our children have grown up within the Internet environment and it has become one of their primary means of communication and entertainment. As of 2010, 75 percent of children between the ages of twelve and seventeen had cell phones. Their ability to navigate through this new world is in many cases vastly superior to ours. It is difficult to admit that our children may know more than we do about a given subject. In many cases, the Internet can provide one of the first tests of a parent's ability to make this admission. Failure to candidly acknowledge their superior understanding of this milieu will immediately affect our level of credibility with our children.

At the same time, an adult parent's view of the predatory environment, however limited, is leaps and bounds beyond a child's perception and comprehension of their own vulnerability. The root of the problem is this dichotomy: Two equally important fields of knowledge, the world of the Internet and the world of the predator, are being viewed through the separate lenses of child and parent. Our children know we are behind them in the digital world and cannot catch up. Worse, they see that we are unwilling to admit it. For our part, we fear they are exposing themselves to terrible risks that they very clearly do not perceive. Like it or not, this is reality. I believe we must begin here.

An internet predator's strategy revolves around a child's curiosity and desire to enter the adult world while being unprepared to navigate its hazards. The efforts we exert to shield and shelter our children from those same hazards, while clear to us, are often interpreted by children as a restriction of their freedom. Predators know this and mold their approach accordingly. So, in actuality, we have a three-way connection between parent, child and predator, rather than the more common and traditional understanding: the two-way relationship between parent and child or between child and predator.

The central and pivotal issue here is also the common denominator: trust. Parents want to give it but are fearful of doing so prematurely; children of all ages want to be trusted, especially in their early teen years, when trust is viewed as a portal to freedom, and predators need it from their targets in order to victimize them. If an internet predator cannot gain the trust of his intended victim, his campaign will be an abject failure. Therefore, *the objective of every successful internet safety program should be to develop a powerful trust relationship between the parent and the child.* Anything that weakens or destabilizes this bond should be avoided like the plague, because the result plays directly into a predator's hands.

The vast majority of safety experts teach that parental control is the Holy Grail in Internet safety. To that end, they recommend a wide variety of "solutions." Perhaps you will recognize some of them:

- "Key Logger" software that allows you to monitor your child's online activity without his or her knowledge

- "Babysitting" software programs that restrict access to undesirable programs

- Not allowing your child to have a computer in his or her room

- Not allowing your child to have a social networking account

While there may be a place for each of these suggestions, it is important to remember that all of them are based on fear that manifests itself as a lack of trust on the part of the parent. Children who are subjected to these "solutions" nearly always resent them because rightly or wrongly, they view them as a lack of respect for their burgeoning right to self-determination. Do not think for a moment that children, especially those connected to their internet-savvy friends, cannot discover your use of hidden programs designed to monitor them. If human beings design it, human beings can discover it, regardless of what the manufacturer says.

Remember, your children and their friends are ahead of you. If they discover that you are monitoring them secretly, trust is blown. They may not reveal that they have discovered what you are doing, preferring to let you think that all is well while they side-step your efforts by establishing accounts outside of your home. They will consider this fair play, since their perspective is that *you* broke trust with *them*. Children uniformly desire respect, trust and freedom. These three values are viewed as the currency of love when expressed consistently by their parents.

In addition, the experts who support parental control as the basis of child internet safety fail to acknowledge the fact that, *without a child's cooperation,* it is impossible for a parent to monitor his or her online activity with absolute certainty. As soon as children reach the age where they can use a cell phone, visit a friend without your company, attend school, have a best friend or join an activity club, you have lost the monitoring battle. When that happens, the focus will shift from your direct oversight to dependence on their obedience when they are out of your view. As they begin to expand their independence and grow their self-concept, it is a foregone conclusion that they will disobey you at some point, especially when children's natural curiosity and need to explore on their own are considered. Parental control is not enough, and trust *by itself* is not enough—they must be delicately balanced, and combined with a third factor, which I will introduce shortly.

The following statement is an example of a blog posting regarding parental cell phone surveillance. It is a typical response from an articulate and normal 16-year-old on the effects of not feeling trusted:

"I was very interested to hear all that was said here, but let me say this: right or wrong tomorrow my parents will be putting tracking software onto my phone. I am a good student. (A's and B's in school) I have a 27 on my ACT, and take all honors and Advanced Placement classes. My parents believe this to be necessary because I, their 16 year old perfect child have been sneaking out of the house and partying.

I have no problem being tracked if it were for some anti-kidnapping precaution; however this is not the case. My parents refuse to give me the responsibility due to me, regardless of achievement. I do not intend to turn off my phone when I go out, or strap it to a dog for a wild goose chase as was suggested. I am tech savvy enough that when I receive my freshly tampered phone I will blatantly delete the app. I have felt violated by this process and while I cannot be used as an example for all kids I can assure you that personally if my parents would handle me more like the adult that I am becoming rather than a pet we would be able to find a safe compromise for both parties.

As a final reinforcement to my position, I would like to also say that the information about my involvement with parties and sneaking out of the house I surrendered willingly two days ago. ...I am interested in any views on this real world situation in which there are no "what ifs."

This student has obviously broken his or her parent's rules. I am not taking sides here. My only purpose is to demonstrate that the *effect of leveraging behavior by eliminating freedom is to remove trust.* One might argue that the student in question caused the breach in trust by breaking the rules, but the punishment meted out only takes both parties further down that path, which is the opposite direction from the one that produces the most positive results.

When considering the available parental alternatives regarding your child's internet security, remember that *it is the predator's objective to sever the bond of trust between you and your child.* From his perspective, if this has happened before he makes contact, so much the better. Like "the Edge" (the composite predator whose mind you peeked into at the beginning of this book), he will exploit their vulnerability. Our victim factory society presents two choices for parents in this arena. The first option is to do very little and play the odds hoping your child will avoid being targeted, which is an abdication of parental responsibility. The second is to take the advice of experts and enforce the rule of law in your home—with the resulting loss of trust your child will experience, when he or she begins to see you as a controlling dictator.

I wish to present a third option: a partnership between you and your child where *the goal is mutually assured trust and respect*. The biggest difference between this method and the other two is that both the parent and the child are bringing something to the table. In return, both will obtain a reward they deeply desire. To make this work, you must start the process by asking your children to teach you what they know about the Internet. This will take time—quality time—but it will also begin to pay you dividends right away. You will know exactly what your children know and you will learn how to navigate the net like they do. If you approach this right, with genuine humility and patience, your children will begin to feel validated, respected and appreciated. They will feel they can open up to you *because you trust and respect them*. Then they will be willing to listen as you trade information: your lessons about how internet predators operate for their navigation skills online. This is the missing third factor I referred to earlier—the unlimited ability for your children to explore new and possibly hazardous venues—in *partnership* with you, their parent.

Earlier in this chapter I mentioned key logger programs, spyware and the hidden liabilities of using these types of programs. Trust and cooperation, the two most crucial factors in the online safety milieu, are significantly diminished by this approach. Yet, intimate knowledge of your children's online activities is important and necessary for success in protecting them. Are there monitoring programs available that promote trust and co-operation between parents and their children? While no software program can guarantee complete coverage of a child's online activity, it would be extremely helpful if parents had a virtual window to look through, provided it could be accomplished without destroying a young person's trust. To throw out normal parental controls in order to establish a better relationship is a strategy that has been tried before and has met with varying degrees of failure.

When we were growing up, we had the family phone, generally located in the living room or kitchen, which allowed our parents to keep a pulse on our social life. It not only helped our parents stay in touch, it also acted as a governor on our behavior. Today, parents can't even hear the near half of the conversations that were afforded them when the phone was the primary source of communication over distance. We have no idea with whom or what our children are talking about.

There is one online service, aBeanstalk.com that I can whole-heartedly recommend. Beanstalk puts the parent back in the driver's seat. It allows you to have your children's back without constantly looking over their shoulder. The main reason why this program works so well is that *it's not designed to be used as spyware.* Parents are encouraged to partner with their children as both become acquainted with Beanstalk features. The idea is to engage and communicate, with the goal of giving children more freedom as they demonstrate responsible online activity.

Linked directly to FaceBook, MySpace and Twitter, Beanstalk filters the content of a child's digital world using thousands of key words. Children spend more than one out of every four waking hours interacting in this medium. When your children (or those they are communicating with) engage in questionable interaction, Mom or Dad receive a real-time notification with the full exchange of what was being said via text message or email. Then they can do what parents do best: parent. With many additional features including GPS location and access to photos posted of or by their child, parents are given the needed window into their children's online world. This allows them to have a much higher level of involvement in their child's life and puts them in a position to give their children effective protection from bullies and unsavory characters. Knowing whom your child "friended" on FaceBook yesterday; who has the biggest voice in your child's digital world, what pictures are posted with your child in them, and their last known location via the GPS are all things Beanstalk can give you. While the program cannot provide complete coverage of all online activity, it is a great place to start building a "safety awareness partnership" between parent and child.

The knowledge that this service is active 24 hours a day, seven days a week has the effect of increasing peace of mind. With the right approach, any action that increases awareness and connection is a powerful indicator to a child that a parent cares. This service is designed to be used openly—scanning your children's digital world much like you did when they were little and you watched them playing in the front yard. They knew you were there, and they accepted this as normal behavior on your part. Childhood hasn't changed, but the tools of childhood have, and we must become familiar with their use if we are to employ them effectively. If used as intended, aBeanstalk.com can help to strengthen trust and confidence between parent and child. Children who have this type of bond with their parents are statistically the most resistant to a predator's advances. Openness and exposure to *potential hazard*, in partnership with a knowledgeable, loving parent, is the best recipe for success.

Massad Ayoob, one of the world's foremost experts on armed self-defense, espouses a similar philosophy in his book, "Gun-Proof Your Children!" He recommends allowing children to handle your firearm whenever they ask, *as long as you are present.*[21] This includes answering any questions they have, instructing them in its safe use and allowing them to examine the gun whenever and for as long as they want. After several investigations prompted by curiosity, most children lose interest because the mystery is gone. Meanwhile, you have trained them to respect firearms and to handle them with safety in mind. If your child should continue to express interest, you will know all about it and can focus the necessary attention on them until you are confident that their curiosity is assuaged. To my way of thinking, this is greatly preferable to treating a firearm as a taboo—out of sight and out of mind until tragedy strikes "out of the blue."

Openness, trust and a shared educational experience produce vastly superior results when compared to rigidly enforced parental controls because they strengthen the bond between parent and child instead of producing resentment, distrust and isolation. With children, whether the subject is gun or internet safety, familiarity with the environment is the key to its safe navigation.

Every time you have an opportunity to express confidence and faith in their abilities, you will capitalize on it. Instead of telling your children they can't have a social networking account, show them how to create one that repels predators and ask them if you can be their first online friend. Slowly teach them the currency of trust—by demonstrating it first, rather than demanding obedience. Trade knowledge, but make sure you do so as an interested mentor rather than a peer or an equal, lest they completely lose sight of your parental authority. Reward them with freedom and only remove it as an absolute last resort. This is not easy, especially at first; nor is it a quick solution. However, over time, a powerful bond of trust will develop and that bond will present an insurmountable obstacle to a predator, whether he makes an approach online or in the real world.

The remainder of this chapter will focus on specifics related to internet safety and is designed to give you a jumping off point as you begin to educate yourself as your child's guide to being a hard target online. My objective is to make this process as simple and effective as possible by focusing on the obstacles a predator must negotiate, as well as the points at which your child is most vulnerable. Surfing the net, doing research, listening to music, communicating with friends they already know in the real world—all these are harmless activities, especially when you know what they are doing. The gray area begins when they engage in chatting with "a friend of a friend," someone they have never met, or when gossip between friends or acquaintances turns into ugly, slanderous rumor mongering. Yet, as damaging as internet sniping and cyber-bullying can be, it is not what most parents fear when they think of the predatory environment that flourishes on the net.

The possibility that your child may be communicating with someone who is disguising his true identity for malevolent reasons is the focus here. In reality, the basic methodology of cyber-space predators is remarkably similar to the tactics used by them in the physical world. We discussed these tactics and their counters at length earlier in this section. What causes the Internet to be so potentially dangerous for young people is that the visual and auditory clues that are part of the physical world—all the normal sensory processes that work together to jumpstart the intuitive process—are absent. Moreover, the predator has almost complete anonymity. What this means is that those who would prey on your child can be more persistent, bold and daring, or they can be much more subtle as the situation dictates. They can bide their time for many months, because they know that they will continue to have access as long as their cover remains intact.

Interaction between predators and children in the real world—especially when they are strangers—usually involves some type of time constraint. The more time he spends engaging in questionable behavior when his identity is known to his victim, the greater his risk. The exact opposite is often the norm with an online predator—his true identity is a secret and therefore, he can spend all the time he feels is necessary to ensnare his young victim. In addition to the absent visual and auditory clues, the intuitive warning which is normally present when the *timing* of the interaction is off—someone wants too much information too fast, for example—is silent, because the predator has the time to cull the information he needs naturally. Because of this, *in the online environment, the specific questions the stranger asks are the most explicit indicators of intent.*

Because the Constitution guarantees the right to freedom of speech and because it is so hard to prove intent when both parties can claim ignorance of the other's identity, it is nearly impossible to convict an internet predator for propositioning a minor. It is only after he has *physically traveled* to meet his intended victim that the authorities have a reasonable chance of obtaining a conviction. That is why on numerous television shows, an arrest is made only after the predator arrives at the home of his victim or succeeds in an actual rendezvous at another location. Make no mistake; these individuals are committing actual crimes when they engage in online interaction with minors with the intention of victimizing them. Unfortunately, cyber–space is a perfect venue for criminals because they are not afraid of what law enforcement knows. They fear what can be proven and used to convict them, and they know that obtaining that proof is a difficult task.

The good news is that online predators have a fairly standard game plan. While the details vary, an online predator must get the right answers to certain questions or he cannot victimize your child. When we properly identify these questions, a series of corresponding red flags become apparent, and we can teach our children to recognize and thwart them. Any attempt to obtain this information by someone whose identity and benign intent are unclear is a serious threat and should be treated as such. *Each question is a test.* The correct answer opens the door for the next question, so that at each stage, the predator's risk is minimized and his knowledge of and influence over his intended victim increase. Together, they form an ongoing, interactive interview consisting of the seven test questions and the red flags listed in the graph below:

THE PREDATOR'S GAME PLAN	RED FLAGS
Test #1 Will they respond to me?	Stranger initiates contact
Test #2 How can I fool them into trusting me?	Persistent questions/attention
Test #3 How do I attach myself to them?	Attempts to form any bond quickly
Test #4 Can I isolate them?	Any suggestion of an exclusive friendship
Test #5 Will they keep secrets?	Attempts to establish secrecy
Test #6 Are they open to a questionable suggestion?	Invitations to view pornography, intimate conversations, sex topics
Test #7 Will they meet me offline?	Any suggestion to meet off line, especially alone

Fig. 9

As you peruse the above information, it becomes readily apparent how simply this can be taught to a child and how difficult it would be for a predator to influence someone who has been trained to recognize these red flags, the issues they reveal, and their pattern. I believe that approaching this topic from the viewpoint of the predator will provide you with a new perspective that is both unique and powerful. Let's go down the list and briefly examine these tests and their indicators:

Test #1: Will they respond to me?

If your child refuses to respond, the predator is dead in the water. This is the simplest solution for everyone. The predator moves on to easier game and your child escapes all the subsequent snares. The fact that a stranger *initiates* contact online does not automatically mean he is a predator or has ulterior motives—but when it happens, this is usually where it begins. Your children may ask you, "If I never talk to someone I don't know, how will I make friends online?" The best answer for this is to teach them that the Internet is a place where you maintain friendships you have already established in the real world. It is a bad place for a child to meet new friends. Once they learn to recognize and respect the red flags, that knowledge will filter their online contacts until the time comes when a casual and harmless online friendship may develop. Take it as a given that your children will eventually interact with a stranger online *and prepare them for it by giving them the appropriate skill-set.*

Test #2: How can I fool them into trusting me?

Trust is given as a direct result of how we feel and how we feel depends on how familiar we are with the person or situation in question. The predator will ask persistent questions and lavish a great deal of attention on his target to gain information he can use to expand the child's comfort zone. Sound familiar? Teach your children that protecting their privacy and guarding personal information are more than just concealing contact information. Especially in the initial stages, it is more about likes and dislikes; it is about knowing where the child's boundaries are, so that *initially* the predator does not cross them. This can be tricky, because predators are adept at the subtle art of getting a child to open up before they realize what is happening. Often they lie about their age. Your children do not realize they are talking to a sweaty, hairy, forty year old man. They think they are talking to another twelve year old: the friend of a friend of a friend, who attends a different middle school. The tart response, "That's none of your business. I'm not telling you that." is not rude; it is an invaluable tool that sends a clear message to a predator and builds a child's self-worth.

Test #3: How do I attach myself to them?

This test is closely related to Test# 2, but with this important difference: A predator will use specific techniques to manipulate his target into a relaxed state of mind where the child will be more accepting of his advances. Using the information he gained when his target passed the second test, the predator will represent himself as *someone just like them* to develop rapport. An important signal is the use of the word "we" early in the communication, or statements that begin with "You and I"— any attempt to form an unsolicited bond. DeBecker refers to this as "forced teaming."[22] His treatment of this particular topic is accurate and thorough. I strongly recommend you obtain a copy of his book for yourself, because the depth of his coverage is beyond the scope of what I am able to present here.

Test #4: Use of any isolation techniques.

If we have arrived here, it is because your child has passed three of the predator's tests— meaning he or she either failed to recognize or ignored three consecutive red flags. This is the predator's version of "three strikes-you're out" and prompts a whole new level of interest and attention. From this point forward, he will seek to have an exclusive relationship with his target because what he needs now is privacy. He needs an agreement based on the consent of his victim—an assurance that no one will be able to interfere with what is happening between them. The good news here is that this is an easy flag to spot. It requires permission to get, and if it is not agreed to, it cannot be enforced. Attempts to cast parents, siblings and friends in a poor light are a sure sign that the predator is trying to isolate a child. Teach your children that no real friend, especially their best friend, is going to try to limit their other friendships. This is *always* a clear sign of an unhealthy interest. At its very best, it is an utterly selfish thing to do. At its worst, it can have deadly consequences.

Test #5: Will they keep secrets?

How does one establish whether or not another will *break confidence?* Tell them a secret—a small, harmless secret—and see if they will respond by revealing one of their own. A predator will pretend to reveal a secret to test the water: to see if their offer of intimacy is reciprocated. If it is not, he can casually withdraw and wait a little longer or until a better opportunity presents itself. The bigger and more private the offered secret is, the more confident the predator is of his success—*or he is in a greater hurry.* Either way, any mention of a secret, whether asked or offered, is a red flag, especially with a new online acquaintance. It is interesting to consider the phrase "breaking confidence" in light of the subject we are discussing. Under normal circumstances, it implies a level of expectation, someone who is confident that the sensitive nature of the revelation will be respected and valued. Mutual trust is the foundation on which this expectation is based. It also implies intimacy.

Test #6: Are they open to a questionable suggestion?

By now it should be obvious why the order in which these tests are arranged is of such importance to the predator. Suggesting a questionable act or behavior exposes him to a previously un–tested level of risk. He must be sure he does not damage the facade of trust and care that he has worked so patiently to establish. Also, someone who will keep his secrets is more likely to give him a second chance, to redeem himself should he misjudge and go too far.

To a predator, the sixth test is of particular importance for two reasons: First, having yielded to a questionable suggestion, the victim will most likely feel guilt and so will become vulnerable to even the most subtle suggestion of blackmail. Secondly, prior to this test, a "No" on the part of the victim would have been viewed by the predator as a rejection. Subsequently, "No" becomes "Yes, with a little more work."

Teach your children that whenever they are confronted with a questionable suggestion, they should ask themselves how comfortable they would feel with you knowing about it and let that answer guide them in their choice of action. Let them know they will never be in trouble with you, should they choose to tell you about it and describe the reward you will give them when they do. Rewards work wonders with children. That's why predators so often give their victims gifts. Be smart and beat the predator to the punch.

Test #7: Will they meet me off line?

This is what the predator's objective has been all along and by this time he has engaged his victim in activity that he knows quite well the child is afraid to reveal to others. He has successfully isolated the victim and has all the power. Having gained the advantage, he will not be afraid to use it. Great pressure can be brought to bear, including threats to expose the victim to others. Perhaps he has persuaded the child to exchange graphic photos. His will be fake, but his victim's will not and fear of exposure can be a powerful motivator. The more pressure he exerts, the greater the risk to the child. This is why your unconditional and non–judgmental support is so vitally important. Without it to fall back on, your child may well go over the edge and never come back. Discuss this scenario frankly with your children and make sure they know that no matter what the action, you will love them and accept them *as if it had never happened*. If there is any silver lining at this point, it is that the predator's true nature is revealed. He is no longer a "friend"; rather, he is revealed as the worst of enemies. The suggestion to meet off-line is the red flag, and pressure is the predator waving it.

Asking the right questions

Your children do not need to possess a large volume of information about the dangers of the Internet. Trust me, they will learn all about it over time. What they need to know all about is your love and interest in them, combined with what is contained in the preceding material. In addition to teaching them to recognize the seven red flags, there are four helpful questions you can train them to ask themselves when engaged in an online conversation with someone they don't know:

- Do I know whom I am talking to? If not, how can I trust him?
- Why is this person asking personal questions?
- Why is he trying to *persuade* me?
- Why is he downing my parents, siblings or my friends?

The habit of critical questioning will prove valuable to them all their life and especially under the circumstances we have been discussing.

Unlike expensive software used to spy on your kids, the strategy I am suggesting does not cost anything to implement. There are no side effects. It does require an investment in time and energy that may not pay you back with immediate results, but over the longer term, it is safer, it is healthier and it will strengthen your personal relationship with your child.

Before we close this chapter, I would like to focus for a moment on a topic we touched on earlier: social networking sites. Parents need to consider and resolve for themselves the issue of age appropriateness. My take on this is that whatever the age of the child, informed parents need to train their children to construct their account according to the following anti-predator subtext:

Repelling an Online Predator

1. I am aware.

(I am street-wise and smart.)

There are a lot of perverts, creeps and sickos online and it is one of the most dangerous environments for kids.

2. I do not easily give trust.

(I am not gullible or easily persuaded.)

Anyone I haven't known for a long time is on a short leash, based on what they do and say.

3. I do not give out personal information.

(I have privacy boundaries.)

Any attempt to get this information is a clear warning of danger, and I will block anyone who tries it.

4. I don't keep secrets from my friends.

(I have no respect for hidden agendas.)

Anything you say to me better be good enough for my friends to hear.

5. I don't do solo meets off line.

(I am careful and cautious. Fooling me will be labor intensive.)

You might not be who you say you are, and I have no way of knowing what your real motives are.

Any social networking page that subtly or overtly sends these messages will be avoided like the plague by predators. This is a person who is quite simply too much work for them. There are many creative ways to cushion this message so that it is not offensive. I suggest making it a family project to find and implement them. Then you can share them with your friends and relatives. What a ripple effect that could have!

Having explored the means to fortify your children's internet presence, let's turn our attention to forging their internal armor—the final step in making them exceptionally difficult targets.

Chapter 22

Adopting the Empowered Mind

"The windows you look through define your horizons, and thus your destiny."

—Unknown

At the beginning of Chapter 19, I pointed out that danger to children comes from five general sources: strangers, familiars, situations, peers and themselves. One by one, we have examined the first four threat sources, and hopefully by now you have a clearer perspective and a firmer grasp of the relevant issues pertaining to them. One last threat source remains terra incognito. It is fitting that we close with this topic, which is the least explored arena, and yet comprises one of the more significant and basic threats to our children. We have touched on the importance of self-image and self-concept a number of times in the preceding pages. Without internal strength, human beings, especially children, are terribly vulnerable to external sources of threat. But what happens when a child's internal defenses implode, and the unseen enemies of the self—despair, discouragement and other joy-killers—assume control?

Most people never stop to consider *that the phenomenon of self-destructive behavior in children is a self-defense issue.* Just as there are ways to train the body and sharpen the senses, there are strategies to fortify the young mind, so that silent and unseen predators like despair, disappointment, resentment, negativity, jealousy, selfishness and hatred find no toe-hold and are repulsed. Society in general—and our educational system in particular—is adept at teaching children what to think in terms of academics, ethics and morals. What has been lacking for many is guidance and training in *how to think regarding their feelings*, so that they grow more and more emotionally powerful—and eventually become impervious to the negative, destructive thinking that produces disempowerment..

Throughout history, great civilizations have had ethical codes of conduct that defined them. All the major religions have moral codes, which are remarkably similar and act as glue, binding the individual believers together. The Judeo-Christian Ten Commandments, the Hindu Four Pathways and the Buddhist Eightfold Path are examples of this. Whatever form they take, without these basic principles, it would be impossible for the individual members of any society to co-exist peacefully and productively. Structure is essential to both individual and social health.

For the past three decades, I have immersed myself in the study of human relationships and conflict. With the passage of time, it has become abundantly clear that the common denominator for every facet of this study is emotional health. I believe that a set of powerful choices defining our emotional integrity is hidden within the basic structure of human morality and ethics. I believe these choices operate in harmony with, but distinct from, any and every social or religious ideology. This means that whatever your adopted faith is, your emotional health, satisfaction and happiness will be significantly strengthened by an understanding of these choices and the principles they are based on. Furthermore, I believe that the earlier these powerful choices are adopted and put into practice in life, the greater the benefit will be.

Children who are emotionally healthy have a correspondingly rich quality of life. All of their systems function smoothly, including the seamless operation of their defensive radar and adrenal abilities when they are needed. They are happy with themselves and are rarely subject to depression and negativity. They are capable of achieving their full potential *at every stage of their growth*. As parents, we hope that our children acquire these benefits and we *expect* that they will, eventually. We assume that the acquisition of this healthy balance, so necessary to a positive outlook, is a natural process. Few, however, attempt to systematically instill a mindset in their children that actively engages the power of their individual choices in regard to emotional health and balance. Some adults are not familiar with this process themselves, even though they have learned to navigate it subconsciously. Others are wholly devoid of the experience and have no point of reference in guiding their children in this arena.

My objective in this last chapter is to identify the principles on which these powerful choices rest and then focus on the choices themselves. This will enable you to begin to plant these wonderful seeds in the fertile ground of your children's minds. Giving them the advantage of knowing by experience how to think from the heart—*how to feel*—in a way that will vastly strengthen their emotional body will be a priceless gift that will pay you both dividends for the rest of your lives.

Principles of Personal Power

1. Tolerance

> *There is no reality, only perception.*

This has proven to be the single most valuable and useful statement I have ever personally come across. Understanding that I am seeing only one side of an issue, and that other human beings, in identical circumstances may have radically different viewpoints—*as real and valuable to them as my viewpoint is to me*—is a powerful and balancing thought. It puts us all on equal terms and promotes respect for important differences. It validates other human beings and opens us to wider horizons.

2. Focus

> *Clarity leads to power.*

The ability to get to the heart of a problem—to extract a core truth and place it in its proper context is the key ingredient in self-determination. Right action is always based on good decision-making and good decision-making comes from clear, focused thinking. To possess clarity is to possess unlimited options, because you can succeed in doing anything you want to. This principle is one of several that link together to define the human emotional circuit. Stated simply:

Grief leads to clarity

Clarity leads to power

Power leads to freedom

Freedom leads to joy

Loss of joy brings us back to grief

3. Association

> *Whom you associate with powerfully influences whom you become.*

All through our lives, and especially during our formative years, our friends, relatives and acquaintances rub off on us. People are sticky. Their habits and character have a direct effect on our own. Some people attract us and others repel us but we are seldom left untouched by them. Whom you choose is what you choose. Knowing this, we can achieve powerful results by executing our choice of acquaintances with purpose.

4. Reciprocity

> *You cannot give a perceived negative and expect to get a positive.*

When it comes to human relationships, this principle is violated more often than any other and leads to untold misery every hour of the day by millions and millions of people. As human beings, we constantly engage in what I call emotional physics—the ebb and flow of energy between us caused by words and actions relative to each other. For example: You have been wronged by your brother and you want him to acknowledge this and make it right. You are hurt and angry. You feel justified in expressing your anger, so you tell him directly and bluntly what he has done and demand his apology. You feel this should motivate him to make a change.

This is a correct thought: It will produce a change—but what will change? More than likely, he will see your anger rather than your reasoning. For him, this is a double negative because like energy attracts like energy. Your anger is added to his anger and compounded with his guilty conscience. He will respond according to what he feels. He perceives negativity and returns it with interest. To reverse this, you must train yourself to ask introspectively, "What do I really want?" To get a positive response, you must consider your words very carefully and address your grievance in a way that produces positive energy. Remember, he will respond according to what he feels from you. You cannot give a perceived negative and expect to get a positive any more than you can expect gravity to reverse itself.

5. Balance

Whoever cares the least controls the relationship.

At first this can sound like a very negative principle. In reality, it is neither positive nor negative, it is simply a fact. For someone to care *less* automatically implies an imbalance. What is important is the linkage between the lack of care and the exercise of control. It works like this: The one who cares the most tries repeatedly to please the other—by offering more time, effort, money etcetera—and thereby becomes dependent on their partner's acceptance or rejection. *By default* power shifts to the other person and this happens because the caring partner allows it to. This dynamic cannot exist in a balanced relationship, any more than darkness can resist the entrance of light. Remember principle number four—reciprocity. It is the key to achieving balance and the goal is *balance in everything*, especially human relationships.

6. Change

> *The one great constant in life is the certainty of surprise.*

We long for stability in our lives and we tend to measure stability by the lack of abrupt change. I once heard someone say, "If you want a good belly-laugh, just tell God about *your* plans!" No matter how much we may want things to stay the same, they never do. Everything is changing, all the time, everywhere around us. We are not the same person we were yesterday and we will be different tomorrow. By accepting this and embracing it, we are putting ourselves in sync with the world around us, instead of constantly fighting against the current. Once this becomes a habit, we can live with a delicious sense of anticipation, knowing we will probably never be bored and we will not be so overwhelmed when life throws us a curve ball. Instead, we will be able to catch it and toss it back.

7. Navigation

> *Re-assess often and make mid-journey course corrections as needed.*

Achieving success in your objectives and living fully while doing it requires a balance between being process-oriented and goal-oriented. Arriving at your destination is not enough by itself; the *real* secret is how you get there. The journey is your life. The problem with long-term goals is that we are constantly changing. Our habits change, our perspective changes, our health changes and we change our minds. Do we stubbornly cling to an objective that no longer fits who we are, because we don't want to be quitters? The answer is yes, sometimes we do and for justifiable reasons. However, to do this *habitually* is unhealthy and leads to a chronically disgruntled attitude; it spoils the journey. Be in touch with your changing self and respect whom you are enough to be flexible. Side trips are fun and often produce rich, unexpected rewards. It may be that they cause you to alter your destination, but since you are in charge of your life, it is your right to do that. *Never confuse giving up with changing course.* One stops progress; the other adjusts your route.

8. Action

> *To survive disaster and maintain an empowered mind, get off your backside and help someone else.*

We touched briefly on this principle earlier. To reflect, focus and act is the formula for solving the problems life presents us with, as a matter of course. When discouragement attempts to detour us into despair, it is usually because we have become bogged down in the reflection portion of the above formula. To pull ourselves out of this mental quicksand, it is helpful to place our focus on other human beings who are in trouble and need our help.

Our own situation may be confusing and overwhelming, but we may be able to see a clear need in another that is not being met. Acting to help them will jump-start our own recovery process because action releases endorphins that counter depression and the joy that results from aiding and caring for others is naturally empowering. It is the fastest and surest way to re–connect to the electricity of life. Having reset your energy and attitude gauges in this manner has a profound effect on how you view your personal situation. The problems that discouragement and despair magnified into overwhelming size have shrunk back to reality and you can begin to successfully chip away at them.

9. Challenge

> *"If you're not living on the edge, you're taking up too much space."*
> –Stephen Hunt

Relishing challenge is, in my opinion, one of the most important secrets of living a powerful life. In this arena, the definition of challenge is *the keenly felt obligation to confront risk*. Without it, life is missing an essential ingredient: All our horizons are reduced and the quality of our existence is greatly devalued. Theodore Roosevelt summed it up best:

"It is not the critic who counts, not the man who points out how the strong man stumbles or where the doer of deeds could have done better. The credit belongs to the man who is actually in the arena, whose face is marred by dust and sweat and blood, who strives valiantly, who errs and comes up short again and again, because there is no effort without error or shortcoming, but who knows the great enthusiasms, the great devotions, who spends himself for a worthy cause; who, at the best, knows, in the end, the triumph of high achievement, and who, at the worst, if he fails, at least he fails while daring greatly, so that his place shall never be with those cold and timid souls who knew neither victory nor defeat."[23]

10. Growth

We live larger only as we accept challenges that expand our comfort envelope.

If you were to step inside my dojo, the first thing you would see upon entering would be three wooden plaques inscribed as follows:

GOOD CLAY   EMPTY CUP   ZEN MIND

This is a poetic way of describing the three qualities necessary for a human being to achieve rapid growth. "Good Clay" refers to the possession of a healthy self-concept. "Empty Cup" is a phrase I use to describe the hunger or eagerness to learn and "Zen Mind" is the capacity to entertain new concepts without being unduly influenced by preconceived ideas. Scientific studies on aging, especially those that focus on the Blue Zones (geographical regions where people live longer with better health) indicate that one of the most important contributing factors is the continuous acquisition of fresh knowledge and skill-sets. These people, many of whom live to be well over 100 years of age, also have a superior quality of life because their mind never stagnates; rather, it continues to expand energetically. They are life–long students, in love with the learning process and life itself.

I have highlighted these 10 principles for you to use as a jumping off place to discover others. Your final list may not look the same as someone else's, but that is normal because they are personal and are uniquely viewed. Based on what I have presented above, I want to offer you the following synopsis, in the hope that you will take every available opportunity to instill it in yourselves and in your children. Teaching them to design their life according to the choices they make—powerful choices that put them in the driver's seat—is preparation for success in whatever endeavor they choose. It will enable them to tap into an unlimited reservoir of positive power, achieve healthy self-esteem and a joyful, balanced and realistic outlook on life. Children who acquire these attributes are the least likely to find themselves in the crosshairs of a predator's scope and prove to be the hardest target, because they possess an empowered mind.

Powerful Choices

Embrace Acceptance

Let acceptance of reality be the mind's default position. Whatever happens, good or bad, start there because it is the best platform to launch effective action from.

Cultivate Gratitude

In every situation, give thanks. This trains a person to see the silver lining, to become a "glass half full" individual, and is an antidote to depression. Happiness becomes a contagious habit.

"The best and most beautiful things in the world cannot be seen nor even touched, but just felt in the heart." –Helen Keller[24]

Live in the Now

Yesterday is gone forever and tomorrow is guaranteed to no one. All we have is today. Learn from the past, plan for tomorrow, *but be here now.*

Seek the Beautiful

This goes beyond noticing beauty; it is an active search for it. Once the mind is trained to do this, every horizon is significant and meaningful; every raindrop becomes a window to vibrant life and color.

Adopt student mindset

Determine to be a lifelong student of yourself and the world around you. Make curiosity a siren song that must be responded to. Never assume you know all about something, because as soon as you do, the shades are drawn and the book is closed: game over.

Expect to Be Surprised

Let surprise be a welcome guest and learn to consider its occurrence normal. This outlook will greatly reduce response time in emergencies because it acts as a buffer for shock and will help you to maintain better equilibrium day to day.

Relish Challenge

Growth cannot occur without an expansion of our comfort envelope, which is a great definition of challenge. Learning to love the excitement of pushing past our self-imposed limits is the key to achieving excellence.

Share Yourself with Others

The more connected we become with our human family, the more influence we have and the more influence we have, the more powerful we become. Sharing your gifts is like planting an acorn. The planted acorn becomes a tree, which in turn produces thousands of acorns. You will become rich in relationships, which in the end is the only wealth that really matters.

*   *   *

The focus of this book has been an exploration of the threatening, violent nature of our world, how we and our children can avoid its adverse effects, and the process by which we are best prepared to survive those circumstances we cannot avoid. We discovered that we have all the advantages nature intended us to possess but in order to activate these gifts, it is necessary to have an experience that changes our personal identity and gives us a working knowledge of these assets. We discovered what it means to become a counterpredator.

The assumption of this new identity is the missing link in forging an unbreakable bond between a parent and his or her child because it restores the parent's rightful position as mentor and hero/protector to that child. We learned about the fastest and most effective way to gain this experience: Survival Response Conditioning and we have studied the principles and lessons that support its methodology. Hopefully you took my advice and obtained the recommended experience before you finished this book or you plan to do so at the first available opportunity.

As we part company, I would like to close with one final thought: Even though this subject matter is crucial to both our safety and peace of mind, it is still only one facet of what it means to be human. Once you have gained the adrenal advantage for yourself and fostered its reception in your children, I hope you turn your whole attention to the subject of this last chapter and secure these benefits for you and yours. You deserve to be happy. I am convinced that the powerful choices we discussed above will eventually lead you there.

~FIN~

Part IV Endnotes

Chapter 16

[1] Published Sept 16, 2007 KOMO-Full length story available at: KATU-TV http://www.katu.com/news/9821817.html

[2] For the full length story contact: Elise Banducci, Mercury News 12/1/02 http://www.mercurynews.com/mld/mercurynews/4645686.html

[3] For full length story and details contact: Ana Facio Contreras CONTRA COSTA TIMES 8/27/2003 http://www.contracostatimes.com/mld/cctimes/news/6628576.html

[4] For full length article contact: Annie Hundley, Greeley Tribune 1/13/03

[5] Source: The Detroit News/Norman Sinclair, Santiago Esparza, Jennifer Mrozowski (This story has been covered extensively by many news networks. I gleaned and condensed details from a number of them. The above source in my opinion best represented the body of facts as they emerged.)

Chapter 17

[6] Dave Grossman, & Loren Christensen, *On Combat: The Psychology and Physiology of Deadly Conflict in War and in Peace.* (Milstadt, IL: Warrior Science Publications, 2007) 72

[7] Howard Hendricks, *Teaching to Change Lives.* (Colorado Springs, Multnomah Books, 2003) 55

[8] Rush W. Dozier, *Fear Itself: The Origin and Nature of the Powerful Emotion That Shapes Our Lives and Our World.* (New York: St. Martin's, 1998) 49-51

Chapter 18

[9] Marcus Aurelius, *Meditations 8:11*

[10] Laurence Gonzales, *Deep Survival: Who Lives, Who Dies and Why.* (New York: Norton, 2003) 182

[11] Howard N. Snyder, PhD, *"Sexual Assault of Young Children as Reported to Law Enforcement: Victim, Incident, and Offender Characteristics,"* National Center for Juvenile Justice, Department of Justice, Office of Justice Programs, July 2000.

[12] Douglas, Emily and D. Finkelhor, "Childhood sexual abuse fact sheet," http://www.unh.edu/ccrc/factsheet/pdf/childhoodSexualAbuseFactSheet.pdf, Crimes Against Children Research Center, May 2005

Chapter 19

[13] Gavin DeBecker, *The Gift of Fear: Survival Signals that Protect Us from Violence.* (Boston: Little, Brown, 1997) 64

[14] http://www.atg.wa.gov/ChildAbductionResearch.aspx

[15] Original source: KOVR 13 / NEWS AND SPORTS / NEWS STORY Posted to the web on 2/23/01 at 7:15 PM http://www.kovr13.com/02feb01/vo022301c.htm

[16] For the full length story see the related articles, dated May 9, 2006, in the Vancouver Sun, the B.C. Almanac, and the National Post.

[17] Details compiled and condensed from the May 23, 1998 Jere Longman article in the New York Times and the December 20, 1999 news release from the Carnegie Hero Fund Commission.

Chapter 20

[18] Martha Stout, *The Sociopath Next Door.* (New York: Broadway Books, 2005)

[19] Used with permission. www.patcondell.net

[20] Brian Schoonover, *Zero Tolerance Discipline Policies.* (Bloomington, IN: iUniverse, 2009)

Chapter 21

[21] Massad F Ayoob, *Gun Proof Your Children.* (Concord NH: Police Bookshelf, 1986) 11

[22] Gavin DeBecker, *The Gift of Fear* 55

Chapter 22

[23] Theodore Roosevelt, "Citizenship in a Republic, "Speech at the Sorbonne, Paris, April 23, 1910

[24] Helen Keller, *The Story of My Life* (1903 Doubleday, Page & Co.) 203 Although this is commonly attributed to Helen Keller, Anne Sullivan, her teacher, is probably the true source. Keller admitted as much in a letter to the Rev. Phillips Brooks dated June 8, 1891. She wrote, ". . . *how happy your little Helen was when her teacher explained to her that the best and most beautiful things in the world cannot be seen nor even touched, but just felt in the heart.*"

List of Tables and Figures

FIG. 1 - The Victim Factory Formula, p. 64

FIG. 2 - Adam's Waterwheel, p. 72

FIG. 3 - Intuitive Responses to Threat, p. 138

FIG. 4 - Intuitive Responses vs. the Rational Brain, p. 140

FIG. 5 - Common Predator Types, p. 148

FIG. 6 - Navigating the Danger Zone, p. 243

FIG. 7 - The Survivor Mindset, p. 274

FIG. 8 - Victor or Victim, p. 275

FIG. 9 - The Predator's Game Plan, p. 309

A Note on Sources

    I am deeply indebted to the authors I have referenced. Each and every one of them has helped to paint my horizon. However, as both a specialist in the milieu of personal safety and a parent myself, certain titles and authors stand out. Any parent who wishes to immerse themselves in this subject and become truly grounded in child safety as I have presented it here should own a personal copy of the books indicated in bold print on the following pages.

Recommended Reading

Ayoob, Massad F. *Gun Proof Your Children.* Concord NH: Police Bookshelf, 1986

Begley, Sharon. *Train Your Mind, Change Your Brain.* New York: Ballantine, 2007

Brown, Sandra L. *How to Spot a Dangerous Man Before You Get Involved.* Alameda CA: Hunter House, 2005

De Becker, Gavin. *The Gift of Fear: Survival Signals that Protect Us from Violence.* Boston: Little, Brown, 1997

De Becker, Gavin. *Protecting the Gift: Keeping Children and Teenagers Safe (and Parents Sane).* New York: The Dial Press, 1999

Doidge, Norman. *The Brain that Changes Itself: Stories of Personal Triumph from the Frontiers of Brain Science.* London: Penguin Group, 2007

Dozier, Rush W. *Fear Itself: The Origin and Nature of the Powerful Emotion That Shapes Our Lives and Our World.* New York: St. Martin's, 1998

Gardner, Debbie, Mike. *Raising Kids Who Can Protect Themselves.* New York: McGraw-Hill, 2004

Gelb, Michael J. *How to Think Like Leonardo Da Vinci.* New York: Bantam Dell 1998

Gladwell, Malcolm. *Blink: The Power of Thinking Without Thinking.* New York: Little, Brown, 2005

Gonzales, Laurence. *Deep Survival: Who lives, Who Dies and Why.* New York: Norton, 2003

Gonzales, Laurence. *Everyday Survival: Why Smart People Do Stupid Things.* New York: Norton, 2008

Grossman, Dave & Christensen, L.W. *On Combat: The Psychology and Physiology of Deadly Conflict in War and in Peace.* Milstadt, IL: Warrior Science Publications, 2007

Grossman, Dave. On Killing: The Psychological Cost of Learning to Kill in War and Society. Boston: Little, Brown, 1995

Hall, Megan Kelley & Jones, Carrie. *Dear Bully: 70 Authors Tell their stories.* New York: Harper Teen, 2011

Kamler, Kenneth. *Surviving the Extremes: What Happens to the Body and Mind at the Limits of Human Endurance.* New York: Penguin, 2004

Kodis, Michelle. *Love Scents: How your Natural Pheromones Influence Your Relationships, Your Moods and Who You Love.* New York: Dutton, 1998

McGraw, Phillip C. *Life Strategies: Doing What Works, Doing What Matters.* New York: Hyperion, 1999

Miller, Alice. *The Drama of the Gifted Child: The Search for the True Self. New York:* Basic, 1994

Miller, Alice. *Thou Shalt not be Aware: Society's Betrayal of the Child.* New York: NAL-Dutton, 1991

Miller, Rory. *Facing Violence: Preparing for the Unexpected.* Wolfeboro, NH: YMAA Publication Center, Inc., 2011

Pipher, Mary. *Reviving Ophelia: Saving the Selves of Adolescent Girls.* New York: Penguin, 1994

Ripley, Amanda. *The Unthinkable: Who Survives When Disaster strikes and Why.* New York: Crown, 2008

Schoonover, Brian. *Zero Tolerance Discipline Policies.* Bloomington, IN: iUniverse, 2009

Sherwood, Ben. *The Survivor's Club: the Secrets and Science that Could Save Your Life.* New York: Grand Central Publishing, 2009

Siddle, Bruce K. *Sharpening the Warrior's Edge: the Psychology & Science of Training.* Belleville, IL: PPCT Research Publications, 1995

Snortland, Ellen. *Beauty Bites Beast: Awakening the Warrior Within Women and Girls.* Pasadena, CA: Trilogy Books, 1996

Spence, Gerry. *From Freedom to Slavery: the Rebirth of Tyranny in America.* New York: St. Martin's Press, 1995

Stout, Martha. *The Sociopath Next Door.* New York: Broadway Books, 2005

Thompson, John W. *Home in One Piece.* Fargo, ND: McCleery & Sons Publishing, 2001

Wooden, Kenneth. *Child Lures: What Every Parent and Child Should Know about Preventing Sexual Abuse and Abduction.* Arlington, TX: The Summit Publishing Group, 1995

Links

Bill Kortenbach
bill@counterpredators.com
Website link: http://www.counterpredators.com/
FaceBook page link: https://www.facebook.com/BillKortenbachAuthor
253-223-6769

Safety First Personal Protection Strategies
safetyfirstpps.org
Ginny Smethers
253-495-2985

National Domestic Violence Hotline
1-800-799-SAFE

Massad Ayoob
Lethal Force Institute
P. O. Box 122, Concord NH 03302-0122
Telephone: (603)224-6814
Toll Free: (800)624-9049
Fax Number: (603)226-3554
E-Mail Address: ayoob@attglobal.net

Gavin DeBecker
Gavin de Becker & Associates, Inc.
11684 Ventura Boulevard, Suite 440
Studio City, California 91604
818.506.0426 (fax)
infoline@gavindebecker.com

Laurence Gonzales
http://bigthink.com/laurencegonzales
http://www.deepsurvival.com
https://www.facebook.com/pages/Laurence-Gonzales/274938225870097

Rory Miller
http://chirontraining.com/

Martha Stout M.D.
http://en.wikipedia.org/wiki/Martha_Stout

Acknowledgments

There are no words capable of portraying the gratitude I feel toward the people who became a part of this book through their mentorship, belief, experience, inspiration, support, advice and most of all, an unbelievable amount of hard work. Although I wrote it, Counterpredators is their book, as surely as the sun rises and sets, because it was created from the tapestry of their combined life force.

To my children Brandon Michael and Alana Marie: I could never have completed this project without your love in my life—the driving force behind every line in this book.

To Virginia Smethers: I would have given this up long ago, had it not been for your strength and patience. Jackie Leavitt, thank you for your savvy advice and on-call willingness to advance this project. I know there were times you wanted to tear my hair out—but you graciously refrained. Jonathan Schedin, for your brilliant execution of the cover; thanks again. To Ben and Heidi Lee—thanks for your integrity and courage; it isn't easy to give someone an opinion that might not be welcome, but is needed just the same.

To my parents, Bernadine and Wolfgang Kortenbach: Thank you for setting my feet on the right path and forcing me to pursue what is real and solid. To Shihan Steve Armstrong: You were the mountain that defined and refined my horizon, whose footsteps none can fill. To Jeff Alexander and the staff of Warrior Spirit: the Big Chief and all his Braves—thank you for your kindness and love while opening my eyes. To Don Wasielewski for your mentoring and friendship: foxhole brothers for life. A very special thank you to Connie Walle, who was there at the beginning and supported me every step of the way.

To those individuals whose words and deeds have inspired me and given me vision and courage: Laird Richmond, whose love of life and humanity I treasure: thank you for your friendship and balance. To Gavin DeBecker, Laurence Gonzales, Gerry Spence and Bruce Siddle, men who I know only through their work, but who have moved me profoundly with their powerful insights: None of this would be possible without your work—thank you.

To Rodika Tollefson, who blessed me with an incredible, pro-bono, chapter by chapter copy edit: Thank you—I learned volumes from your effort and this project is cleaner, tighter and more professional because of it.

To Violet Tveit, your formatting was a Godsend.

George Warnell, Tim Carter, Mike O'dell, Steve Taylor, Mic Stumpf, Narva Walton, Pat and Christine Osburn and Chris Arena: All of you believed in me and you believed in this project from the moment you were introduced to it—words are not enough, but thank you. I received excellent advice and technical support from John Kouklis, Alan Wheeler, Bill McCabe, Kris Wilder, Rudy Burkin, the Baker family, Rachel Wellman, Wren Rocacorba and Hannah Masters.

Special thanks to Randall Murch for extremely professional, helpful critiques in the midst of a very aggressive schedule.

The following people read my manuscript at various stages and gave me invaluable advice and counsel: Bennett Fors, Dale Heidal, Johnny Hester, Bob Ingram, Kim and Ray Kerkof, Le Nguyen and Sharla Mitchell. I greatly appreciate your efforts to keep me honest, focused and accurate.

I want to acknowledge and thank the entire staff at Safety First Personal Protection Strategies. Without your tireless and altruistic service, this story would continue to remain untold. In particular I would like to mention Dotti Monjaraz, Taryn Smethers, Shila Bachelor, Linda Sharp, Debra Lanning, Shanti Kortenbach, Steve Roberts, Kim Meyers, Kaye Hoke, Jasmine Anderson, Toni Mackintosh, Kim Mackintosh and Mary Pimentel.

Last, I wish to acknowledge a very special group of men, every one of them a Praetorian: the spiritual Sons of Leonidas. This began with them and it is fitting that it ends with them.

George Warnell
Brandon Kortenbach
Decarlo Brown
Marcus Glasco
Brad Bachelor
Allen Wheeler

Steve Taylor
Richard Lanning
Duke Needham
Ben Goucher
Hal Bennett
Joe Baker
Jonathan Schedin
Kris Barnes
Paul Sioda
Jon Crain
Darrin Tollefson
Doug Ward
Joe Murphy

About the Author

Photo Credit Jackie Leavitt

Bill Kortenbach is a lifelong martial artist with over 35 years of active experience. He is the founder and CEO of Safety First Personal Protection Strategies, a 501c3 dedicated to the safety and empowerment of people of all ages. He holds a 7th-Dan in Isshinryu Karate and has trained extensively in a number of other disciplines including the Filipino stick and blade arts, Aikido and Pentjak-silat. He has served as a Board Director for the Sexual Assault Center of Pierce County, Washington. Bill specializes in reality-based training. He has trained hundreds of students and is an accomplished writer, speaker and seminar leader. He currently anchors "The Street Wise Forum" on KLAY 1180 AM; a weekly morning radio program which airs every Saturday at 9 a.m. Bill lives in Tacoma, Washington and enjoys hiking, woodworking and knife design in his spare time.

Made in the USA
Middletown, DE
18 May 2024